ESTHER'S TOWN

A BUR OAK BOOK

Esther's Town

DEEMER LEE

UNIVERSITY OF IOWA PRESS
IOWA CITY

University of Iowa Press, Iowa City 52242
Copyright © 1980 Iowa State University Press
University of Iowa Press paperback edition, 2013
All rights reserved
www.uiowapress.org
Printed in the United States of America

The University of Iowa Press is a member of Green Press Initiative
and is committed to preserving natural resources.

Printed on acid-free paper

Library of Congress Cataloging-in-Publication Data
Lee, Deemer, 1905–1979.
Esther's town / by Deemer Lee.—University of Iowa Press
paperback ed.
p. cm.
"A Bur Oak Book."
Originally published: Ames: Iowa State University Press, c1980.
Includes bibliographical references and index.
ISBN 978-1-58729-572-0, 1-58729-572-5 (pbk)
1. Estherville (Iowa)—History. I. Title.
F629.E7L43 2012
977.7'125—dc23 2011049772

CONTENTS

PREFACE

URING the more than forty-four years that I gathered and wrote news—forty-one of those years as editor and publisher of the *News*—many persons impressed me as exciting characters in the cast of a continuing drama of small-town life. Each community has its own dramatis personae, and yet I suppose there may be considerable similarity in the pattern of small-town life, wherever it is lived in rural America.

Upon retiring from my newspaper, I finally found the time to recreate some of the scenes recorded for newspaper print and to recollect especially episodes that were precious in my memory of Estherville life. To these recollections I have added some of my father's and also his father's. To fill in the story of Estherville, I have drawn on newspaper files, biographical sketches of pioneers, and historical material available from previously published books.

I have told the story the way it was, or the way it was told to me. It is history, not fiction, to the best of my ability to learn and record it accurately. I am grateful for the help of the members of my family in the painful task of transcribing my scribbling and my error-prone typing into readable copy, and for making welcomed suggestions. Appreciated also is the lift given me by Dorothy Story in reading some of the endless columns of newspaper microfilms to glean history that otherwise could have been missed. Several other persons in the community made contributions from their records and their memories.

Because my paternal grandparents settled on a farm a few miles from Estherville in 1870, only fourteen years after the first white settlers arrived in the county, the history of Estherville and the history of the Lee family are intertwined. We Lees are among the characters in the cast. The material accomplishments of the community in which we have lived all these years are for me of interest that is secondary to the fascinating people I knew and who moved in and out of the Estherville narrative.

If those who venture to read these pages about Esther's town find them uninteresting I shall be deeply disappointed. For all of its ups and downs, life has to me been exciting and fun.

Deemer Lee

ACKNOWLEDGMENTS

Very special thanks are due Henry Larsen and the Emmet County Historical Society for the pictures used in this book.

My thanks go also to my sons, Robert and William, for their support and faith in helping me carry on their father's last writing effort. Bob, with his journalism education, was especially helpful in the final editing of the manuscript.

Everyld Lee

ESTHER'S TOWN

An Era of Bootlegging,
Culture under Canvas,
and Arson

BACK when the Chicago, Rock Island and Pacific Railway was operating between receiverships, passengers who paused at the depot for a change of crews saw a half-block-long signboard painted in man-high lettering:

WATCH ESTHERVILLE GROW!

It was an impressive and challenging advertisement, but one that did not emphasize the most notable characteristic of Estherville.

The town was making some growth, but not at the speed of light or at a rate readily noticed by the naked eye. A brisk trade in bootleg alcohol negotiated between the interested parties at two Lincoln Street pool halls and a parade of male visitors up and down an open wooden stairway that led to Mabel's parlor of pleasure above Frank Carpenter's *Democrat* office were considerably more evident than any increase of the town's population.

The *Democrat* office was superbly located because it was close to the newspaper's prime news sources. In fact, the noisy traffic up Mabel's stairway was a disturbing annoyance when the editor tried to concentrate on turning a neat phrase. In the roaring twenties the meanest toughs, the bloodiest fistfights, and the liveliest trade in booze and commercialized love saw action in the *Democrat* block — until the aldermen relocated crime and sin a block away. There it was less visible and more remote from trade in fashionable dresses, men's clothing, groceries, meats, drugs, and other reputable commerce.

At about the same time, city legislators, upon instigation of the

3

Chamber of Commerce, changed the names of east-west streets.
Lincoln Street metamorphosed into Central Avenue and more
respectability, while the WATCH ESTHERVILLE GROW sign
was torn down or fell down. By then attrition of patronage had
deprived Chicago-bound passenger trains Nos. 19 and 20 of
revenues adequate for support of dining car service. Edwin A. Boss,
later to become a hotel baron in Des Moines, was the first Rock
Island dining steward. William Moore, whose family was one of
only two Negro families in Estherville, presided as dining car
steward on the run out of Estherville. The word "black" in those
days was useful in describing nighttime, dark closets, woods, and
chalk boards—not people.

As more passengers deserted the trains, the railroad also
removed Pullman cars. And finally the only live bodies riding past
the depot were a few pigs and Hereford steers on their way to
slaughter. And shortly these creatures, too, would abandon the
C.R.I.&P. in favor of block-long leviathans thundering down the
highways. When that time came, Estherville had gained a few more
souls but had shed some of the lively color that Frank Carpenter
reported with tact and sympathy for readers of the *Democrat* during the first two decades of the new century.

Carpenter's printshop was as immaculate as his person and his
bachelor kitchen. But the drum cylinder press of his shop was not
quite new enough for handy printing of his weekly paper nor quite
old enough to qualify yet as a museum antique. But, by the time it
was retired by Frank's successor in the late twenties for a two-
revolution press, it had recorded through the *Democrat*'s pages fifty
years of joy, anguish, hope, and sorrow. Frank had penciled his last
galley correction and won mortal peace.

My first newspaper assignment, in 1924, was to cover for the
Democrat the town's annual week of culture and enlightenment
under a Redpath Vauter chautauqua tent. Chautauqua programs
had been going on since almost the beginning of the century. This
forerunner of the astrodome was a tent pitched in a vacant yard,
which bred nine trillion mosquitoes a year, each of which matured
to the full vigor of life for the express purpose of perforating the
hides of season-ticket holders of chautauqua programs.

Chautauqua week was carefully timed not only to mature the
mosquito crop but to assure the summer's most scorching weather

Chautauqua, 1909.

of about 169 degrees Fahrenheit and the certainty of at least one barn-burner of a thunder and lightning storm that ripped holes in the tent and scared hell out of the assembly. But these bombardments, which served to remind God's creatures of their vulnerability, always fell short of maiming or massacring prisoners of the tent. Because of the sober, spiritually refreshing, and educationally beneficial nature of chautauqua programs, divine intervention may have spared mass annihilation during storms of monsoon dimensions that rent holes in the canvas, swayed the poles, uprooted stakes, and charitably scattered lantern-slide pictures of uncomely naked African savages. Drenched and trapped, the local ticket holders sat there thirsting for culture while hungry mosquitoes feasted on their flesh.

I never quite understood why Frank Carpenter was willing to pay me the extravagant weekly wage of $15 to write him on-the-spot chautauqua coverage of such thin-soup fare as Filipino music that was louder than it was melodious, concerts of caterwauling sopranos, assorted lectures, travel narrations, and other tripe. But due to the regularity with which various acts of God put the chautauqua tent in jeopardy, despite the sublimity of its purposes, Frank obviously thought staff coverage was a sound investment in case the affair lost its providential priorities and developed into a full-scale catastrophe.

On no other basis than that of news preparedness could an exorbitant fee of $15 to write a week of chautauqua chitchat be justified. In fairness, it must be admitted that Vauter inserted a gem here and there on the program. For example, there was the time that the perspiring William Jennings Bryan orated "The Cross of Gold." This was the loss leader of one year's tent seminar. On one other year the thick-maned Bohumir Kryl thrashed the air with his baton as he waved the orchestra through Verdi's "Anvil Chorus." His virtuoso production included spectacular showers of sparks from an electric anvil that provided enjoyment for both those who thirsted for musical entertainment and those allergic to it. A performance of Gilbert and Sullivan's *The Mikado* was another oasis in the Redpath desert.

Toward the end of each chautauqua week, when the mosquitoes had gorged themselves to satiety, and preferably on some evening when the climate relapsed to something under 115 degrees Fahrenheit, and when the tent was not heaving and threatening to blow away or fall down—that was the time to do something about the next year's campaign. This painful but necessary procedure to assure culture and enlightenment for the following year began with a statement by the Redpath manager. He tantalizingly hinted at the bright prospects for an even more palatable menu of mental improvement for the coming season.

Such a program promised for the town next year would meet community needs to prevent stagnation, lassitude, intemperance, ignorance, indifference, narrow-mindedness, cussedness, moral depravity, and other symptoms of a decaying society. An effective and attractive statement of program prospects always prompted L. L. Bingham to find his feet and offer to head the subscription list of guarantors. Mr. Bingham, a tall, gaunt figure who wore facial shrubbery with great dignity, was a man of unimpeached community standing, dependably generous in support of all causes he endorsed. He also taught the First Presbyterian Church's Sunday school class—the Friendly Fellows Club—of male youths who had attained an impressionable age. With the support of Mr. Bingham and Mayor B. B. Anderson, the chautauqua advance guaranty was invariably subscribed, sooner or later, right on down to the very last year—when the tent wore out and the prospects for a week of intellectualism thinned. The inhabitants had become preoccupied with riding in their automobiles or listening to "Amos and Andy," "Fibber McGee and Molly," and other classics on the radio. They forgot about improving their minds and their morals.

I do recall two special ecumenical occasions, during a period when I was yet too young to be worth a salary of $15 a week, that provided members of the community unusual opportunities for spiritual refurbishment. One of these missionary efforts, in 1915, was conducted in a 2,000-seat tabernacle that the upstanding citizens erected in two days on Main Street, across from the old courthouse. What I remember about the revival meeting there was the baptism of my friend Jim White, who carelessly overlooked that he had already been washed of original sin during infancy. So when Jim responded to the emotional call for "finding the light" and marched up front for baptism, it was entirely superfluous. Later, someone revealed to Susan White the news of her son's redundant salvation that perhaps jeopardized the original proceedings in Grace Episcopal Church. She was less than pleased and rebuked him warmly. But as always, she forgave him. It is questionable that double immunity ever did Jim any harm, although proof in these matters is never easy to establish.

I remember more distinctly than the meeting highlighted by Jim's renouncement of sin the proceedings of another summer revival, conducted in a wooden tabernacle. It was also located on Main Street, but east of the old courthouse square. The home of Hugh Greig, a wealthy grain buyer, was on the north side of that street, not far from where the tabernacle platform was erected. One evening our family attended the revival session and sat near the rear of the building, as was father's preference. When the sermon had been preached and enthusiasm for Christianity was at high fever, the divine invited members of the audience to step forward and be saved. At that point a voice boomed into the building through a knothole on the north side of the tabernacle. "Go on up in front, Nels," yelled Greig, who then stepped back, tripped over the pail of water he had just pumped a few feet away and sprawled pratt down in the water bucket. Mischief often finds quick reward. Father stood pat on his early Lutheran baptism and kept his seat. He saw no need to supplement or duplicate his baptism by joining the processional up front to the sawdust, notwithstanding Hugh Greig's personal invitation.

Without tents, Estherville would have been a disadvantaged community. Canvas supplied the kind of civic wants that in much later years would be satisfied only in brick and mortar. Under canvas Esthervilleans listened to music, lectures, travelogues—even fervent evangelistic preaching—and they experienced the entertainment of Broadway stage plays. Regularly each summer the Aulger Brothers brought a troop of stock company players to town for such lively amusement as the 1926 program that included "Cat and the Canary," "The Goose Hangs High," "Meet the Wife," "Lazy Bones," and "The Love Nest" at 25¢ or 50¢; ladies were admitted free of charge. The price included a full band concert overture at 7:15 p.m. by the versatile cast. The Aulgers brought their own canvas theater, along with collapsible seats and a plank stage. Who needed to risk being fleeced by New York city slickers to see Broadway drama? The Aulger Brothers willingly brought Broadway to the prairie.

There was Lyceum, too, to improve and amuse the mind. These programs of the twenties were held at the theater or in a church. In 1925 Judge Ben Lindsay spoke, the Cathedral Choir sang, and actors performed "Two Fellows and a Girl." Opportunities to soak up culture went on year round, but in summer, when tents could be pitched, the tempo of entertainment quickened.

When Barnum & Bailey, Ringling, Barnes, Sells Floto, and lesser circuses came to town, the much smaller tents used for road shows, roller skating rinks, and religious revival meetings were dwarfed by the massive circus canvas tops. These portable hippodromes were raised by roustabout circus workers, elephant power, and by willing, ecstatic youngsters eager to carry water for the elephants. They pounded stakes and ran errands. Their rewards were tickets to see what would go on in the big tent. However, admission to the menagerie tent and sideshows to see the snake charmer, the fat lady, the dwarfs, freaks, and other curiosities required cash—unless one could belly under the edge of the tent. This was a maneuver at which future Estherville lawyers, plumbers, storekeepers, farmers, and bankers developed promising skill.

Unloading circus equipment, with calliope drawn by eight horses, 1916.

Weeks before the circus, advance men plastered board fences and the sides of buildings with colorful posters and they deluged newspaper offices with photos and stories of what would happen in the big tent, handing out generous supplies of complimentary tickets. But the most effective attention compeller was a parade that preceded the afternoon performance. Brightly painted wagons hauled wild animals, while girls in tights rode on the elephants as the huge animals tromped down the street. Clowns cavorted and a steam calliope brought up the rear. Who could resist buying a ticket after that sample?

Whatever the circus confection known as cotton candy lacked in sanitation was made up in sheer delight of the eating. Circus peanuts and hot dogs dripping of mustard and garnished with piccalilli were also special. These delicacies of the circus tent were consumed in an atmosphere redolent of galloping ponies, plodding elephants, and giraffes. While some of the spangled, scantily attired female performers rode the ponies and others were perched high on the elephants' backs, an animal trainer entered the cage of a roaring man-eating lion or a snarling tiger. The chair that the trainer held in one hand was seemingly protective, but it was unclear whether the blank cartridges he fired were intended to tame the beast or incite it to remember its jungle role.

This exciting episode had to share attention with flying acrobats who performed amazing feats of death-defying skill on high trapezes, sometimes without the consolation of a net below. Down on the ground, and close to the spectators, clowns in roguish and grotesque costumes and wearing false faces paraded their antics and pranks in easy view of the peanut and candy eaters, bringing shrieks of laughter. In one of the rings a barefoot clown, standing atop a pony, divested himself systematically of twenty-nine vests, more or less. In another circle trained dogs went through their acts, all while a brass band, assisted by the steam calliope, made the merriment even more thrilling.

Almost as exciting as what went on under the big tent at both the afternoon and evening performances was the loading operation afterward at the Rock Island railroad yard, when three special trains carrying the animals, tent equipment, and circus people were put aboard the cars for departure to the next show town. Under the light of red flares, this remarkable feat of organization and discipline astonished the hundreds of young and old circus fans who gathered close to the railroad tracks. Most of these spectators had been too sleepy to watch the early morning unloading, but they cheerfully watched late into the night until steam locomotives, with a two-whistle blast warning, began pulling trainloads of tented adventure across the Des Moines River bridge and slowly up through the hills west of the town. In another favored community, it would next day fulfill the promises of its color-saturated billboards.

Air conditioning is a modern invention that aggravates the energy problem, runs up extravagantly expensive light bills, and plugs my sinuses. The air conditioning of my youth was simple, inexpensive, and left me unaware that I had been born with sinuses. In those days the practical air-conditioning contraption was a dried palm leaf, powered by a slight rotation of the wrist—either one. The users created their own breezes that were easily regulated by the vigor with which they waved the fans. Fashionable ladies, however, eschewed palm leaves in favor of artistically decorated folding models equipped with a colorful loop of cord and a tassel. Some came from Japan. Carried in their purses, the fans were taken out, unfolded, and waved in graceful gestures. Without fans only hardy specimens could have survived an Estherville summer, particularly while they sweltered under tents in search of amusement, culture, or regeneration of the soul.

Long before I became acquainted with Frank Carpenter and began to haunt his printshop to admire such treasures as his old-fashioned platten "snapper" presses, along with a miracle known as a typesetting machine and cases of movable foundry type, the drama of small-town happenings began to absorb me. This interest may have been first aroused by a series of impromptu urban-renewal projects undertaken by a mentally deprived young man who set about putting a match to various structures in town he considered suitable tinder. This amateur arsonist found rewarding thrills at the fires he started with his mother's kitchen matches. He also enjoyed hearing the horrendous siren that always blew to summon hose and ladder volunteers to the scene of each blaze. They usually arrived in deliberate haste in time to cool the embers.

Roy Blazer's barn on South Tenth Street produced a particularly attractive blaze, as did firing of a feed shed on Lincoln Street. In each of those two incendiary accomplishments, there was on hand a generous supply of flammables to assure effective fireworks. The firemaker through faulty judgment set fire to John Wesley's Methodist Church, a sturdy structure of brick and mortar. It fizzled. Perhaps the venerable edifice enjoyed a special immunity not understood by the naive arsonist. Ultimately the town marshal realized that the firebug was a person of unsound mind. Thus the list of suspects could be narrowed somewhat. Also, the firemaker made the mistake of showing up so promptly at his productions that his perfect attendance record attracted notice and led to his identification.

By the end of November 1914, the firebug had in two months achieved the impressive box score of burning seven barns and one feed store and had made an unsuccessful attempt on the Methodist Church. When the confused sixteen-year-old high school junior finally acknowledged authorship of the fireworks and was commit-

Coon Block, three-story building at Central and Sixth streets.

ted to psychiatric treatment, the town became calmer, but the younger generation of spectators thought it also less interesting. Youth did not invariably root for premature quenching of flames by the volunteer fire laddies.

Costly fires were endemic in Estherville as early as 1904, a year before I was born, when ten buildings at the center of Estherville trade and commerce were consumed by a fire that put a whole new look on the downtown scene. Hotel guests fled in their nightclothes from rooms in the old Lincoln House when the entire Coon block burned one subzero night. Losses to H. C. Coon, Shadle & Sons, the *Vindicator & Republican* office, and Bemis Brothers were put at $160,000 to $200,000 by the *Democrat*. Firemen became discouraged in 1910 because of low water pressure that thwarted them and they objected to unsanitary fire quarters. When they went on strike, they left the 3,401 inhabitants temporarily vulnerable. The volunteers were happier when a city hall was built in 1914, but it was by no means the end of disastrous fires. In 1914 the *Enterprise* office was consumed by fire, and that made the score even with all three newspaper plants. Henry Graaf's theater, finished in 1916, was destroyed by fire a year later, along with losses incurred by Hugh D. Lawrence's clothing store, Carl Olson's jewelry store, Art Erickson's photo studio, and Dr. A. Ivey's dental office—a total of $175,000 in property gone up in smoke. In 1917 alone, new construction totaled a half-million dollars.[1]

The arsonist's series of efforts, while charged with suspenseful guessing of which premises would be scorched next, were unmatched for sheer magnificence by some of the infernos arranged by acts of God (or produced by faulty flues or crossed wires) that came off during howling blizzards in the dead of night.

Burning of the Opera House, Henry Graaf's movie theater, Harry Toll's livery stable, and the Gronstal & Leiren paint store and other Estherville spectaculars produced volcanoes of smoke and belching flame that enraptured relaxed young viewers and embarrassed the volunteer fire department, often hampered by frozen

Enterprise *office.*

fireplugs, bursted hose lines, and lack of special equipment. Estherville surged far ahead of the times in practicing its own version of
urban reconstruction. Improved buildings always filled the burned-
out cavities.

The town's wailing siren, which conceivably disturbed not only
the quick but also the dead, was ordinarily used to signal the out-
break of a fire. But it also sent fire volunteers to the Des Moines
River bank whenever some youngster was reported to have gone
under the current. In those prepollution, plentiful-water days, the
river commanded respect and was deep enough for fair pike and
catfish sport. The deep holes were treacherous to those youngsters
who disobeyed their mothers to seek relief from sizzling summer
heat and to enjoy good fun skinny-dipping in the cool stream. Each
summer claimed one or more lives, until the town in 1928 spent
$9,000 to build a swimming pool and $5,000 for a bathhouse.

It would be unreal to conclude that Estherville youth found
entertainment only at fires and naked bathing in the river. There
were movies at the old King Theater on Saturday afternoons,
fistfights, marbles, baseball, kite flying, and other simple pleasures.

When Henry Graaf's movie palace burned down in 1917, he
promptly rebuilt it with a better one, which awed the entertainment
patrons with a huge music box. This was a Rube Goldberg–inspired
arrangement of horns, cymbals, drums, strings, pipes, and other
noisemakers that automatically cranked out waltzes, symphonies,
dirges, marches, and other music suitable for listening as one
watched silent flickers on the screen. The room-sized music box was
enclosed by colored glass at the back of Henry's confectionery store,
where the music could clearly be heard both in his Grand Theater
next door and in the presence of patrons lured by gleaming cases of
homemade candy to sip sodas and eat sundaes. The music box put
the ordinary player piano contraption to shame for the output of
sound. It must have been the forerunner of both the computer and
electronic amplification.

On special occasions, Henry shut off the music machine as his
wife and two sons entered the theater pit to play live piano, fiddle,
and horn. He brought vaudeville to the Grand occasionally. It was
on the stage of the Grand that the Benevolent and Protective Order
of Elks, Lodge No. 528, produced its annual edition of the Minstrel
Show, always a sellout. As I recall, the 1921 production was billed
as "The Jollities" and the 1923 show was called "The Frivolities."

Graaf's Ice Cream Parlor on Sixth Street.

The audience was invariably suitably barbered, curled, pressed, and scented for the occasion. Few notables of the town were absent—or were spared the mordant wit of the minstrel players.

When the interlocutor asked the banjo-playing and tambourine-equipped minstrels if anyone knew Mack Groves, one of the soot-faced endmen quickly raised a white-gloved hand: "Why boss, he's dat big bluff overlooking da city." Mayor Groves then glanced at his wife, Marietta, squirmed, and laughed as comfortably as he could manage. Minstrel show soloists were recruited from the town's most accomplished voices and the chorines were chosen from among the town's least awkward and most comely volunteers.

It was an inconsiderate or impoverished father or beau who left the theater by the front entrance rather than guide his loved ones through the side door to the Graaf confectionery and expose them to the provocative smells of candies and pastries. Anyone with money in his pocket was certain to yield to a soda, a sundae, or a sack of sweetmeats.

Fearless Settlers
and Rampaging Indians

ED SILLGE, when I first knew him in 1922, was no longer Frank Carpenter's partner, compositor, and *Democrat* pressman. He was semiretired and a part-time printer at another shop in town, the *Vindicator & Republican*. Ed was the most distinguished-looking printer I was ever to know, as well as a talented one. We became best acquainted under traumatic circumstances. It was soon after I began frequenting the *V&R*'s printshop to proofread and supervise a monthly high school publication known as *The Pepper* that I came to admire Ed and share his misfortune.

A slender man, Ed wore gold-rimmed half-moon spectacles, the first I had ever seen, to aid his expressive brown eyes. These curious aids to vision enabled Ed to look down at his type with convenient magnification or he could easily glance above the lenses at whatever was out of close range—including the tall, scrawny kid from school who probably tried his patience on those Saturday mornings when *The Pepper* was being put to press.

Ed wore black sateen sleeve protectors over his white shirt. These were held in place by elastic, just above the elbow. A long, black, bibbed apron spared his front side from printer's ink as he set type and assembled columns of it in page forms. Then he presided with dignity at the feedboard of a two-revolution Campbell flatbed press that magically transformed scribbling into magnificent printed pages.

Soft speaking, reserved, and kind, Ed Sillge personified to me the image perfect. He could do no wrong. His advice on how *Pepper* stories should best be arranged and displayed in type was infallible. Of course I had scant experience. When I knew him, Ed was getting old, and age destroys not only muscle fibre but one's memory cells as well. Ed became acutely aware of this one Saturday morning just after he had finished arranging galleys of *Pepper* type into four page forms and carried them to the bed of the press. Ed then lowered the feedboard, placed a pile of bookpaper sheets in front of him on the board, rubbed his fingers with glycerin to make them tacky, and threw the switch Releasing the clutch, he slipped the first sheet against the cylinder gauges and the electric motor set the press in motion.

Oh, my! Having set up the press many hundreds of times before, Ed knew that upon placing the heavy steel framework of forms holding four pages of lead slugs and type on the bed of the press, one more detail must not be omitted. The mass of steel and lead must be secured by using a wrench to lock two sturdy lugs in place. It was this detail Ed forgot. What happened on that Saturday morning when Ed set the press in motion and the motor started to chase the iron bed of the press and its type forms forth and back under the impression cylinder was too awful to think about. Although nothing unusual happened when the precious cargo of *Pepper* type

Print shop of the Vindicator & Republican, *1919. From left: Caroline Myhre, Vincent Maloney, Ed Sillge, Adelaide Nichols, George Nichols.*

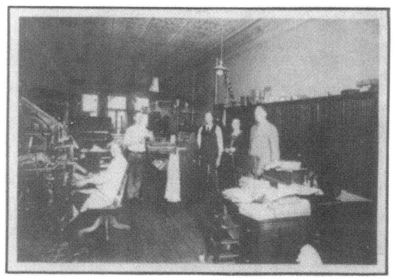

lurched forward on the "forth" motion, when the mass of metal
plunged back under the cylinder on the reciprocal action all hell
broke loose.

Type slugs, handset foundry type, borders, column rules, logo-
types, and stereotypes were hurled to the printshop floor in a vast
heap of scrambled wreckage. Looking back from where he stood on
a platform at the feedboard, Ed peered above his spectacles in
speechless disbelief. He never did explode in the anger typical of
printers I was to know later, who lacked Ed's poise and tranquility.
If St. Peter qualifies any printers or reporters for admission to the
promised land, we're sure that he'll homestead Ed on one of the
lusher pastures.

Ed's and my friendship became well cemented that Saturday
when together we spent the afternoon redoing what had been done
and undone in the morning. Ed, I'm sure, never accepted a cent for
his painful afternoon's work. I learned something about printing
that Saturday, but it was not until about fifty years later that I came
to understand fully the ravages that time inflicts to deteriorate one's
memory cells.

The *Vindicator & Republican* shop, in which the pied type
episode occurred, published a newspaper that had the longest history of any Estherville publication. Eaton Northrop and O. C.
Bates, in a spirit of pioneering enterprise, began publishing the
Northern Vindicator just twelve years after the first white men arrived to settle the county. When an act of the Iowa legislature in
1851 established Emmet County, named for Robert Emmet, the
Irish patriot, only Sioux, Fox, and Sac Indians and wild game in-
habited the area. It wasn't until 1859 that the county was actually
organized. That was three years after the first white men, Jesse
Coverdale and George C. Granger, settled down in June beside the
Des Moines River in a wood thicket three miles south of the Iowa-
Minnesota line. They were joined by D. W. Hoyt, William
Granger, and Adolphus Jenkins. In August John Rourke and his
wife—along with Thomas, William, and James Mahar, Patrick
Conlan, and Edward Conlan—put down Irish roots in High Lake
Township in the shelter of timber near two lakes, then known as
High and Mud, nine miles southeast of the future Estherville town-
site.

Thomas Mahar was a colorful Irishman whom I remember see-

Tom Mahar at Ingham cabin, 1870.

ing at his log cabin near the shore of Mud Lake when I was a boy. After coming to America in 1846 from Ireland, Mahar was working in an eastern mill when seized with a desire for adventure that took him by train to Dubuque, the end of the railroad. There he set out afoot with an axe and a gun. Arriving in High Lake Township, probably early in 1856, he staked out claims for himself, his brothers, and friends. When his relatives arrived from Ireland, he met them at Dubuque with an ox team. His cabin served as the Island Grove post office until it was closed in 1874. It was when Mahar made a trip to Estherville to replenish his supply of tobacco that the Robert Ridleys, who arrived in 1857, saw him for the first time. But it wasn't the last they saw or heard of him. He was one of the volunteers who a few years later joined the Northern Border Brigade to defend settlers against warring Indians.

Nels Peter Bruhjeld and his wife Britha were probably the first of the Norwegian settlers to arrive from Wisconsin at the High Lake area. They settled east of the Des Moines River in June 1860, at about the same time Peter's brother Botolf also came there. The Lars Paulsen family chose a location west of the river a few miles away. Ole and Turi Flatland took a claim on the river to the southeast of Bruhjeld. Other Norwegians continued to settle the area, the biggest flux of Norse coming to the county as the new decade opened.

There is no accurate record of who inhabited Emmet County before white settlers began arriving in 1856. Several different tribes of Indians roamed the plains. Mound Builders preceded them. Only one mound was found in the county, five miles south of Estherville on Colonel Allen's farm. The mound, about thirty feet in diameter, contained tomahawks, other weapons, pottery, and human skeletons. Two mounds had been leveled and broken into. Of the many tribes, including Iowas, who inhabited the state, the Sioux, Sacs, and Foxes were the bands who hunted, fished, and camped in Emmet County. The last intertribal battle in the area occurred in 1852 in nearby Kossuth County, where the Sacs and Foxes defeated the Sioux. About seventy braves fought on each side. The Sioux became increasingly hostile to the settlers, whom they harassed on several occasions.

Indians found the area that became Emmet County attractive for reasons different from those that impelled white settlers to stake out claims and establish themselves. Before it was drained in later years, much of the land was covered by small lakes and swamps that yielded fish and game. Many of the lakes—such as Crane, Elmer, Birge, Eagle, Cheever, Ryan, Four-Mile, Clear, and Twelve-Mile— would largely disappear when bull ditches and trunk tile lines converted the haunts of beaver, muskrat, and pickerel into black, rich Webster soil to produce heavy yields of grain. Two branches of the Des Moines River and the larger lakes—High, Mud (Ingham), Tuttle (Okamanpadu), Swan, and Iowa—would continue to provide sport and recreation in the years to come.

Marshy areas covered much of the area until drainage made the soil highly productive agriculturally. Along the lakes and streams were hardwood trees such as oak, walnut, maple, hickory, and elm. There were wild fruits as well—gooseberries, crabapples, grapes, and plums. But most of the county was a treeless native prairie culture that flourished on the drift soils from Pleistocene glacial deposits. Although the prairie was flat, the area was actually of relatively high elevation—1,298 feet above sea level. Fresh water, both surface and at deep levels, was plentiful. The settlers chose well, as had the Indians, in seeking an environment that would sustain them. And it was the fertility of the soil, the dependable annual rainfall, and the ultimate abundant harvest of grain that sustained the county's trading center, Estherville, which had its beginning only a few months after the first white men arrived in the county.

Robert E. Ridley and A. H. Ridley who came from Maine by train as far as Dubuque, together with a Graves family from Winneshiek County, Iowa, began a settlement on the river that became Estherville. The Ridleys made the twelve-day trip from Dubuque (first written DuBuque) by ox team and covered wagon, the usual mode of travel. Inauspiciously, Esther Ridley arrived only a month after tragedy struck the sparsely populated area and drove fear into those who survived massacre. Peter Rourke, the first white child born in the county, was only two months old when his parents wondered if they and their infant would be spared from Sioux tomahawks.

A renegade Indian, Ink-pa-du-ta, who had been banished by his own tribe of Wahpeton Sioux, led a band of 50 to 150 reckless Sioux Indians who experienced deprivation as a result of the severe winter of 1857. The tribe went on a rampage in March, twenty

Esther Ridley.   Robert Ridley.

miles west of Granger's and Coverdale's camp and also the Ridley group. They attacked settlers living in an area close to three lakes—Spirit and East and West Okoboji. In settlements along those lakes, Ink-pa-du-ta's warriors slaughtered forty settlers—men, women, and children—destroying and plundering their buildings and possessions.[1] During a six-day rampage caused partly by anger that white men had invaded the lakes area which they treasured as chosen hunting and fishing grounds, the Sioux left a bloody trail through three sparsely settled groups of cabins. Joseph Harshman of the Estherville settlement, who chose an unfortunate time to go to the lake settlement for flour, arrived at the height of the massacre. He was murdered. Among those attacked was a girl of fourteen, Abigail Gardner, who was kidnapped. She was finally released more than two months later at St. Paul. Although the Indians were pursued by volunteers from 100 miles away at Fort Dodge and Webster City, the scent was lost and the war party escaped into Dakota territory and was never overtaken. Two of the pursuers froze to death during a raging snowstorm when they became separated from their party.

Although they had not been regarded as warlike, the Sioux gradually became more hostile as white men moved onto their lands. The hard winter, when Indians had to subsist largely on fish, may have been the immediate cause of Sioux discontent that resulted in their vicious attack, but there was a background incident that had occurred several years before. In February 1854, a few miles south of Algona in Humboldt County, a whiskey peddler and horse thief, Henry Lott, treacherously murdered Si-do-min-a-do-ta, a Sioux Indian, and all the members of his family except one son.[2] After the murder of Si-do-min-a-do-ta, known as "Old Two-Fingers," Lott carted the body a few miles away and thrust it under the ice in a creek that understandably came to be known as Bloody Run. Later, at Homer, in Webster County, travelers came across a gruesome scene—the head of an Indian on top of a pole leaned against a cabin, where someone had placed it after finding it in Bloody Run. Chief Ink-pa-du-ta, who had threatened and brutalized settlers at Algona and places nearby, evened the score in the Spirit Lake Massacre. It is believed by some historians that Si-do-min-a-do-ta was his brother.

Like settlers farther west, south, and north of the Spirit Lake bloodletting, the few new residents of Emmet County were struck with terror and armed themselves as best they could against further attack. In response to the appeal of settlers in northwest Iowa for some security against Indian attacks, of which the Spirit Lake incident was only one of many in the region, a company was recruited from Hamilton and Webster counties to protect the area. Second Lieutenant Jewett was placed in charge of a small group in Estherville. Protection was abandoned shortly, but the company had to be called out again a year later. In 1860 a company of "Minute Men" was authorized by the legislature to be in readiness whenever they might be needed to meet Indian threats. Despite all the dangers and the gruesome casualties at nearby Spirit Lake, the hardy groups of settlers that had arrived in Emmet County at Emmet Grove, at High Lake, and at the site of Estherville prepared themselves to stay—Indians or no Indians. And they did stay, including the newly arrived Esther.

Along with Jesse Coverdale and George C. Granger from the Emmet Grove camp just up the river three miles, Robert and Esther Ridley and A. H. Ridley from Maine, and Adolphus Jenkins, John Jenkins, and George Jenkins from New York laid out and platted a town they called Estherville, named for the lady who defied hardships and fears to join her husband in starting a new community. Although many hardy settlers declined to stay through the winter of 1857-58, Esther opted to stick it out. And the schoolhouse the Ridleys and their fellow townsmen built bespoke permanence. Esther's daughter, Anna, firstborn of the town in 1858, would have a place to study her R's, along with what she was to learn about life in the timber along the river and on the prairie close by. After repeated failures to harness the Des Moines River rapids for power, the settlers finally built a sawmill, and it became easier for those following them to get lumber for their cabins. The infant Peter Rourke at High Lake and all the other Emmet County residents escaped Indian scalping knives but there were frequent disquieting incidents. Fear of the redskins remained for several years.

To supply spiritual needs of Esther's town, a Methodist circuit rider, Cornelius McLean, began making regular calls on alternate Sundays at Estherville and Spirit Lake, and also at adjacent communities. The schoolhouse served as a sanctuary as well as a class-room. It would be another eleven years before the Free Will Baptists would offer the settlement a choice of worship.

The county's modest population of 105 in 1860 by no means neglected its privilege of suffrage. Unanimous in its political sentiments, the settlers gave Abraham Lincoln all their votes and then supported the Union's call to arms. Emmet County men the next year joined a cavalry unit organized at Fort Dodge. They served with the Army of the Potomac, attached to the Eleventh Pennsylvania Cavalry. The Emmet enlistees, estimated at 40 percent of the population, created a vacuum in defense when they left. To meet that need, a company of cavalry was recruited in 1861. A year later it dispatched thirty men to the Estherville-Okoboji area in temporary defense of the settlements, until a Northern Border Brigade was recruited.

By 1861 the town got around to formally platting a townsite into blocks and lots as the settlement moved confidently to build a peaceful future. Stagecoach delays were annoying, and the congregation was disappointed when Preacher McLean's biweekly visit was thwarted by a swollen creek, a raging snowstorm, or a fatigued horse. Regardless of the rigorous climate, hostile environment, and other irritations, the Ridleys and their neighbors felt secure. They were not prepared for the news that suddenly burst upon them in August 1862. A fifteen-year-old boy, bleeding and barefoot, struggled into the village bearing frightful tidings.

Suffering from gunshot wounds, the boy related that a band of Sioux Indians had murdered his parents and other settlers north of Jackson, Minnesota. Despite his injuries, the boy had managed to travel afoot thirty miles along the Des Moines River to Estherville to spread the alarm. The 200 aroused townsmen, led by Jesse Coverdale, immediately threw up a rough stockade around the schoolhouse for protection, and they dispatched word to Governor Kirkwood asking for help. Led by Chief Little Crow, the Sioux had massacred 700 settlers north of New Ulm and close to Jackson, just across the state line from Emmet County. The Indians had made no serious threats in the Estherville area since the Spirit Lake Massacre five years before, but the New Ulm and Jackson uprising rekindled fears of settlers in Emmet County and those farther south and east as well. Many families fled, leaving their possessions behind.

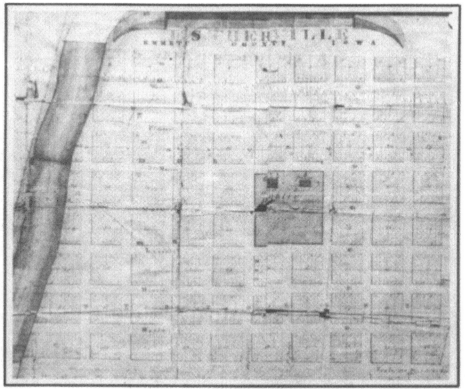

The first map of Estherville, 1861

Two companies of militia, on orders of the governor, organized in the four counties of Kossuth, Palo Alto, Humboldt, and Emmet under William H. Ingham of Algona, who was named captain of Company A, known as the Northern Border Brigade.[3] Taking up station at Estherville, the company by fall had erected a fortification of four-inch planks in the shape of a stockade on ground provided by Robert Ridley. Commandeering timber anywhere it could be found, regardless of who claimed to own it, Captain Ingham took over the Ridley and Jenkins sawmill, which had been operating for only a few months. Located three blocks from the settlers' homes, the stockade included barracks, officer quarters, a commissary, a guardhouse, and a well.

The settlers moved inside the stockade, which was buttressed by a sod wall five feet thick at the base. When the fort's water supply was contaminated by a dead horse that fell in the well, the occupants were still so frightened they were reluctant to seek good water available only a few blocks away. The fortification, which never suffered an attack, was named Fort Defiance at the suggestion of Howard Graves, who fourteen years later decided to establish a bank in the town. When conservationists in 1931 set aside 185 acres of native timber and wildlife as a state park, they named it Fort Defiance.

Captain Ingham's disregard for property niceties in pressing teams and timber into fort service earned him the title of Dictator among unhappy settlers, and his quartermaster, Lewis H. Smith, got him into further trouble. Hearing reports that Smith was serving rations of overly ripe beef to the company while reserving more

Company A, Northern Border Brigade, in a parade, 1911.

Fort Defiance, built in 1862–63, for housing Company A, Northern Border Brigade.

Fort Defiance Park entrance, dedicated May 24, 1936.

wholesome and tastier victuals for himself, Lieutenant Colonel James A. Sawyer drove to Estherville from Sioux City to investigate the complaints. Shabbily dressed in civilian garb and admitted to the fort so that he ostensibly could prepare a meal in an old skillet, the colonel carefully observed the company mess. His verdict was that complaints were justified. Revealing his rank, the colonel then dressed down the quartermaster and censured Captain Ingham as well. Admittedly, good provisions were scarce. Fortunately, there were no digestive casualties as a result of the quartermaster's faulty stewardship.[4]

Some of the tension at the fort and among the nervous settlers was relieved by First Lieutenant Edward McNight, who was as talented in quoting gems from Shakespeare as in handling a brigade musket. The settlement was not easily diverted from its apprehensions, although by the next year it was clear that the Indian menace had passed, and the company of militia was mustered out. Captain Ingham returned home to Algona with his family, which included his eldest son, five-year-old Harvey, who was to become the talented editor of the *Des Moines Register & Leader.*

After the Border Brigade abandoned the fort, it was used as a temporary residence for newcomers and for a time housed the *Vindicator.*[5] When the palisade and buildings were dismantled, the timbers were sold to those persons building new cabins and barns. The site a few years later became the concrete block and tile yard of L. L. Bingham.

Three months after the New Ulm massacre, thirty-eight Sioux Indians who had participated in the bloodletting were hung by the neck around the perimeter of a square, elevated stage erected in Mankato. The Sioux Indians blamed their behavior on the United States government, preoccupied by the Civil War. The government had neglected to pay for Indian lands and annuities promised them. Angry and hungry, the Sioux had retaliated with a vengeance that threw all southern Minnesota and northern Iowa into a state of shock.

After the New Ulm uprising, the Indians proved much less a hazard and concern to pioneer settlers than the unpredictable climate, prairie fires, and insects. When in April 1871 O. C. Bates couldn't think of a word forceful enough to describe a brutal snowstorm that lashed the open prairie and imperiled the settlement, he invented one. He described the seasonally late, blinding snowstorm as a "blizzard," giving meaning to the word from that day forward. In such a storm two years later, County Supervisor O. E. Prosser lost his life while driving a team of horses home from a board meeting. There were other fatalities among those who lost their way in blizzards. Many of the area's most ferocious storms occurred as late as April.

Editor Bates conceded that his newspaper might not be the best publication in the world but he claimed it was the best in the county—a statement he could prove. It was the only one. A supply of ink for his press was apparently less a problem, he found, than locating an easy source of dry wood to heat the printshop boiler. The editor wrote that he would gladly trade a subscription for wood. Although payment in greenbacks was preferred, Bates invited subscribers to trade hay, turkeys, melons, fish, game, vegetables — even baked goods — for the privilege of reading the *Vindicator*. Besides local news, the paper included ready-print "boiler plate" literature, such as the sayings of Josh Billings, instructional articles on the science of prairie farming, and even the texts of new laws enacted by the state legislature.

Although the hungry editors and printers were eager to swap subscriptions for whatever would keep them warm and fed, they laid a dark curse on "stingy readers" who borrowed copies of the paper from their neighbors. "Come right up like a man and subscribe," editor Bates demanded of his sponging readers. After all, the per-annum price of the worthy *Vindicator* was a mere two dollars. Bates also expressed disrespect for loathsome infidels who stopped their subscriptions simply because they disagreed with editorial sentiment. Such a practice has been an annoyance to outspoken editors and publishers throughout the history of dedicated journalism.

In explaining why he and his partners had named their journal the *Vindicator*, Bates told his several readers that the name referred to the recent Civil War, in vindication of the rights of the laboring and producing masses. There would be few "masses" in Estherville, even long after the publishing days of Northrop and Bates. The publishers reminded themselves and readers that the newspaper's economy was fragile. Trying to publish a newspaper "on the borders of civilization — remote from commerce centers and business thoroughfares" — was not easy, they said. Bates promised himself more toil and trial than reward or compensation. His prediction that scarce money, remoteness from supplies, and other hardships would augur days of thanklessness and unprofitability proved prophetic. Hardship abounded on every hand.

The pieing of type, as printers referred to scrambled messes, apparently had a long and exasperating history in the *Vindicator* shop, beginning with the paper's founders. But the struggling Bates was unwilling to shoulder all the blame for some of his shop's mishaps. "Those do-nothings who warm themselves at the editor's stove, read news items over his shoulder, and scatter type about the premises with their clumsy feet and elbows" were a trial. The loafers who soaked up precious printshop heat were obstacles to the production of readable prose. He had troubles enough without awkward louts spilling his type and bumping his elbows.

His troubles were many. Noting that others seemed to be able to travel the roads, poor as they admittedly were, the irritated Bates, short of paper, complained in print, "so why can't the stage get through?" Publication had to be interrupted for several weeks during the summer of '69 for lack of paper. That blasted stage. And it didn't make the Bateses' summer any sunnier when the *Humboldt Independent* unfeelingly told its readers that apparently the *Vindicator* had "given up the ghost." Such nonsense, stormed publisher Northrop, who boasted that subscriptions of his journal had become so popular, the need for print paper so great, and the distances from a source of supply so remote that the newspaper's popularity had led to a shortage problem. However, subscribers were free to decide for themselves whether the naked truth about interruption of publication was being embellished by the brave publishers, who conceded that there was no editorial bliss in trying to establish a paper "100 miles from a railroad—or anyplace." No-good loafers who soaked up printshop heat and pied the types, and stingy settlers who borrowed the paper, or stopped it, or didn't read it all, were annoying frustrations. The publishers said, "it costs a small fortune to pay the running expenses of the *Vindicator* for a year." Editors as well as sodbusters had problems.

Blizzards, Prairie Fires,
and Grasshoppers

MY father's parents and their daughter Nettie arrived in Emmet County two years after Northrop and Bates gave birth to the *Vindicator*. When Joseph and Christie (baptized as Kjesti) Lee arrived in 1870 with their infant girl in an ox-drawn wagon from Leeds, Wisconsin, it was too late in the season to build a log house. They fashioned a dugout and sod structure six miles south of Estherville in the side of a hill, sheltered by timber, near the east bank of the Des Moines River. In the same brutal year that a fourteen-year-old neighbor boy froze to death in a blizzard, the Lees spent the first winter in a new, crude home. They made it do until spring, when a log cabin could be started. Four years before, my grandfather had visited the county to survey the prospects of staking a claim.

During 1870 and 1871 a stream of Norwegian migrants from Wisconsin to Emmet County settled largely along the river in the native oak timber near the Lees and in woodlands around High Lake and what was then called Mud Lake, later named Ingham, in memory of the captain of the Northern Border Brigade. Danish families began homesteading a few miles farther east in Emmet's southeast township, which they appropriately named Denmark. A settlement at Armstrong Grove, straight east of Estherville near the county line, began developing as early as 1864.

The Lees were among a steady stream of immigrants who arrived in Emmet Couny during 1870 and 1871. Some of the newcomers came by the way of Emmetsburg, which, to the confusion of many persons, is not situated in Emmet County but is rather the county seat of Palo Alto, the first county south of Emmet. In explaining why settlers moved on north through Palo Alto County instead of settling there, the *Northern Vindicator* exulted that "Em-

Joseph and Christie Lee.

met has more dry land, and has twenty acres of timber where Palo
Alto has one." Settlers valued timber for fuel, for logs to build
cabins, and for shelter. The *Vindicator* further irritated Emmetsburg readers by adding that Emmet soil "is of better quality." Who
knows but what such odious comparisons may have set the stage for
a long-standing football rivalry that bloomed when that rough sport
came into vogue?

Teams of oxen drew prairie schooners to Emmet's thick black
soil. They came from the east, southeast, and south in growing
numbers during the early seventies. It cost only $70.75 to travel
from Christiana, Norway, to Fort Dodge, Iowa, according to a
newspaper statement attributed to Peter Larson. Inexpensive
transportation encouraged many immigrants to take potluck on the
prairie — to till its soil and seek prosperity.

When with my father I visited Tom Mahar's dwelling not long
before he died in 1915 at the age of ninety-four, Mahar was living in
the same cabin he had built forty years before, close to the shore of
Mud Lake. Wanting to be hospitable, he sent home some pieplant.
I was not favorably impressed with the comforts of Mr. Mahar's
quarters, probably typical of the dwellings in which all the early settlers made their homes. Tom's place was nothing novel to my

father, however, because he had been born and reared in just such a primitive cabin. Many of these early structures had been erected without benefit of a plumb bob. As a result, many of them leaned one way or another. The builders apparently just eyeballed their work. The luxury homes afforded floors of timber slabs axed as smooth as possible. Sod roofs were later supplanted by clapboards when sawed lumber became available. There were no bricks for building fireplaces; logs or sod plastered with clay sufficed.

House raisings were social occasions that climaxed the tedious work of notching logs, fitting them together, caulking the cracks, and roofing. A deerskin thong, the latchstring, took the place of unavailable hardware. The latchstring was withdrawn inside the cabin only at nightfall; the rest of the time it hung outside to welcome visitors. This was a practice of which marauding Indians sometimes took stealthy advantage. Crude benches and stools were common articles of furniture. Bedsteads were fastened in a corner, partially supported by the log wall. A straw or feather tick was a luxury.[1]

A fireplace provided the heat and was the stove to bake bread and prepare the meals. No family intentionally allowed the fire to go out, even in the heat of summer, when a bed of coals was kept outdoors for use when needed for cooking. There were no matches. A trestle-like table and a cupboard supported on one wall were provinces of the housewife. On another wall a rifle, bullet pouch, and a powder horn hung from pegs. The luxury of kerosene lamps was to come later and electric lights much later yet. A shallow dish of lard or other grease with a loosely twisted cotton rag in it for a wick provided illumination of a sort. More sophisticated and somewhat scarce were candles fashioned from a mold that was shared by the settlement—an improvement upon dishes of grease. But often an open fireplace provided the family's only lighting on winter evenings.

When settlers shared harvest work or the building of a cabin, women prepared joint meals and made such occasions festive social events that relieved lonesomeness. Footraces, horseshoe pitching, target shooting, and wrestling were common diversions when settlers gathered. Dances at which men and women in their homespun clothes responded to the fiddling of "Irish Washerwoman" or "Turkey in the Straw" were gala events. Husking bees, quiltings, spelling contests, and housewarmings were other excuses for social-

izing. A wedding or a "shivaree" was extra special. If the cider got
hard, perhaps the housewife fretted, but at least some male Norwegians did not lament. What rose to the top of the cider barrel was
a popular beverage when farmers celebrated. Manufactured goods
were expensive and remote; the settlers made do with what they had
and they did not mourn their shortages.[2]

Many Scandinavians, including my grandparents from Norway—my grandfather from Voss, and my grandmother from Bergen—stopped first in Chicago, and then in Wisconsin before ven-
turing to the raw prairie to become agriculturalists, livestock
raisers, and dairy farmers. The flow of wagon traffic slowed in 1872
and 1873, however, for many were ready to quit and seek more suitable homesteads elsewhere. Grasshoppers were devouring the crops.
The nation foundered on a financial panic. It was a savage winter,
and grasshoppers ate so much of the crops the following summer
that the board of supervisors reduced taxes.

Settlers in large numbers abandoned their homes and moved
on; they felt they could endure no more of Emmet's hostile environment. It was in this year of adversity that my father was born—
March 11, 1873. The family lived then in a cabin close to where Joseph and Christie first lodged three years earlier after they un-
packed their possessions and took shelter in a cavelike hut.

Christie and her husband found a measure of diversion in the
seclusion of their crude home when by 1871 they were able to borrow books from a lending library organized by the Progressive Society and Library Association. The Estherville doctor's wife, Mrs.
E. H. Ballard, the librarian, found a convenient location for the
books in the Haskins and Ballard drugstore. At first the library
books were few, but within ten years a twelve-volume Froude's History of England had been added. By a slender majority, the townspeople in 1897 voted a library levy, which supplied money for books
to stock the library. After subsequent moves, first to the S. E. Bemis
store, then to a Lincoln Street location, and then to a second-floor
location in the Coon block, the library finally found a permanent,
solidly built home in 1903, when W. P. Ward and E. E. Hartung
announced a $10,000 gift from a foundation funded by Andrew
Carnegie's steel empire. It still stands in the public square, bursting
with stacks upon stacks of books on crowded shelves.

Estherville Public Library.

Although Christie Lee enjoyed reading, particularly the weekly edition of the *New York Tribune,* she performed many household chores. Christie's mother, Grandma Grothe, made her place useful in the family cabin by knitting necessary items of warm clothing. Although she could communicate in English, Mrs. Grothe preferred her native tongue. When at a meeting of Lutheran Circle a neighbor and friend offered to lend her a Bible, Grandma Grothe politely declined. She explained that she preferred to read it in the original Norwegian.

The High Lake area, south and southeast of Estherville, attracted Petersons, Paulsons, Oshers, Olsons, Sandos, and Johnsons. Many Norwegian names resulted from baptizing the offspring as John's son, Paul's son, or Peter's son, written as Johnson, Paulson, and Peterson. The Danes used many similar names but they characteristically wrote the final vowel in their names as an "e" rather than an "o," as the Norwegians did. Those who migrated to Emmet County from the valleys of Hallingdal and Gudbrandsdal, and from

Bergen, Oslo, Stavanger, and other Norway localities, found ship passage as soul trying as it was economical. Sailing ships were painfully slow and uncomfortable.

When Gro Svendsen, a bride, finally reached America after a dreary voyage in 1862, she wrote her parents in Hallingdal of the trials she experienced.[3] Sailing down the fjord from Askarstrand, Norway, on April 22, the ship didn't land at Quebec until June 19, after storms, sickness, violent waves, and iceberg floes. By steamer, Ole and Gro Svendsen reached Hamilton, Ontario, June 27. They then rode by train through Detroit and Chicago, arriving at St. Ansgar, Iowa, July 7. Many Norwegian immigrants paused there before moving farther west.

The exhausting trip across the Atlantic in crowded quarters was boring, often nauseating, and at times frightening. It was no luxury cruise. The lure was promise of fertile land of rich glacial soil and economic opportunity, which Ole and Gro sought in a quarter-section of Emmet County land. "It's a fine piece of land," Gro Nilsdatter wrote her father, Nils Knudsen Gudmundsrud, in Hallingdal the year after they sailed and Ole had staked out their claim to prairie wealth. The Svendsens' experiences were typical of hundreds of other Norse settlers in the High Lake region and also of the Andreasons, Jensens, Christensens, Nielsens, Petersens, and other Danes who imported not only themselves but even a name for their village—Ringsted. They called the township Denmark.

Scandinavian immigrants found Emmet winters more severe, the snow deeper, the wind more violent, the thunder and lightning more terrifying, the dew wetter, and the countryside more desolate than their native lands. They thought their old-world clothing of wool much warmer than American-made garments, largely of cotton. Moreover, they choked easily on a strange language. The name of the Des Moines River, close to their homes, was often pronounced by the newcomers from Scandinavia as "DisMines" River. Such words as "slough," "Sioux," and "Dubuque" were also twisters. My father often amused me when I was a boy by telling of the Norwegian who reported that on a trip across the state his wagon "got stuck in the slutch, halfway between SI-ox City and DUB-kwee."

But Norsemen weren't the only ones who did violence to the language. Many persons misspelled the name of the county by adding a redundant second "t" to Emmet. Such error has persisted through the automobile, radio, airplane, television, computer, and space ages, despite early efforts on the parts of Northrop and Bates, who dealt sternly with this inexcusable blunder. Affixing an extra "t" in a name honoring "the illustrious patriot and noble martyr is too glaring to be longer tolerated," thundered Bates in print. "Therefore we have dropped this orthographical superfluity and request all who revere the memory of Emmet, or have any regard for their reputation as spellists to follow suit." Notwithstanding this caveat, some "spellists" have stumbled blissfully on in ignorance through a century of "orthographical superfluity."

Few if any settlers were financially well situated. However, they did not think themselves "poor." They simply made do with remarkably little actual cash. A wagon in 1864 cost $35, a plow sold for $26, a kitchen stove was worth $25, and a full-grown ox brought $120 to $130.[4] Farmers raised sorghum—which they used for sweetening—melons, turnips, and other vegetables. They produced potatoes, corn, wheat, oats, barley, sheep, pigs, calves, and colts. Sometimes there was wheat, corn, or barley to sell for cash—as far away as 100 miles, in Waseca, Minnesota—but when the grasshoppers laid the ground bare, as they did for five straight years, there might be only enough grain to mill into flour or cereal, and no more.

On occasion, the community's bounty of wildlife was more generous than the settlers could use, as in 1868 when so many red-wing blackbirds flew in for a visit there was no grain left in the fields to harvest after the little creatures had appeased their appetites. The blackbird invasion drove the price of flour up to $12 a hundred pounds.

After her arrival in Estherville, Gro Svendsen wrote home to Daddy Nils that prices were high. But she did not dream how much higher they would rise in the mass-production age, when farmers began driving powerful tractors, trucks, multi-row plows, planters, and combines. The Svendsens, Lees, Petersons, and Sandos paid high prices, and they received cheap prices for their produce, if there was any crop left to sell. But they fueled their horses and other power with pasture grass and oats—not precious petroleum from Saudi Arabia.

Prairie grass, rich in the nutrients on which cattle thrive, was a menace to settler life, limb, and property when it caught fire, as frequently happened. Fire was a hazard more feared than tomahawks. In 1872 the *Northern Vindicator* warned against the "prairie fire fiend," which the year before inflicted terrible losses, consuming $10,000 of farm property on twenty homesteads. "No one should kindle any unnecessary fire on the prairie; when one is started it should be backset or otherwise kept in due bounds," the newspaper warned. "Plow plenty of furrows around exposed buildings and stacks," the paper added.

In 1876, however, after five years of insect devastation, farmers cautiously set fire to their fields in an effort to destroy the grasshoppers, which every year laid eggs that produced the pests in devastating numbers again the next season. The effort was only partially successful, but the 1877 crop improved over the previous one, starting an era of less insect destruction. Settlers were annoyed by billions of hungry mosquitoes, but at least these insects didn't devour the crops.

Often it was the lot of the boys in a family to herd cattle over largely unfenced prairie lands rich in native grasses, succulent and nutritious. The boys took their cattle out to graze in the morning and returned only at dusk. Sometimes boys would merge their herds and then separate the cattle as they returned to their own yards. When he reminisced many years later, father would still mourn the "hundreds" of jackknives he said he lost while herding cattle on low grasslands across the river from the Lee homestead. But more than the exaggerated number of knives he claimed to have misplaced while whittling sticks as his family's cattle grazed, father lamented new-century devastation to the prairie he had tromped. Diesel shovels and bulldozers made huge, ugly spoilbanks of riverside pastures as they quarried rich glacial gravel deposits for use in surfacing roads and manufacturing concrete. The pits not only yielded salable sand and rock but must have provided a rich harvest of father's jackknives as well.

Each year prairie-fire danger diminished as settlers turned over the native soil on which elk and buffalo had once fed and used the land for grain crops. Although farmers continued to graze and milk cows, they gave increasing attention to agriculture. They started orchards and replanted woodlands destroyed by fire or taken for lumber and firewood. Once the native grasses had been plowed, it proved difficult to produce good pasture and meadow on the same soil, so as early as 1870 farmers began experimenting with the seed-ing of timothy. Yields of as much as two tons an acre were reported. By 1872 a "herd law" was proposed to make fencing mandatory, and Emmet farmers wondered whether they ought to support such legislation. Some viewed such an act as class legislation to protect established settlers by fencing their land and timber acres against use by the poor, but fences became the rule. By 1872 Emmet farmers were already beginning to think collectively. They organized the Emmet County Agricultural and Mechanical Society a year after the first annual county fair was held.[5]

In 1871 the *Northern Vindicator* estimated that between Jack Creek and the Des Moines River the county contained sixty square miles of good prairie ground, 3,000 acres of heavy timber, and the valuable asset of a chain of lakes in the High Lake area. Settlers knew that the area's richest assets were its deep, black soil—largely Webster and Clarion—and its timber. But the woods and lakes also yielded rewards to hunters, trappers, and fishermen. As Indians drove the buffalo west ahead of them, most big game disappeared from the area. But when the settlers arrived they found plentiful small game and fish. They tapped these resources as the Indians gradually abandoned them. John H. Jenkins and Charles H. Keith in two months of trapping in 1860 took 27 otters, 142 mink, 2 beavers, 5,318 muskrats, 51 wild geese, 1 swan, and 3 black-tipped cranes. Jenkins said this was not his biggest haul. The settlement staged a grand rabbit hunt in 1862. The following year an elk was found, trapped in swampland, and shot. In 1871 a hunter shot 26 wild geese. Hunters bagged an eagle and a blue crane in 1872, and they took prairie chickens by the hundreds and gave them away to those who wanted them. Hunters shot a crane in 1873 and in 1874 killed a wildcat near Estherville.

Although the *Vindicator* published no stock market quotations, it did keep trappers informed on what they could get for skins. Muskrats were worth 15¢ to 18¢; mink, $2; beavers, $3.50; and otters, $5 to $7. As late as 1886 an otter weighing forty pounds was trapped by Richard Dundas. During the scarce-money days of 1868 and 1869 some of the settlers raised their only cash from pelts. Trappers said that they could trace a well-worn otter trail from Emmet Grove east to a chain of sloughs and small lakes and south to Swan and High lakes.

Fishermen caught pike, pickerel, bass, perch, and catfish in huge numbers, particularly in the Okoboji lakes and in Spirit Lake. In 1868 the *Vindicator* said that "one man with an ordinary pitchfork can secure a wagon-load of fish within a few hours." In 1870 Peter Larson caught a wagonful of fish at Okoboji. In addition to Okoboji, Spirit, and High lakes, fish were caught plentifully in the west branch of the Des Moines River running through Estherville, the east fork of the Des Moines through Armstrong, and in some of the creeks.

But by the time father and I — during my teen years — were dipping our lines in the Des Moines River in search of walleyed pike and blue-channel catfish and rowing our hands sore probing the rushes and rock piles of Angler's Bay at Spirit Lake, we were grateful for modest catches. We had to employ more subtle lure than a pitchfork. Despite our fancy tackle and carefully selected bait, we were often "skunked," as my maternal grandfather described failure. Mother had to find substitute protein for the fish we planned to catch and she planned to fry.

A law passed by the state legislature in May 1872 forbidding seining and netting, but with no mention of banning pitchforks, was long in coming. Conservation measures to protect game came too late to prevent extinction of prairie chickens, carrier pigeons — once so numerous that flocks of them hid the sun — and certain species of waterfowl. Game disappeared. Overfishing and pollution thinned out the fish.

One of the last Indian visits to the High Lake timber, in October 1874, triggered a brief panic — twelve years after the New Ulm massacre. A boy discovered a group of Winnebagos three miles from his home and became frightened. Not having seen any Indians before and assuming that all Indians were dangerous savages, he spread an alarm that led an experienced Indian fighter, Orson Rice, to organize a spontaneous group of brave volunteers to prevent a massacre. There was no violence. The Winnebagos were both friendly and harmless. The vigilantes were embarrassed.

A few years later my father, then a young boy, observed two Indians, Chief Moon Eye and his squaw, coming up a hill from the river toward the Lee cabin. The chief drove a rickety buggy drawn by a white Indian pony as his squaw trudged up the hill afoot. Father said that Indians often traded baskets they had woven for food, some of which they disliked but seldom refused. Settlers often found butter, too salty for Indian palates, plastered on trees. Many Indians relished muskrat dishes.

Winnebagos who continued for several years to make occasional visits to the High Lake woods were without guile. But some of the whites who stalked the region lacked neither cunning nor deceit. Fear and hardships that caused settlers to become discouraged and leave the prairie, sometimes for only a breathing spell, provided opportunities to swindlers. They moved in to jump the claims of honest but harried homesteaders. Most homesteaders had arrived in the county with little more money than enough to cover fees of the Homestead Act. To remain on the land, erect a cabin, and support life with food, shelter, and clothing made it difficult for settlers to comply with requirements of the act to establish title. Pirates, as the settlers called claim jumpers, lurked in the brush to seize land they construed as abandoned. Such sharks incited the contempt of the *Vindicator,* which characterized land pirates as possessing the instinct but not the manliness of highway robbers.

What encouraged the "lot of shiftless, sharklike robbers prowling the county" to seize settlers' claims was the increasing value of prairie land as settlers tilled the soil. As many as 200 claims were jumped in one season in Jackson County, Minnesota, just north of Emmet. Farmers also needed to be wary of land offices ready to swindle them in one way or another. Editor Bates referred to the crooks as "a stench in the nostrils of all honest men."

Distraught settlers sought comfort from adversities of weather, sickness, swindlers, and swarms of locusts (as Gro Svendsen described the grasshoppers) that descended on the fields and farmyards like blinding snowstorms. They found a measure of this solace in the visits of preachers, who revived their faith. Christmas of 1872 was an occasion for special rejoicing by the numerous settlers of Lutheran persuasion. The Reverend H. H. Hande came from Norway in answer to a request of Estherville Lutherans for a pastor. He preached on December 25, 1872, at the Estherville Lutheran Church. As early as 1861 the Reverend C. L. Clausen of St. Ansgar had preached a Lutheran service, the first in the county. Other such visits followed.

Preachers of various faiths came after the Methodists, Free Baptists, and Lutherans to take up residence. The religious selection expanded during the ensuing decade to include Presbyterian,

Christian, Baptist, Episcopal, Christian Science, and Catholic faiths. Representation of such churches as the Free Methodist, Calvary Gospel, Fellowship Tabernacle, Church of the Nazarene, Church of the Bible, and Jehovah's Witnesses came in the new century to provide the community with an unusually high ratio of church to population. Regardless of the availability of spiritual guidance, however, the settlement managed to diversify in sin and vice.

The Reverend W. W. Mallory frequently gave wickedness and the devil a wallop from the pulpit in a one-room building that served the causes of learning, justice, and theology. "It is no more possible," the pastor assured his congregation, "for a sinner to enter the kingdom of heaven than for a shad to climb a greased pole, tail foremost, with a loaf of bread in its mouth." The Reverend Mallory, who was the first regular Methodist preacher in Estherville, received reinforcement from the Reverend Peter Baker in a religious revival meeting they thought the settlement needed for spiritual regeneration. Since both preachers shared a taste for chewing tobacco, the Reverend Baker made a supreme sacrifice when he drew a plug of tobacco from his pocket and deposited it on the altar, explaining, "I hereafter consecrate my tobacco to the Lord." The Reverend Mallory, as quick-witted and resourceful as he was devout, promptly rose from his seat, proceeded to the altar, pocketed the tasty plug, and announced, "As a servant of the Lord I will take care of it." At least that is how a *Vindicator* editor, A. B. Funk, remembered the incident many years later.

Preachers received vigorous support for combating intemperance from a group of women. They mobilized to take a firm position against infringement of the law regulating the dispensing of booze. Twenty-five women of the town's 300 population became the precursors of Carry Nation as they burst upon Estherville's two saloons February 16, 1872. Startled customers looked on in anguish while the ladies of temperance poured whiskey on the floor and dumped spirits outside in the gutter. The ladies smashed tumblers, decanters, and bottles, and split kegs, leaving a scene of desolation and ruin. They spilled 200 gallons of refreshments.

A disgusted editor of the Jackson *Pilot* referred to the raiders as Amazonian shrews. The Emmetsburg *Democrat,* of predominantly Irish Palo Alto County, viewed the raid as an attack on Irish settlers, known to have a particular taste for whiskey. But the *Northern Vindicator* approved what the reformers did, labeling their brother newspaper critics "champions of whiskey, harlots, obscenity, falsehood, crime, and every wickedness known to the devil's catalogue." This indictment, however, may have included more sin than the temperance ladies had in mind to eradicate.

The *Vindicator* managed to survive its broad denunciation of wet sympathizers despite the resentment it stirred up among some subscribers. Twenty-five angry patrons of the paper reportedly stopped their subscriptions. But Frank Day, who was by then editor of the newspaper, branded this an exaggeration of the truth. Only four subscribers terminated, he said. Supporters of sobriety quickly rounded up seventeen paid new readers among upstanding residents to replace those discontented patrons of booze who quit the paper.

The following week the sheriff decided on a stand for law and order and uncovered another fifty gallons of liquor the ladies had missed. Newspaper pen-and-ink artists as far away as New York employed their imaginations to depict the exciting scene of Amazonian shrews expressing righteous agitation over deportment in the settlement's saloon. A few years later Estherville voters dried up the town watering places, and the booze trade went underground.

An Invasion
from Outer Space

ALTHOUGH the Emmet Grove settlement was little more than a camp, it produced a first-rate murder mystery in 1858.[1] Two trappers, one by the name of Dodson, and another known as "Dutch Charley," came from Mankato during the winter of '57 to trap. Later they were joined by a young Englishman by the name of Metricott, supposed by some guessers to have a substantial independent income. When Dodson established himself at a camp down the river beyond Estherville, Metricott loaded a canoe with supplies and headed down the Des Moines River for the Dodson camp. He was observed in Estherville as he paddled past the village, but that was the last anybody saw of him until several weeks later when A. H. Ridley, Adolphus Jenkins, and another Estherville companion discovered Metricott's body on a knoll two miles south of Estherville. His canoe had been discreetly hidden nearby. An inquest yielded mostly mystery and supposition. "Dutch Charley" was a prime suspect in Metricott's murder but there was stronger suspicion that a band of Sioux Indians was responsible. Four years later, when the Sioux went on their rampage in 1862, the Indians murdered "Dutch Charley." As for Dodson, he survived the inquest and the Indians. He lived to become active as a scout in the Civil War, in which he was a casualty.

When George C. Granger was appointed postmaster of the little Emmet Grove settlement begun in 1856, there was a mail route from Mankato, Minnesota, through Jackson to Emmet and on to Spirit Lake, Peterson, Cherokee, Melbourne, and Sioux City. Hopefully, mail arrived once every two weeks. When Granger decided to give up the duties of postmaster, which must have been modest, Henry Jenkins took his place. He served until the Emmet Grove office was abandoned, somewhat before a post office was established in 1860 at Estherville. Adolphus Jenkins was post-master.

Neither the post office at Emmet Grove nor the one later in Estherville did a flourishing business during the early years, but by 1873 postal communication had picked up. The newspaper boasted that on one certain Wednesday 125 letters were mailed to Algona. That made it, the paper insisted, a fourth-class office.

Just a few years before, it was not fourth-class or anything approaching it. Lewis Paulson would long remember the miserable journey he made as postman in February 1861 when during a raging blizzard it took him five days to make the forty-five mile trip from Estherville to Algona. The public rewarded him with a $9 contribution for the trip he made on snowshoes. At one point he was temporarily blinded by the snow, lost his way, and wandered in virtually a circle for one whole night. He didn't stop to rest for fear of freezing to death. Stumbling accidentally near a cabin when he thought he heard someone calling hogs, he found hospitality that saved his life.

Travel and settlement living were not luxurious even during the seventies, but the trails were becoming more familiar and the homesteads closer together. By the seventies there were such diversions as baseball games played by the Northern Blizzards against nearby teams. By 1873 enough musicians had been found in the community to form a brass band.

As for industry, the community offered only bare essentials. Eleven years after the settlement began, R. E. Ridley built a dam across the Des Moines River and set up a gristmill that ground grain from the farms of a seven-county area. The mill was situated on the west side of the stream, across from where the town later built its electric power plant. A second flour mill to provide settlers with ingredients for baking the staff of life, pancakes, and other items of the simple diet on which prairie and small-town life subsisted was built somewhat later by Adolphus Jenkins, B. F. Jenkins, and J. A. Hagadorn.

A sawmill built soon after the Ridleys and their companions arrived on the Estherville site served the settlers building cabins. Products became available to builders also from a clay brick and tile factory started in 1871 that operated until 1900. Discovery of coal in 1870 led to a dead end, however, as quality of the fuel

Gristmill shown during the highest floodwater. The
mill was owned by Mr. Ammon.

proved disappointing, especially to the group that subsidized the
venture with capital of $100,000.

Publishing a newspaper also proved discouraging, just as Bates
and Northrop had predicted when they opened shop in 1868. The
seventies witnessed a succession of hopeful journalists trying to live
by their wits. Northrop relinquished his type stick to Frank Day
after only a year of suffering. Bates stayed on two more years, when
the masthead became Frank A. Day and H. G. Day. They were
replaced by Henry Jenkins and Charles W. Jarvis, followed in '76 by
Frank Davey. In eight years the editors and publishers had come
and gone with amazing frequency. My own tenure of forty-one
years, much later, appears something of an eternity by comparison.
I was either more stubborn or more durable.

Newspaper advertising had not yet appealed to the imagination of Estherville merchants in the seventies — or for that matter

until considerably later. But entrepreneurs of the big cities recommended their wares in generous use of *Vindicator* white space. Metropolitan advertisers recommended Estey organs, Bradbury and Story & Camp pianos, Wilson sewing machines, Dr. E. B. Foote's services in New York for cure of various chronic disorders, and Dr. Walker's Vinegar Bitters.

Dr. Ballard, one of the town's most energetic and useful personalities, was more aggressive than most other local ad users. He advertised that paint, tobacco, stationery, medicines, and drugs were available on his premises. An 1875 issue of the *Vindicator* published a notice by the Emmet board of supervisors that offered a $50 reward for apprehension and conviction of anyone setting a prairie fire in the county. James Maher advertised groceries and cigars. E. S. Wells reminded readers of his livery stable services, and W. H. Davis offered to repair worn boots and shoes.

The decade that brought a stream of settlers to the county beginning in 1870 was one of hardship on the prairie. Farmers were buffeted by blizzards and saw their crops eaten by the locusts. They harvested little surplus grain that they could sell and convert to cash. They suffered as well from the nation's financial panic. They feared Sioux Indian depredations, and finally, before the decade ended, were scared out of their wits by an intrusion from space. They may have wondered if someone was trying to tell them something.

As farmers struggled for survival on the prairie, town dwellers found life less traumatic, although the residents suffered some interruptions to peaceful socializing such as when the Ladies of Temperance spilled saloon whiskey in the gutter and gave rude notice that laws were meant to be obeyed. And the town was aware of a significant shortcoming; there were not enough women to go round. Many of the settlers had not brought wives or girl friends with them. "Young unmarried ladies are as scarce in Estherville as they are abundant in Massachusetts," complained the *Vindicator*. Worst of all, "There are not enough [ladies] to organize a quilting or a cotillion party, or to go home from church with the young men," the editor wrote November 11, 1871.

But during the decade the town did do something about a problem that was to trouble it for a long time to come—destructive fires. A group of public-spirited men in 1870 organized a bucket

Dr. E. H. Ballard,
first doctor and first
mayor.

brigade, which later sported a hose cart and even a hand pumper that forced water from a well in the public square to quench unwelcome blazes. Within a year the enterprising brigade added a hand-pulled chemical wagon and three more hose carts. It was a banner day when a horse-drawn hook and ladder truck was purchased. The first volunteer to arrive at the scene of a fire when the village whistle blew received the handsome reward of a dollar bill. And dollar bills were scarce. Draymen of the fire department hustled from the fire station at "top speed," whatever tempo that was. It was surely more deliberate than when the town became sufficiently affluent to support a motorized, bright red, chain-driven Wilcox truck in 1913.

Ed Sillge's brother, Oscar, who was a harness maker and who crafted descriptive prose to fit his mood when moved to irritation, took a leading role in fighting fires during the department's early days. I remember him very well, but by that time Oscar, A. O. Peterson, and other veteran fire fighters were past their prime. Oscar, however, who was unlike his soft-spoken printer brother, had in his late years lost little of his mastery in the art of colorful profanity that erupted whenever a customer complained about the high cost of outfitting a horse in suitable raiment.

Although the seventies in Estherville brought no great

sophistication in the quality of life, some improvements came along. Wooden sidewalks were better than no walks at all. When the last of these booby traps were disappearing during my youth, about 30 years later, they were a formidable hazard. Rotted boards and those loose at one end produced annoying casualties to the limbs of unwary pedestrians who didn't know the territory.

Log houses were supplanted by better-looking, more spacious, and more comfortable frame structures. Hitching posts arranged conveniently around the square were the precursors of parking meters. Corner horse fountains preceded gasoline filling stations. Social life became gayer; dancing to fiddle music was more relaxed than when Sioux Indians were thought to be lurking nearby. Frame store buildings afforded wooden walks in front of them, shielded with wooden canopies that protected customers from rain, snow, and sun. Items of hardware, a selection of fabrics, and other goods began to appear on store shelves to enhance the quality of life. However, nature was about to spring a spectacular surprise.

Father was six years old when he and his family on their farm in High Lake Township were frightened by a dismaying meteoritic disturbance. What mystified and terrorized them proved to be one of the most significant meteorite falls on record. Farmers and Estherville townspeople on a clear Saturday afternoon May 10, 1879, heard a screeching roar that approached from the southwest toward the northeast, accompanied by several deafening detonations that terminated in a resounding crash. A quarter of a ton of dense ore plummeted to earth a mile north of Estherville.

Terrified women drew their children close to them on that May afternoon in 1879. The Blizzards interrupted their baseball game at Estherville when the meteorite streaked through the sky. Mrs. George Allen, driving across the prairie a few miles west of Estherville, watched the visitor from outer space pass directly above her buggy and she observed it breaking into fragments. Mrs. Sever Lee saw dirt fly in the slough on the Lees' farm when the largest segment of the meteorite slammed to earth. S. W. Brown, who farmed north of the Sever H. Lees, saw the exploding rocket as it fell to earth.[2]

Hundreds of others who did not actually see the meteorite were awed by thunderous rumbles, punctuated by detonation. Eyewitnesses described a long trail of whitish smoke that reminded them of the exhaust from the smokestack of a steam locomotive as the projectile descended earthward. S. W. Brown described what he saw as a red streak, emitting smoke as though fired from a cannon. Each of the three separate main fragments of the ore body radiated ribbons of smoke that hung glistening in the bright sunshine, tracing in the sky the outline of a gigantic crow's foot. Others described the occurrence as "brilliantly white, like the light of the sun, dazzling in appearance, sputtering like iron heated white-hot in a forge." Reports of those who viewed the phenomenon came from as far as 100 miles. Three generations later vapor trails from the exhausts of jet aircraft would fascinate viewers but not awe them; only supersonic jets would startle the inhabitants.

Those who did not see the meteorite traveling in its path at three miles a second but who heard the commotion were particularly frightened because it was a mystery why there should be "thunder" and explosions on a cloudless day. The end of the world, maybe. Doors and windows rattled. Dishes shook in the cupboards. Window lights shattered. The earth itself trembled. Housewives who had not noticed that the sky was clear hastened to drop their chores with pots and kettles to close windows and doors against rain from a threatening thunderstorm. Farmers looked up, unknowing, and stopped their plowing. A heated rhubarb in the Blizzards' baseball game came to an abrupt halt. Domestic animals, chickens, and dogs behaved strangely. A boy herding his father's cattle looked up to see a shower of stones falling out of the sky that stampeded his cattle in four directions. Concussion of the fall was felt fifty miles away, while the shrill tornadolike roar and the noise of the hissing and bursting fragments carried a much shorter distance.

Several youths of the neighborhood rushed to explore a funnel-shaped hole 10 or 12 feet in diameter on the Sever Lee farm, several miles north and west of the unrelated Lees, my grandparents. Slough water and mud covered the bottom of the hole below which the mysterious projectile from outer space was buried. Outside the pit lay great chunks of earth and mud that had been excavated by force of the ore body. Splintered fragments of metallic stones were scattered about, as far as 100 yards. Laboring all the next day, Sunday, eight young men—Sam, Bob, and Jim Weir; George and Charlie Barber; Elmer Crumb; Elmer Barrett; and Chester Rewey—made little progress. They decided to mechanize their task by using a well-water digging outfit. Then they found the need for a block, tackle, and a windlass.

By Monday night they had recovered a piece of ore about a foot square that weighed 32 pounds. The next day's dig uncovered the main body of the meteorite. It measured 27 inches by 22¾ inches by 15 inches, weighed 431 pounds, and the edges were jagged, according to Ben Hur Wilson, writing years later in the Iowa *Palimpsest*. The meteorite had buried itself 14 feet into the ground. A second fragment of the object from outer space was found a few days after it fell on the Amos A. Pingrey farm north of Estherville close by the Des Moines River. The piece on the Pingrey farm weighed 151 pounds and was buried 4 feet in the ground. A third segment weighing 92½ pounds that had split off in flight was not discovered until February 23, 1880, more than nine months after the fall. It was found in an unidentified slough by the Pietz brothers while trapping. Probing a rat spear into a hole, the trappers struck a hard surface that proved to be a piece of the meteorite, buried 5 feet in the edge of a marshy area. Smaller fragments were found nearby.

Bits of meteorite soon became popular keepsakes and favorite material for rings, stickpins, and various ornaments fashioned by the blacksmith. When a large portion of the meteorite was displayed on a packing box in front of the Emmet House hotel, it attracted so much notice and interest that the youths who had excavated it decided to seek a fortune, à la Phineas T. Barnum, by exhibiting the strange intrusion from the sky to those curious enough for a peek at the object to risk the price of a look. Protecting their treasure in a strongbox, the young men loaded it on a wagon and started across southern Minnesota to earn a fortune. A sign on the wagon told what it held.

"I am the Heavenly Meteor/I arrived May 10 at 5 o'clock/My weight is 431 lbs./From whence I came nobody knows/But I am en route for Chicago." But the boys never got there. Warned that they might not have clear and legal title to their heaven-sent treasure, the young men decided that while contemplating their rights, or lack of them, it would be discreet to hide their find. Wrapping it in an old quilt, Chester Rewey and his pals buried their piece of sky in George Osborn's cornfield, marking the spot with stakes, as they

supposed pirates did. There the hunk of meteorite lay incognito all
summer, shielded by Osborn's growing stalks of corn.

Rewey and his companions ultimately sold their piece of
meteorite to Charles Birge of Keokuk, a lawyer, who had obtained
the segment found by the Pietz brothers and previously disposed of
to Dr. E. H. Ballard and George Allen. Birge also accumulated
about 100 pounds of smaller pieces picked up off the prairie. Finally he acquired title to the large sought-after specimen of iron,
nickel, phosphorus, sulphur, and other elements. Contending that
Sever Lee was behind on payments for the land he had acquired
from him on contract, Birge insisted that Lee had forfeited his right
to title. Birge's claim on the meteorite was sustained by the district
court. Lee later gained title to the farm but sans meteorite.

Pieces of the outer-space curiosity, identified as mesosiderita
(ironstone), brought as much as 75¢ an ounce to the finders. The
total mass of the meteorite was estimated at 744 pounds, largest of
all falls recorded in Iowa. It was estimated that as many as 5,000
bits, some as small as a pea, were found in the countryside. Amos
Pingrey, a pioneer schoolteacher, gave the chunk that fell on his
farm to a neighbor, John Horner. Pingrey later regretted doing so
and brought suit, unsuccessfully, to recover it. Before disposing of
the segment he received from Pingrey, Horner concealed it in a
cave on Ab. Ridley's farm. Horner later sold the piece of meteorite
to Dr. E. J. Thompson, professor at the University of Minnesota,
who had been instructed by Gov. John S. Pillsbury to acquire as
much of the meteorite as possible. Reportedly, Thompson carried
the governor's blank check to make the purchase.

Although a slice of the meteorite is on display at the Estherville
Public Library, the largest piece went to the British Museum of
Natural History, London, where I viewed it with understandable
interest in the summer of 1964. After purchasing the meteorite
chunk from Charles Birge for a reputedly worthwhile sum, the
museum sawed the stone into three sections. Two smaller pieces
went to the Musée National d'Histoire Naturelle in Paris and the
Naturhistorisches Museum in Vienna. Pieces of meteorite are ex-
hibited in the Field Museum, Chicago; the United States National
Museum, Washington, D.C.; the American Museum of Natural
History, New York; the Peabody Museums at Harvard and Yale;
and a meteorite collection at Amherst. The only Iowa display is the

one in the Estherville library, less than two miles from where the meteorite struck the ground. Small fragments and ornaments fashioned from them have largely disappeared. In 1929 the Okamanpado chapter of the Daughters of the American Revolution identified the spot where the meteorite fell by placing a slab of native stone with a bronze plate on a road west of where the fall took place. It was subsequently relocated east, along Highway 4.

Late in 1858 the inhabitants had become restive over not having an independent county government. Acting upon approval of their separation by the Webster District Court, they called for the first election February 7, 1859. One of the first acts of the county board of supervisors after Emmet was formally organized in 1859 as a county separate from its attachment to Webster was to arrange for both a schoolhouse and a courthouse.[3] The board of supervisors contracted with Logan and Meservey of Fort Dodge to build the schoolhouse, where Mary Howe presided, and also a courthouse— which was never built. That is why the schoolhouse put up by Davis and Spinney on the contract made by Logan and Meservey had to double as a hall of justice as well as a school. And therein lies a tale of skulduggery.

The county government expected to pay for both the schoolhouse and the courthouse by trading to the contractors swamp and overflow acres in three sections of land presumably owned by the county. This procedure of swapping land for new buildings was common in other counties, but the Emmet plan backfired. Although under the acts of Congress swamps were county property, the surveyor general rejected a survey of the land made by C. C. Carpenter, who had been appointed by County Judge Adolphus Jenkins. As a result of the rejected survey, Emmet County had no title to the land it had agreed to use as payment for the schoolhouse and for a courthouse.

But the schoolhouse by this time in the proceedings had already been built. Work had started on the courthouse but the contractors simply ordered the carpenters to pack their hammers and saws and be on their way. However, the problem of how to get paid for a schoolhouse by a county that had no money or swamplands to swap called for a resourcefulness of which Logan and Meservey proved capable.[4]

Invalid though the deeds were, the contractors nevertheless used instruments based on the Carpenter survey as a basis of giving title to parcels of land that they sold through land agencies in eastern states to purchasers who would in time discover they had been defrauded. When they arrived in Emmet County to take possession of their purchased property, purchasers found they could obtain it only by securing government title under the Homestead Act. The county's swampland transaction stigmatized the area for some time and gave Emmet a shabby reputation of fraudulent real estate transactions.

When Mary Howe started teaching the first Estherville school in 1859 — two years after the settlement began — she held class in a log house owned by E. A. Ridley. The next year classes met in the structure built by Logan and Meservey in the public square. Carpenters finished the school in time for a nutritious housewarming on Christmas Eve, 1860, when village women cooked a free supper to celebrate the prospects of education and enlightenment — swampland difficulties notwithstanding.

When Mary Howe's desk wasn't in classroom use, it served as a pulpit, a lectern, or a bench of justice. The schoolhouse was a classroom, community building, church, courthouse, lecture hall, political forum, and social hall — all in one modest edifice that stood in the square, until it was moved across the street in 1876. There it went the way of numerous other town structures — a victim of fire.

In 1871 the county arranged for D. W. Lane to build a suitable schoolhouse two blocks south, at Fifth and Howard streets. This was described as "a noble structure" by local journalists. The new seat of learning was thirty-four feet wide, fifty feet long, and twenty-nine feet high. Two stories, no less, it was capped by a fourteen-by-fourteen-foot tower for a bell to remind youngsters when it was time to shape up and fold their hands at their desks. Professor J. W. Cory was the principal. The teachers were Edna Barker, Minnie Belle (Neville) Lough, Grace Agnes (Bemis) Brown, and Orlando Lough. The *Vindicator* boasted that the new building was the finest school structure north of Fort Dodge, but that statement probably was not meant to include Minneapolis and St. Paul. Two years later the county found it necessary to purchase still another building in which to educate the Estherville young. Mary Jenkins was in charge.

In the Lane building, pride of the town, the arts flourished. A. P. Wilkins of Emmetsburg established a singing school and Minnie Howe undertook to teach youngsters five to nine years of age to read and write. Although education was the primary purpose of the elegant school building, the structure's spacious classroom and lecture hall invited assorted uses. The Reverend Hallward Hande, for example, taught singing there to a class of Norwegians.

The burden of early schooling was on learning the three R's. Visual and audio aids were unknown to nineteenth century schools in Estherville. If Mary Howe and her contemporaries had decided to make Iowa history a subject of study, as chauvinistic legislators later required, the subject could not have absorbed many hours. There wasn't much of it to learn.

It was June 17, 1673, when Joliet and Marquette viewed Iowa along the west bank of the Mississippi for the first time. William Des Lisle, who mapped the state in 1718, noticed an Indian village on Lake Okoboji, the scene 139 years later of a massacre. First a possession of Spain and then of France until 1804, Iowa didn't become a separate territory until July 4, 1838. The state took its name from the "Iowa" or "Ioway" Indians. Iowa was admitted as the nation's first free state in the Louisiana Purchase on December 28, 1846. Although a fort was erected at Fort Madison in 1808, there was no permanent Iowa settlement until June 1, 1833 — about twenty-three years before whites began settling Emmet County.[5]

By 1876 Esthervilleans and their customers enjoyed access to library books, weekly news in print, a mill to grind their grain, a mill to saw their timber, bricks from a local kiln, shelves of merchandise, a harness maker to serve them, and a moneylender to round out the essentials of prairie civilization. Howard Graves, a native of New York State, obliged the settlement by establishing a private bank that remained a privately owned institution until 1886, when it was incorporated as the Estherville State Bank, with Mr. Graves as president. His death in 1913 spared him the pain of knowing what would befall the bank when a wave of speculation, falling grain prices, and loose banking practices toppled the institution ten years after his death.

Although not as spectacular as the pyrotechnics of the meteorite that fell in '79, another event that same year shook the town of Estherville more resoundingly than a chunk of ore descending from outer space. The town lost its designation as county seat — no small matter. Not only was this event consequential economically and as a matter of convenience to merchants and other business interests, it was an affront. This loss of face and prestige resulted because the school building that doubled as community center and courthouse had burned down three years before — in 1876. Compounding the problem was the rejection of a survey to authorize sale by the county of swamplands depended on to finance the building of a new courthouse when a school was built in 1871. But the plot that deprived Estherville of the county seat had been hatched long before the fire of '76.

Because Estherville is close to the west border of the county, many of those residing farther east thought a more central location would be preferable. Such sentiments were popular even before the county commissioners contracted for facilities in 1871. But once construction of the schoolhouse began, the movement to relocate the county government subsided. When the school-courthouse went up in flames in 1876, however, agitation for a move eastward was enthusiastically renewed. A petition to the board of supervisors on July 7, 1879, asked for an election to submit the proposition of county-seat relocation.[6] When three weeks later the supervisors met to weigh the proposition, they faced a 165-name petition favoring a change and a remonstrance signed by 151 objectors. That was the count after removal of the names of 14 persons who were either so confused or so undecided they signed both petitions.

On the motion of J. H. Warren, supported by Matthew Richmond, A. Christopher, and Henry Barber, the board voted to hold an election. A dissenting vote was cast by Jesse Coverdale, whose identity with the founding of Estherville impelled him to vote loyally in favor of Esther's town. But his cause lost the election, held October 14, when a majority voted to locate the county seat north of Swan Lake in a village by the same name.

At its zenith, Swan Lake included two saloons, a Presbyterian Church, livery stable, hotel, print shop, post office, schoolhouse, a building used as a courthouse, blacksmith shop, merchandise store, bank, drugstore, a number of houses, and a cemetery. Andreas's map of 1875 showed a proposed railroad routed from the southeast to the northwest through Swan Lake. It never developed into actual ties and rails, but the proposal contributed to the brief existence of Swan Lake as the county seat and as a town.

There was scant joy among the county's officers when six days after the election the supervisors ordered officers to move themselves, their possessions, and their records close to the shore of a shallow lake. This pastoral setting made Estherville seem metropolitan. In the language of a farmland realtor, the county board described the new county seat location as "the northwest quarter of section 25, township 99, range 33 west of the 5th principal meridian." The board made it clear where the officers could

Emmet County, as depicted in A. T. Andreas's "Illustrated Historical Atlas of the State of Iowa," 1875.

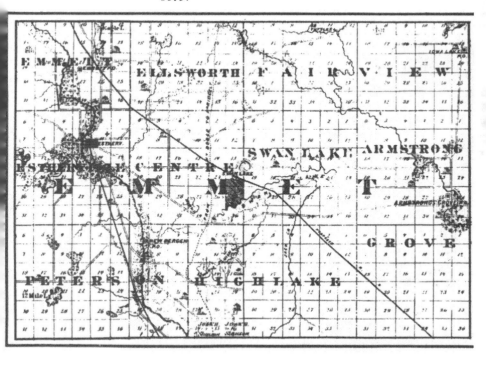

find Swan Lake and told them to show up there within six days. But nothing happened.

On October 25 the board ordered the county auditor to issue the sheriff a copy of its order and serve notice on the foot-draggers — just in case they had forgotten or had misplaced the first order. Even a writ of mandamus sought by Supervisors Warren and Christopher and signed by Judge E. R. Duffie in district court at Emmetsburg failed to budge the reluctant officers. When on January 9 the board ordered action "at once," all the officers obeyed except the independent-thinking county treasurer, Dr. E. H. Ballard, who defiantly remained in Estherville until the expiration of his term of office.

A case filed in Cerro Gordo County District Court, testing legality of the vote that put the county seat in Swan Lake, was still pending in 1882, when a movement was begun to reverse the transfer by holding a new public election. Just three days before Estherville became a rail point, attorneys Soper and Allen, in behalf of R. E. Ridley and others, presented a petition to the county board signed by 276 voters asking resubmission of the relocation question at the next general election.

The building of a railroad line into Estherville infused Estherville with new confidence and influenced the outcome of the squabbling over where the county seat ought to be situated. At the general election in November 1882, the tide turned 348 to 177 in favor of a return to Estherville. But the minority alleged that workmen employed in building the Burlington, Cedar Rapids & Northern railroad had cast unqualified votes in the election. Upon canvassing the votes, however, the board declared the result correct, as reported. By January 15 the county had reseated itself where Doc Ballard had held his ground all along. But it would be almost another three years before a suitable courthouse was provided.

The board chose Foster & Liebe as architects to plan a suitable structure to house the superintendent of schools, sheriff, auditor, clerk, recorder, treasurer, records, a courtroom, a heating plant, and a space in which to lock up the criminally inclined. The quaint building, which was completed and accepted November 22, 1884, stood in the center of a public two-block square donated to the city of Estherville by the Ridleys. By resolution, the city council permit-

Courthouse and Square, about 1890, before library was built.

ted the county to share space in the park for its New England flavored courthouse, which did service until 1958. It was then replaced by a building that cost twenty-nine times more than the one constructed by the Zerbe brothers.

To make sure of a sound foundation, F. E. Allen, Charles Jarvis, and Adolphus Jenkins—the board's building committee—appointed B. Lardig to oversee the stonework. A cupola on the building became a favored nesting roost for pigeons, which were annually thinned out by the sheriff's artillery. This pigeon haven also proved to be useful in A. A. Halleck's perennial efforts to make panoramic photographs of buildings surrounding the square. These mementos of early Estherville were snapped before trees in the park were tall enough to obstruct the view of clapboard store buildings, horse fountains, and hitching posts.

Mr. Lardig's stonework gave stubborn resistance to bulldozers seventy-four years later when sentimentalists lost their cause in behalf of preserving the cute little courthouse as an antique relic. Zerbe Brothers, the low bidders, built the courthouse for $11,718. The board thus discomfited second-guessers who predicted the county would be $600 short in trying to provide a building with the 6 percent $12,000 bond issue voted by the electors. The county officers, finally provided with a courthouse, moved into the new building in December.[7]

During the brief time that the county seat was at Swan Lake, the residents of Estherville formalized a town government. Samuel Wade in 1861 surveyed the townsite, platted back in 1858, when Robert E. Ridley laid out a town on 160 acres of land he had acquired. Ridley and others of the platters, following the New England pattern, set aside four blocks for a square. But the town later decided four square blocks to be twice as much as needed. Two blocks to the west went into commercial and residential use. Ridley, Adolphus Jenkins, Jesse Coverdale, Gaylord Graves, and their wives, accepting the Wade survey as correct, granted and deeded "to the loving public all the streets of said village and the public square as designed on the plat."

Early in the same year a movement began to incorporate the village, which according to the 1880 census contained about half of the county's 1,550 inhabitants. A petition for incorporation was presented September 1, 1881, to the district court.[8] Judge John N. Weaver granted it, and in an election a month later, October 4, twenty-eight persons voted for the proposition and sixteen opposed it. The light vote left both sides claiming much more support than expressed in the poll. There was apparently substantial sentiment for the town continuing as an unincorporated village. But Judge Weaver settled the issue at the next term of court by declaring Estherville to be an incorporated town—Esther's town.

The county treasurer, Dr. E. H. Ballard, who had refused to move his office to Swan Lake when Estherville lost the county seat in 1879, was the popular choice for mayor when incorporated Estherville held its first election.[9] L. S. Williams was named recorder and Knuet Espeset, R. E. Ridley, John Ammon, F. E. Allen, J. H. Barnhart, and Frank Davey were elected trustees. At their first meeting, December 6, 1881, four days after the election, the trustees appointed a marshal, A. K. Ridley.

As the village became an incorporated town and moved into the eighties, more and more store buildings began appearing, giving company to the early nucleus of sawmill, gristmill, newspaper, private bank, two store buildings, blacksmith shop, and multipurpose school building. In 1882—the year Estherville won back the county seat and when first officers of the newly incorporated town began serving their terms—an event changed many aspects of the community. The first train whistle was heard.

New Life in the Town

As early as March 19, 1869, Howard Graves sought to interest a railroad company in building a line into Estherville. After thirteen years of frustration, problems of finance, reorganization, litigation, and head-to-head competition, Graves and his fellow townsmen finally realized their hopes. And then, as fate arranged it, two railroads fought over which of them would serve the town. Both of them built into the newly incorporated community, connecting it at last with the rest of the nation by reliable transportation.

When Graves first undertook to put Estherville on a railroad line, intercity commerce was carried on in part by a two-horse spring wagon, which operated on a weekly schedule under auspices of a firm with an imposing name, the Fort Dodge & Spirit Lake Lawe Stage Line, W. K. Mulroney, proprietor. Another connection was made with Fort Dodge, the nearest rail point from Estherville, via Dakotah, in Humboldt County. The Northwestern Stage Company provided daily service, when not interrupted by harsh weather. The Northwestern Company enjoyed connections with Dubuque and Sioux City.

A railroad line held promise of much more dependable service than a stagecoach and a spring wagon, but it was nearly a year before the Graves effort stirred enough rail action to result in even the survey of a rail route that included Estherville. Then interest resulted from activity on the part of local residents to seek defeat of state legislation proposed by Galusha Parsons of Webster County. This legislation would have deprived the Des Moines Valley Railroad Company of the financial support of 100,000 acres of land that had previously been granted to build a line from Fort Dodge, up the west branch of the Des Moines River, to Estherville.[1]

Defeat of the Parsons Bill put plans back on the track. But they were washed out later in the year when the company became financially strapped and was sold under foreclosure. The company's line from Keokuk to Des Moines became Chicago, Rock Island & Pacific property. The track from Des Moines to Fort Dodge was taken over by the Minneapolis & St. Louis company. Estherville continued to depend on undependable service by stage and spring wagon.

Perhaps fate was telling the community that the Lancaster, Ohio, school board was right when, in righteous indignation back in 1828, it had refused to permit even debate on the subject of whether railroads were a feasible means of transportation.[2] "We are willing to allow you the use of the schoolhouse to debate all proper questions, but such subjects as railroads we regard as improper infidelity," the school board pontificated when asked for the privilege of using an auditorium to discuss railroad plans. "If God had ever intended His creatures to travel over the face of the country at the frightful speed of fifteen miles an hour, he would have clearly foretold it through His holy prophets. It is a device of Satan to lead immortal souls down to hell." Insolvency of the Des Moines Valley Railroad at least temporarily saved the souls of Estherville from damnation. Their intercity transportation continued slower than a disreputable speed of fifteen miles an hour. But Graves, Ballard, Bates, et al. were willing to risk divine displeasure.

It was another two years before a ray of hope shone through the clouds to renew the prospect of a railroad into the town. On March 27, 1872, a city committee met to hear General Lindsay Seals of the Twin Cities explain plans for building a line of the St. Paul & Union Pacific Railroad Company from Minneapolis to Omaha via Estherville to connect with the Union Pacific.[3] Any sort of rail connection would be preferable to none, the townsmen thought. A committee of Adolphus Jenkins, R. E. Ridley, H. G. Day, I. Skinner, and G. M. Haskins undertook to select a depot location. In five days optimistic townsmen pledged a $5,000 bonus to the company, under the condition that trains would be running to Estherville by July 1, 1874. They promised the railroad company a freight and passenger station within a half-mile of the public square. More than that, special elections held in eight townships resulted in voting to levy a 5 percent property tax to produce $75,000 for assisting construction of the line. Hopeful residents could almost see smoke pouring out of locomotive stacks and hear the clackity clack of cars rumbling through the town. But not a penny was spent, or even raised. The deal was off.

The general had transferred his loyalty to an entirely different concern: the Fort Dodge & Northwestern Railroad Company, of which John F. Duncombe was president, General Seals the secretary, and O. E. Palmer the treasurer. The company conditionally purchased large tracts of Des Moines Valley Railroad land, some of it in Emmet County. Special tax funds levied in Clay County, which corners Emmet, were later lured to divert to the Iowa & Dakota Railroad Company. But no plan stayed glued very long. When Esthervilleans quizzed the general about what had happened to plans for a Minneapolis-Omaha line to join the Union Pacific, he met them with silence. Not only had Seals switched his interest, but the company he joined, the Fort Dodge & Northwestern, was not to build that line either. The company folded and the Fort Dodge & Fort Ridgely assumed its assets.

Meanwhile, passengers and freight moved by stagecoach and wagon. But two years later more dreaming took place. Responding to a request for financial assistance to aid a Fort Dodge & Fort Ridgely planned line, Emmet County held elections in Armstrong Grove, Center, Ellsworth, Emmet, Estherville, Swan Lake, Iowa Lake, and Twelve-Mile Lake townships to vote on a 5 percent levy. Voters approved the levy but the board of supervisors on January 5, 1877, cautiously ordered the county treasurer to collect the tax only when the company had complied with the stipulated conditions. No compliance and no railroad, then no funds. Again the taxpayers kept their money; one more discouraging disappointment. But when one plan evaporated another always seemed to appear.

A company that called itself the Cedar Rapids, Iowa Falls & Northwestern proposed a line from Cedar Rapids to Worthington, Minnesota (50 miles northwest beyond Estherville), and on June 23, 1880, it issued $825,000 in bonds to finance the project. The company earlier in the year had completed the line between Holland, in Grundy County, and Clarion, in Wright County. Via Estherville, it proposed to reach Worthington, 177 miles from Holland, the following year. This news spurred the old Des Moines Valley Railroad to revive plans for a line from Fort Dodge through Emmetsburg to Estherville and perhaps beyond.

Lukewarm on the plans, Estherville men attended tardily a meeting (after it had adjourned) at Emmetsburg called by Robert Shea, Palo Alto county treasurer, to discuss prospects. They learned that on March 9, 1881, bond and stockholders of the company at a meeting in New York City had agreed to extend the company's line into Minnesota. But the local leaders, who had been burned, opted to throw in their lot with the Cedar Rapids, Iowa Falls & Northwestern. That seemed more promising than plans of the Des Moines Valley group, especially after the personable S. L. Dows, representing the Cedar Rapids company, appeared at a meeting April 28, 1881, at which Howard Graves presided. The Estherville group was sufficiently well impressed by Dows's presentation of proposed action that a committee of Frank Davey, E. H. Ballard, F. E. Allen, David Weir, and Knuet Espeset was appointed.

Already experienced in railroad dreaming and planning, the committee drew an agreement between the people of Emmet County and Dows's company. It called for the railroad to pay the expense of an election on a 5 percent levy. By then the local residents had become wary of incurring election expense for plans that never got past the paper stage. Five of the six townships involved—Center, Estherville, Emmet, High Lake, and Twelve-Mile Lake—voted in favor of the levy.

Two months later, June 23, 1881, the railroad agreed to issue $4,000,000 in bonds for construction upon leasing the proposed line from Holland to Worthington to the B.C.R.&N. (Burlington, Cedar Rapids & Northern). Work actually began and construction proceeded rapidly. Track was laid as far as Emmetsburg and grading was nearly completed into Estherville by the end of the year. But trouble, as usual, lay ahead. Plans of still another company collided at Emmetsburg with those of the B.C.R.&N. What next? Esthervilleans asked themselves.

The Chicago, Milwaukee & St. Paul railroad, which had extended its line from McGregor through Mason City and Algona, reached west to Emmetsburg in early 1878. By the time the B.C.R.&N. track layers coming from the south arrived in early 1881 the Milwaukee had put down track west of Emmetsburg as far as Spencer. Though not announced, the plan was for the Milwaukee to reach Estherville with a branch north from Emmetsburg. Expecting trouble in making a crossing over the Milwaukee, top brass of the B.C.R.&N. appeared on the crossing site to guide action. Judge Tracy, president; general superintendent Ives; S. L. Dows as construction officer; and chief engineer White occupied a private car from which to offer direction and support of the crew. A rail crossing iron was ready for installation.

Between 10 A.M. and noon one Sunday, track layers put the crossing in place and proceeded north toward Estherville. But the issue was unsettled. At midnight Milwaukee workmen began removing the track crossing. By morning, when B.C.R.&N. crews came to work, a string of freight cars stood where the crossing tracks of the B.C.R.&N. had been removed. Milwaukee superintendent Sanborn had hastened from his office at Mason City when informed of the B.C.R.&N. crossing and had directed its removal. The Milwaukee effectively kept the crossing location blocked; upon allowing a train through the junction point, it replaced the string of cars to prevent further work.

With a choice of dynamite or litigation, the B.C.R.&N. chose the courts. Judge Weaver, after considering a restraining order asked by one railroad and a cross complaint filed by another, ruled in favor of the B.C.R.&N. Although the Milwaukee appealed to the Iowa Supreme Court, the railroad agreed to settlement before a decision was handed down. The Milwaukee consented to the crossing and paid $1,000 for delaying B.C.R.&N. work.

However, the Milwaukee did not abandon its idea of a line to Estherville. It chose a route along the east side of the Des Moines River, rather than the west, as the B.C.R.&N. civil engineers did. The Milwaukee line passed through High Lake Township, then across a corner of Center Township, into Estherville. The town contributed $180 for depot grounds and right-of-way. Dr. E. H. Ballard and Knuet Espeset acted as a committee in charge, appointed by Mayor F. E. Allen. Because the B.C.R.&N. reached Estherville ahead of the Milwaukee, arriving June 8, 1882, it received the patronage upon which survival depended.

The Milwaukee tore up its tracks in August 1889, leaving a vacated railroad grade through High Lake Township that yet today leaves traces of the exciting railroad building race between the Milwaukee and the B.C.R.&N. My grandfather was postmaster at the Milwaukee's New Bergen station in High Lake Township during the short time that the Milwaukee operated trains. As a young boy, my father picked up mail from the Milwaukee during its brief Emmet County history and delivered it to the nearby Wallingford community, situated on the B.C.R.&N. The abandoned Milwaukee de-

C.R.I.&P. depot during the Age of Steam; built in 1910.

pot in Estherville, subsidized by the town's donation of $180, served as a residential property on North Eighth Street until it gave way to an offstreet parking lot about seventy-five years later.

After reaching Estherville in June 1882, the B.C.R.&N. completed its track as far as Spirit Lake during the same summer and then pushed on to Sioux Falls and Watertown, South Dakota. Following the purchase in 1885 of the majority of stock in the B.C.R.&N., the Rock Island and Pacific took over the line. That railroad mushroomed into a vast network of track in the Midwest and Southwest. A branch line of the Rock Island, built in 1892 as the Chicago & Iowa Western, added an additional rail connection. From Estherville the line extended through Gruver, Armstrong, Swea City, and Lakota to Dows. Also it connected Lakota to Albert Lea on a Rock Island line from Des Moines to Minneapolis.

As a division point for the line from Cedar Rapids to South Dakota, Estherville nurtured a new industry that spawned others. The railroad breathed new life into the town, which began the fairly rapid expansion that inspired some local wit to order a sign near the depot: WATCH ESTHERVILLE GROW.

Two months after trains began running into Estherville, a sec-

ond newspaper, the *National Broad-Axe*, began publication under
the proprietorship of Reynolds, Lough & Co. It represented the
English American Land Company, with addresses in both Estherville and in London, England.[4] Under the ownership of F. B.
Woods, what had been the *Broad-Axe*, then the *Republican*, and
then the *Herald* became once again in 1887 the *Republican*.[5] In
1902 George Nichols merged the *Republican* with the *Northern
Vindicator* and thus the *V. & R.* was born, with George A. Nichols
as editor and publisher.[6] He and his daughter Adelaide continued
to own the paper until my brother and I bought it on October 4,
1944.

During the brief editorship of C. J. Reynolds, 23, the *Broad-
Axe* fearlessly chopped away at whatever offered a suitable target,
including the hide of Frank Davey, the county auditor. Reynolds
claimed to fear no politicians and promised to expose corruption as
he saw it. "We call a cat a cat, a dog a dog, and a rat a rat,"
Reynolds boasted. He promised to swing the blade of the *Broad-
Axe* until it "hews down every corrupt politician."

His challenge to those who disagreed with him to withdraw
their support was soon answered. Reynolds announced after a year
of publication that the paper would no longer solicit advertising or
subscriptions. Lough & Son took over; Reynolds disappeared, and
Frank Davey slept easier when he became the editor. J. W. Lough
and A. F. Lough soon announced that they would operate the paper "as a business—not for glory." Although the more conservative
Davey took over as editor and the Loughs let it be known they did
not mind dollar patronage, the *Broad-Axe* blade dulled and soon it
ceased to hew, to chop, or even to print.

But the *Broad-Axe*, during its brief history, had at least
visualized the hazard of pedestrians walking the long, high, steel
railroad bridge that spanned the river. The editor warned young
people to quit using the bridge because, after all, trains did also
cross it. No deaths occurred, however, as the residents of Estherville
adjusted to the sophistication of the railway age. This new era
brought such remarkable improvements, noted in the *Broad-Axe*,
as a concrete crossing over street mud at the principal downtown intersection. The aldermen considered other possibilities—such as
electric, gas, and coal oil street lamps—but all the options seemed
foolishly expensive to the careful council in 1882.

The coming of the railroad created immediate demand for more hotel rooms. The town's first hotel was The Estherville House, which in 1869 offered "commodious accommodations for stabling 30 horses in the rear, with stages departing from the House in all directions, making excellent connections." Host G. M. Haskins assured readers of the *Vindicator* that "tourists and emigrants" would receive satisfactory attention. When in 1882 trains started puffing into Estherville, visitors were welcomed by H. C. Coon's Lincoln House, on Lincoln Street east of Sixth, which offered free bus service to and from trains and "conveyance to any part of the county at liberal rates." Or weary travelers could sleep on North Sixth Street at The Emmet House, which was originally the Fortner Hotel, dating back to 1870. In 1882 J. W. Ridley turned The Emmet House proprietorship over to Isaac Mattson, who promised "meals and clean beds." The Burlington and Crawford hotels came later. Al Holtzhauser's Orleans Hotel provided convenient service just across the street from the railroad station after the Rock Island took over the line from the B.C.R.&N. at the turn of the century.

Emmet House on North Sixth Street.

Orleans Hotel.

Railroad payrolls, later important to the local economy, were modest at the start. When Tom Brand started as an engineman in 1885, he earned $1.65 per 100 miles, which took him from eight to as many as fifty hours.[7] By 1889, Brand, who moved to Estherville in 1894, earned $2.50 for 100 miles. In the early days of diamond-stack coal-burning engines, there were no such things as patent couplers, air brakes, or cab protection from snow, sleet, cold, rain, and dust. When the engineer hit a string of cars too hard, he had a fight on his hands with the brakeman. Coupling cars required more delicacy than the engineer could sometimes manage.

One of the hardships endured by railroaders was battling winter snows, such as those that fell in the winter of 1883–84 closing the track of the B.C.R.&N. two miles west of Estherville at McCulla cut. A photographer preserved for posterity the scene of a Civil War type locomotive submerged by snow as high as the base of the smokestack. The crewmen posed atop the drifted-in engine before shoveling it out. But railroad transportation thrived and the industry became the life and blood of the Estherville community.

Peter Johnston, a lawyer, who four years before had become briefly involved with H. I. Wasson in the *Broad-Axe* as it metamorphosed into the *Herald*, started the *Democrat* in 1888. The paper fell victim to a disastrous fire in 1895, but Johnston rebuilt and re-equipped it, only to sell the next year to Frank Carpenter (my first newspaper employer) and a partner, Ed Sillge, whose skills in typography won my lasting admiration.

If nothing else of note happened in the year 1888, when Johnston started the *Democrat,* a certain death and burial occurred that stirred at least parochial interest, particularly among the numerous Norwegian-born and their families. For about a year Nicolai Ibsen, an obscure brother of the famous dramatist, Henrik, lived with the pioneer Michael Berhows family. Nicolai, a sheepherder, died April 25, 1888, and was buried in the Norwegian cemetery a short distance north of Estherville. Today a modest, weathered stone in the cemetery marking Nicolai's grave is inscribed: "By Strangers Honored and By Strangers Mourned."

Tombstone of Nicolai Ibsen in Norwegian cemetery north of Estherville.

The decade of the eighties brought more than trains to Iowa. The county seat returned from Swan Lake, Estherville incorporated into a city, and business flourished. More newspapers started, trade became livelier, new industries arrived, more hotels sprang up, and a need for capital emerged. On November 27, 1886, Howard

Graves, along with F. E. Allen, John M. Barker, T. W. Burdick, and A. Bradish as directors, incorporated the Graves private bank as the Estherville State Bank, with a capital of $25,000. Graves, logically, became the bank's first president and J. H. Bradish its cashier. First to serve the community, the bank was also the first to succumb to economic disaster in the twenties. Today a new, airy Federal Savings & Loan office building stands where the Graves bank once did business.

In 1890 a second bank opened on North Sixth Street at Lincoln Street as the Emmet County Bank, with a capital of $25,000, incorporated by F. E. Allen, S. T. Meservey, E. S. Ormsby, Webb Vincent, and E. B. Soper. Two years later it became the First National Bank.[8] In 1894 a third bank, privately owned, was started by Frank H. and Will T. Rhodes, on Lincoln Street, east of Sixth Street. It was incorporated in 1916 as the First Trust & Savings Bank with a capital of $35,000.[9] The fourth bank to serve the community was not incorporated until 1901. It was the Iowa Savings Bank with a capital of $20,000 and E. J. Breen, president; Mack J. Groves, vice-president; Frank P. Woods, cashier; E. E. Hartung, John Montgomery, C. M. Brown, and L. W. Woods, directors.[10] The bank was across the street south of the First National and west of the Rhodes bank. A year later a fifth bank was organized as the Provident Trust & Savings Bank, with E. B. Soper, president; Webb Vincent, vice-president; John P. Kirby, cashier; and Mart K. Whelan, E. I. Sondrol, O. Neville, and H. G. Graaf, directors. The bank was later to have the same officers and occupy the same building as the First National Bank.

During the nineties and in the early years of the next century, banks would spring up in other towns of the county, some of them affiliated with Estherville banks. The twenties wiped out all of them. Today pharmacists who fill prescriptions for pills to relieve the bellyache and rheumatic pains stand at counters where the Iowa Savings and the First Trust & Savings once cached their legal tender in walk-in vaults.

As the community began to flex its economic muscle, leaders saw the need to incorporate it as a second-class city. This was accomplished in October 1892, after a census taken by W. S. Jones reported a burgeoning population of 2,185. Governor Horace Boies dutifully signed incorporation papers, and the secretary of state affixed his signature with distinct pleasure. William M. McFarland, who had represented Emmet County as its first member of the legislature, from 1887 to 1891, served as secretary of state from 1891 to 1897. Making Estherville a second-class city was a joy, not a duty, for that active and respected Esthervillean. The first mayor of the "city" of Estherville elected in March 1893 was A. W. Dawson.[11]

A year before the 1892 census, when Estherville became a "city," the inhabitants expressed dissatisfaction with having to pump their drinking water from private wells. They also wearied of reading by kerosene lamps and tallow candles. An 1891 ordinance created the Estherville Water Company but nothing got done until 1894, when A. D. Root proposed a municipal waterworks and light plant. At a special election in June, the proposal received overwhelming approval. Tired pumpers voted 282 to 12 for a waterworks and those in favor of Mazda lighting won 264 to 18.

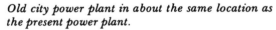

Old city power plant in about the same location as the present power plant.

For $3,562 the General Electric Company installed a generator, but for the $1,574 agreed upon, the Sioux City Engine & Iron Works didn't perform its contract to provide an engine and boiler. Adams, Green & Company took over the job, although some of the work didn't meet approval. The waterworks cost $10,594, bid by C. W. Hubbard of Sioux Falls, South Dakota. L. R. Woods was the first commissioner. Both plants were completed early in 1895. The kerosene lamp and the water pail were on the way out.

However, the day of the water closet was yet to come. The first Esthervillean to abandon the privy was one William Harrabin, first user to connect to a sanitary sewer. The engineering firm of Wardle & Yeager, whose proposal was accepted by the city fathers October 5, 1899, built the line. Instead of depositing sewage in privies, the city began pouring it untreated into the Des Moines River from a network of branches that fanned out across the town. In my youth ten and fifteen years later, there were still sufficient numbers of one- and two-holers to amuse Halloween pranksters who reveled in upsetting outdoor relief stations. Occasionally such mischief surprised an unwary patron sitting on a chilly pine board with a mail-order catalogue for company.

At about this same time the desire for telephone service materialized in the corporate shape of the Estherville Telephone Company, organized October 31, 1895, by Charles W. Crim, Mart K. Whelan, E. J. Breen, and F. E. Allen. But by the first of the year 1901 there were only twenty-four subscribers who had installed big wall contraptions equipped with dry-cell batteries, a crank, and a noisy bell. The discouraged company sold out to the Western Electric Company, which reduced the rate by 25¢ a month and had soon connected a total of 250 users. The telephone habit was catching on. Three years later the Emmet County Telephone Company was incorporated. A company followed in 1912 at Armstrong and in 1914 at Ringsted.

To protect expanding ownership of property, the citizenry voted in 1888 to upgrade the volunteer fire department with the acquisition of a building to house the new hand engine and the hook-and-ladder truck purchased in 1884.[12] But the department had to put up with rented quarters for four or five more years. Importuned by officers of the frustrated volunteer company, the city council on November 20, 1893, finally appropriated $800 to build an engine house.[13] But that wasn't the end of fires or complaints of the fire fighters, whose problems grew even more troublesome in the new century.

Aside from industry involving division-point activity of the B.C.R.&N. (the Rock Island, after the turn of the century), Estherville payrolls have largely been those of firms directly or indirectly related to farming. This pattern began developing as early as 1889, when L. W. Mitchell began making English cheddar cheese from milk brought to town by farmers. Estherville men, aware of the importance of assisting agricultural movement and improvement, participated in the incorporation June 1, 1893, of the Emmet County Agricultural Society.[14] On June 6, 1894, dairymen organized the Farmers' Cooperative Creamery. The first creamery of the county operated only a year, beginning in 1881, at Swan Lake. During the nineties creamery associations sprang up all over the county.

A modest growth in population induced by railroad transportation set in motion the building of new schools, including the Washington building in 1891, originally used as a high school, which was centrally located on North Sixth Street. The community built the Jackson school on the south side in 1895 for $11,000, followed in 1900 by McKinley school west of the river on a hillside, and Lincoln school in north Estherville. To raise money for school buildings the county sold three sections of land in 160-acre tracts. The land brought $6 to $10.60 an acre. Farms such as those auctioned brought as much as $300 an acre during the 1920 land boom but as little as $60 when the bubble burst. Prices of $2,500 an acre and more became commonplace in the 1970s.

New residents moving to the community built more churches to supplement those already functioning before 1890. (See Estherville Churches in the Appendix.) At the same time, churches were springing up in the surrounding neighborhoods. No one in the county had far to walk or ride to find a house of worship, all of one or another Christian persuasion. During the last two decades of the century the inhabitants also found sociability and stimulation in meetings of lodges and fraternal associations that fifty years later would languish from the competition of motoring, radio, movies, stereo, TV, and sports events. (See Fraternal Organizations and Societies in the Appendix.) Thomas Sammons tantalized readers of the *Northern Vindicator* with the lore of riches in the far north. Olaf Johnson was chosen among eight willing applicants to repre-

*High school built in
1912.*

sent local shareholders in a Klondike company formed in January
1898 to attempt to obtain some of the wealth from the promising
area. Shares were sold at $50 per speculator to E. J. Breen, J. B.
Binford, C. P. Clay, A. J. Penn, J. P. Kirby, Frank Bullis, C. R.
Ammon, and J. J. Klopp. Some of these "investors" were among the
town's elite, conservative businessmen who could not resist temptation to seek quick fortune, which only a very few would find.

Another event of 1898 was more far-reaching in its impact on
the community. The ten Estherville members of Company K of the
Iowa National Guard who responded to a call for volunteers in the
Spanish-American War found disillusion and misery. They assembled enthusiastically April 24, 1898, at Emmetsburg for drilling,
then went April 30 to Camp McKinley at Des Moines, and a month
later left for Camp Thomas at Chickamaugua, Georgia. From news
reported in a weekly column written for the *Vindicator* by W. T.
Haecock, a partner in the paper with George W. Gruwell, readers
gleaned disheartening tales related in Haecock's "Extracts from a
Volunteer's Diary."

Disease, fever, homesickness, privation, and death were not
what the enlistees had in mind when they volunteered after the sink-
ing of the Maine. Haecock reported that the men were terrified of
being taken to the camp hospital, because conditions there were so
frightful that a man could die without anyone becoming aware of
it. Members of the GAR could supply little more than sympathy.
Camp miseries ceased only in August, when the war ended. A
month later the soldiers were home on furlough. The last Emmet
County volunteers were discharged November 3. Eight returned to
Estherville, one was still in the hospital, and another went visiting.

Four schools, about 1910: Top left, Lincoln; top right, Jackson; bottom left, McKinley; bottom right, Washington Building.

A few days later, at the general election, voters of the county defeated a proposal, 196 to 180, to erect a monument commemorating deeds of Civil War veterans. Voters did not choose to levy a one-mill tax for a memorial, as permitted in 1897 by legislative act.

In 1898 the *Northern Vindicator* gave publicity to a movement among physicians to establish a hospital. But it bore no fruit, partly because the railroad declined to support the project. A hospital would have to wait until 1908, when physicians established the Estherville City Hospital. A poor farm also would come later, in 1913, after Mrs. J. P. Littell organized Estherville Associated Charities to assist needy persons.

But the community had made adequate provision for the dead. An Eastside cemetery dates from 1866 and Oakhill Cemetery, in a wooded area west of the river was started in 1889. Slumbering under these acres and in the burial grounds of Norwegian Lutherans and Roman Catholics are the remains of many remarkable persons. The chiseled inscriptions on their marble and granite markers are a Who's Who of rugged people who pioneered, persevered, innovated, and collaborated to build Esther's town.

Progressives
versus
Standpatters

AS the twentieth century opened and Edward VII succeeded Queen Victoria to the throne of England, Estherville began a new period of development. The town welcomed another railroad line and, whether needed or not, a fourth newspaper opened shop. A second railroad line was certain to improve the town's transportation link with the rest of the country, but publishers of the *Vindicator,* the *Republican,* and the *Democrat* wondered if the already sparse pickings might prove too meager a support for so many journalists. Maybe they all would starve. However, the tension eased a little two years after A. F. Lough started the fourth paper, the Estherville *Enterprise,* when George Nichols thinned the field by consolidating the *Vindicator* with the *Republican.* Then there were three papers once again, but still two more than perhaps anybody needed.

In the early days of newspapering, editors as well as readers were especially conscious of politics, and the three Estherville papers reflected three distinct flavors of political persuasion. The climate was warmed by a bitter struggle within the Republican party between standpatters and progressives, while Republicans of whatever preference vigorously opposed Democrats in the general election. Upon acquisition of the $5,000 *Enterprise* plant in October 1907 by George E. Patterson, the county attorney, the paper became a staunch supporter of Republican progressives.

This stance included endorsement of my father, who was elected county attorney in 1900 and who by 1906 was ready for the state legislature. (See Emmet County Men Elected to State Office in the Appendix.) When father was reelected to the legislature in

1908, the *Democrat* reported he spent $52.61 campaigning, while Frank P. Woods spent $328.75 in getting elected congressman. It was the year William Howard Taft was elected president. Father was deeply involved in the intraparty scrap between conservative standpatters and the progressives, led by Albert B. Cummins. At stake were such issues as railroad regulation, the use of passes to woo newspaper support; and matters of railroad accident safety and liability. Bitter fights developed in precinct caucuses as progressives sought stricter control over the railroads. Besides their opposition to railroad reform, standpatters also resisted a movement to take the nomination for United States senator out of state convention control. Father wrote the primary law, which removed nominations from convention rooms.

He was also deeply involved in writing and passing legislation that made it easier for farm owners to organize drainage districts. Bull ditches—so-called because the power to dredge the early ones was supplied by oxen—and large-diameter tile lines that fed into the ditches, lakes, creeks, and rivers made Emmet County's vast swampland some of the most fertile soil in the state or in the world. When provided with adequate county tile and ditch outlets, farmers were able to drain their rich, black soil. Iowa land became more valuable than many farms in neighboring Minnesota simply because of legislation in Iowa that encouraged organization of drainage districts empowered to levy taxes for improvement.

With Albert B. Cummins in the governor's chair, progressives of the legislature won contests to regulate railroad stock security "watering" practices and abuse of free railroad passes to win political favor. Legislative acts fixed liability for fires caused by locomotives, required protection of railroad crossings, and dealt with other problems affecting the public interest.

Frank P. Woods of Estherville, who served from from 1909 to 1917 as representative of the Tenth Congressional District, and Dr. E. W. Bachman, who served in the state senate from 1901 to 1905, were among the active progressives, along with father, who supported reform legislation. They helped Cummins in his race for governor and then later in his successful campaign for the United States Senate, where he became a leader in the writing of railroad legislation. Audiences at Emmet County political rallies heard such orators as United States Senator Jonathan P. Dolliver and Cummins. But oratory had to be supplemented by in-fighting at precinct caucuses and at county conventions to win delegates.

Shrewd maneuvering and carefully planned strategy by local politicians often captured delegates to the county convention or to a state convention. Some of the tensest moments occurred in precinct caucuses when factions vied for the chair. And once in it, the chairman often virtually dictated who would be named as delegates to the county convention. Before anyone could propose a democratic method of choosing a selection committee, the chairman might announce who would serve on the committee to name delegates, carefully selecting his partisans. A burly chairman, according to legend, shouted down one of the voters attending the caucus. "Sit down," he ordered an upstart who proposed that a committee on delegates be elected, "I already have the list of delegates here in my pocket." The story was little exaggeration, if any, of what did happen frequently.

At one second-ward caucus in Estherville there was a heated discussion of whether a certain voter was entitled to vote in that precinct. He lived on the west side of Sixth Street, which was in the old first ward. Just south of the man's house the street bends thirty degrees to the east, and he insisted that the ward boundary followed a straight north-and-south line. The ward line did not bend with the street, he insisted, and because the bedroom in which he slept was east of a straight north-south line he should be counted as a resident of the second ward. The chairman ruled that the resident should be seated in the caucus; after all the man was of the chairman's own persuasion. Where a man slept was where he lived, the chairman said. On a voice vote a caucus chairman seldom lost his cause.

Often the members of a political clique were less than happy with one of their group. Whenever someone would complain that so-and-so of the party was really a son-of-a-bitch, father would remind him, "Yes, I know. But remember he's our son-of-a-bitch."

Among leading conservatives — standpatters — of the community were Mart K. Whelan, Charles W. Crim, and George Allen, who with his son G. K. (Kirt) Allen, purchased the *Enterprise* in 1913. The Opera House, the Woodman Hall, and the courthouse provided settings for political pyrotechnics that drew packed audiences. The day of distractions from radio, TV, and daily newspapers was a long way off during electioneering excitement from 1900 to 1912. The Republican party in 1912 split over the nomination of William Howard Taft, and Theodore Roosevelt ran as a Bull Moose candidate. Neither won; Woodrow Wilson was elected president and the *Democrat*'s publisher, Frank Carpenter, became postmaster.

At about the time father was becoming interested in state politics, the *Democrat* was not only using its ink to report political goings-on but had become successful in persuading local entrepreneurs to use generous blocks of white space to inform readers of their wares. For an appropriate Christmas gift, Jay Johnston's drugstore suggested hat pins from 35¢ to $2, while H. H. Tosdal recommended a meerschaum pipe at $1, or a better one for $5. Beymer & Hendershot were selling Christmas ties at 25¢ to 50¢, or somewhat fancier ones for as much as $1.50. At Nau Brothers store in the bitter weather of January 1907, Chris and Knute Nau told readers they could find Coon, Wombat, Russian Buffalo, Bulgarian Lamb, and other suitable warm fur coats. West of the square, Herman Graaf's Eagle Clothing sold Hart Schaffner & Marx suits at $15 and $25. Patent leather shoes could be found at F. M. Shadle & Sons at $2.98 a pair. Over at Herman Oransky's store, ladies coats sold at $6.95.

Bill Foshier offered his auctioneering services. Drugs could be found at F. S. Shadle's drugstore and also at J. J. Klopp's pharmacy, which advertised that its "black oil for barbwire cuts is best." P. L. Christensen made Baltimore oysters available at 40¢ a quart and Ohio maple syrup at $1.35 a gallon. For divertissement at only 10¢, 20¢, and 30¢ a seat, the Trousdale Brothers, Winn and Boyd, offered three nights of repertoire at the opera house. Customers got a dollar's worth of whatever for a dollar in 1906.

When in 1899 the Minneapolis & St. Louis railroad built a line from Winthrop, Minnesota, to Storm Lake, Iowa, via Estherville, boosters rose to the occasion by raising funds for ground on which to build a depot, a roundhouse, and machine shops. No shop was ever built, but Estherville was a division point, except for a brief period in 1909. The line south from New Ulm into Estherville was delayed a year because grasshoppers ate the crops that the M.&St.L. had planned to haul.[1] The line proved expensive to build and maintain because it had to provide trestles over many streams and gullies. South of Estherville the surveyors sent track builders on a horseshoe route a mile and a half to cross a half-mile slough. Farther down the line toward Storm Lake a spindly three-deck wooden trestle, built on a curve, quivered every time a train crept over the bridge. Even though the railroad between Peoria and Chicago had to bridge the Spoon River and climb Kickapoo Hill, it carried the Cannon Ball Express and the North Star Limited from Minneapolis to Chicago in thirteen and a half hours.

On the line to Minneapolis was a news butcher known as Smitty who was a ventriloquist. He entertained travelers with such exciting impersonations as mock prizefights, arguments, and the imitation of animal noises. On the main lines, the railroad's deluxe service included dining cars and sleepers, drawn by colorfully appointed locomotives.

During the winter of 1917 a section of the M.&St.L. was closed for a month because of snow. Twenty boxes of dynamite were exploded to open the tracks. The line south from Estherville to Storm Lake was intended to reach Omaha, but like countless other railroad plans it got there only on paper. Estherville passengers reached Minneapolis on a line from Dakota via Winthrop. The Chicago and Northwestern took over the railroad in 1960.

By 1915 Rock Island passengers who were invited by Estherville's mammoth billboard near the depot to WATCH ESTHERVILLE GROW enjoyed the convenience of as many as ten trains a day, two of which even ran on Sunday. Through-service to Chicago, via Cedar Rapids, included sleepers and dining cars. The M.&St.L. took passengers comfortably in sleepers to Minneapolis via Winthrop. Travelers enjoyed accommodations to Sioux Falls, Albert Lea, Storm Lake, Fort Dodge, Des Moines, and dozens of intermediate stations. In 1916 the Rock Island railroad supported about 500 workers in Estherville who drew $50,000 in wages.

Frank Carpenter's newspaper carried a regular column—"Links & Pins"—to record the weekly happenings of conductors, engineers, roundhouse mechanics, car-shop workers, section hands, and white-collar employees. Anyone boarding a passenger train or arriving on one might likely encounter news-hungry Carpenter. "Where you bound?" or "Where you been?" Carp would ask, and he usually found out. He was tireless in collecting what he called "locals" for personal mention columns of the *Democrat*. George

Nichols or his daughter Adelaide also circulated at the depot to keep abreast of what their readers were doing.

A huge tinted photograph of the Golden State Limited tempted those who came into the station with a desire to board that luxury train for a trip to California. Upstairs in the $26,000 Rock Island depot were offices of the division superintendent, the division freight agent, the trainmaster, section master, and the dispatchers. With their telegraph keys the dispatchers kept in constant touch with various passenger and freight trains operating on the division's main line and also on the branches. Trainmen received orders of where to pass or meet another train. These orders were relayed to trainmen by station agents who received them by telegraph from the dispatching nerve center.

Telegraphers in the depot provided the town's only up-to-the-minute news of the outside world. First news of who won the prize-fight in Chicago, who was nominated for president, which horse won the derby, and other hot news came to Estherville by railroad wire and then spread by grapevine through the town. Dispatchers worked around the clock to keep railroad traffic unsnarled and to avoid collisions. I remember best of all among those responsible individuals chief dispatcher Ed Callendar, G. H. Morse, Joe Orvis, and Ed Broms, along with telegrapher Jack Cramer.

The M.&St.L. line gave rise to Billy Baker's colorful store near that line's depot, accommodating travelers with guest rooms above the store. A steaming bowl of Billy's oyster stew revived circulation of the blood after a long, cold journey in January or February. The train from Des Moines, due early in the evening, might arrive at midnight or even later. Stoves in the coaches could not be depended upon to keep the passengers snug when blizzards howled. On coaches assigned to the Des Moines run, the red plush cushions were not always in the best of repair. A passenger took his life in hand when he ventured to go from one car to the next across open platforms as the train lurched down uneven, poorly ballasted track. But Charlie Keeting presided as conductor over a voyage on the Estherville-Des Moines run with as much dignity and grace as though he were in charge of the Twentieth Century Limited.

Oil lamps hanging from the center of the coach afforded uncertain illumination and sometimes spilled oil, when the engineer took his train over a particularly rough stretch of track. In the spring, when the frozen roadbed thawed, runoff water endangered the track. On occasion, in bitter winter weather the locomotive might run low on steam and the fireman and brakeman would forage fence posts and discarded ties to fire up the boiler.

But riding the M.&St.L. to Des Moines to visit Grandma and Grandpa Deemer was a supreme experience for me. My parents did the worrying; I enjoyed a shoe-box lunch of fried chicken and apple pie (eaten in the fingers, upside down). Never once, however, was I able to glimpse a telegram being sent down the wire along the railroad track. I later learned telegrams didn't flit along the wire like the messages I sent skyward up waxed string to one of my homemade kites.

Visiting my grandparents in Des Moines was a fascinating adventure, because grandfather was my hero. He was an expert shot with a 22-caliber rifle. With the .22 he thinned out rats in his barn, which had been converted to house his Model T after old Fred passed on to horse heaven. Grandfather's rifle aim had been sharpened at Corinth, Vicksburg, and Missionary Ridge. He also was highly skilled at horseshoes and beat a mean tenor drum in the GAR drum corps that paraded on special occasions.

I was awed by the steam engines and generators in the electric light plant he superintended, but nothing of Joe Deemer's mechanical talent rubbed off on his grandson. When he acquired a Model T, the old engineer performed all his own surgery and service on it. He also had the knack of knowing just how to adjust the spark level so it would fire the gasoline to start the engine but without so powerful a jolt that it would backfire and break his arm while trying to crank it. He was not pleased with the gas headlamps, fueled from a small tank fastened to the running board. Joe always aimed to arrive wherever he was going before nightfall.

When Grandpa Deemer came to Estherville, he and I would often sit in the north end of the park on a green bench, close by a bubbling fountain with tadpoles in it. There we ate pears, which grandfather peeled with his pocket knife—the same one he used to cut bait when we fished for bullheads on the rock dam built by the Ridleys in the dim, early days. The gristmill on the west side of the Des Moines River was long gone.

After grandfather bought a Model T and began driving it to Estherville instead of taking passage on the poky M.&St.L., we ex-

*Joseph and Lillian Deemer
with grandson Deemer Lee.*

panded our fishing expeditions to include such promising pike holes
as those near the Tom & Jerry bridge. Sometimes we drove into
Lars Herem's pasture and down to a quiet bend in the river north of
Emmet bridge. Grandfather possessed inexhaustible patience and
unbeatable optimism. Our catches — if any — were modest, but we
watched the flight of birds and we whittled whistles out of green
willow branches. Only the crows, the splash of a fish, or the croak of
a frog broke the river stillness.

My grandmother had no interest in such experiences. She preferred telephone conversation in Des Moines with her Woman's Relief Corps friends, but she won my friendship, when I visited her,
with caraway-seed cookies, peach pie, and chicken with dumplings.
When I wasn't hungry, though, I chose the company of grandpa
and a pet chicken that sat on his knee — until Aunt Millie became
confused about which hen in the chicken yard she had been directed to harvest for Sunday dinner.

For about one year, in 1901, the town of Estherville enjoyed
reading the *Daily Tribune,* published by Frank Carpenter and Ed
Sillge at their *Democrat* printing office. Half the paper was ready-
printed, sent down from Minneapolis on the afternoon M.&St.L.
passenger train. The daily concept, about thirty years premature
for Estherville, did not pay its way, attracting only a limited
number of paying subscribers. Uncle Robert, a reporter for Carpenter and Sillge, had conceived and carried out the idea. Carpenter had given Robert a job when he noticed that the young man was
more engrossed in reading books than delivering groceries. The

Robert M. Lee.

Tribune expired when Carpenter's protégé was lured to E. P. Adler's *Davenport Daily Times.*

When Uncle Robert died in 1939, after jobs in Des Moines, Milwaukee, Denver, and on three Chicago newspapers, the town's lazy delivery boy was once again the managing editor of a newspaper called the *Tribune,* Colonel McCormick's, with about a million more subscribers than the *Estherville Tribune* could attract. A quarter of a century after the 1901 daily venture, I reversed the progression. Starting as a part-time reporter for the *Chicago Tribune,* I settled down in Estherville to buy the *Democrat* and start a daily newspaper that survived the depression, press accidents, typographical errors, irritated subscribers, unhappy advertisers, the competition of radio and TV, and all the other pitfalls and frustrations that beset newspaper publishers.

Uncle Robert never lost his love for the Emmet County community, and he gave support and encouragement to my venture. He cherished recollections of incidents that occurred during his boyhood and while working for Frank Carpenter. He liked to tell of an Estherville saloonkeeper on South Sixth Street who employed two of his customers to clean out the privy at the rear of the spa. The two men in charge of deodorizing and unburdening the premises became irritated with each other and began hurling missiles of whatever most conveniently came to hand. When these besmeared, unperfumed custodians of the privy entered the saloon shortly for rest and refreshment, the barkeep's paying customers fled in panic.

Their retreat was reminiscent of the saloon raid in earlier days when Estherville ladies of temperance smashed bottles and poured sipping whiskey in the gutter as parched patrons agonized.

The community's spiritual needs were abundantly supplied by a wide choice of Christian denomination churches, but, as the new century opened, Estherville lacked a suitable hospital. Even incorporation of the Northwest Iowa Hospital Association July 14, 1898, by Dr. Albert A. Anderson, Dr. C. E. Birney, Dr. C. B. Adams, and Dr. M. E. Wilson did not result in a hospital. For a brief time in 1906 and 1907 Mrs. Cora Rhodes operated a hospital during a diphtheria epidemic, but Estherville City Hospital was not established until April 1908.

First located at Seventh and Howard streets, the hospital later moved to a large residential property at Eighth and Des Moines streets. It was there, my lungs clogged with ether vapors, that Dr. E. W. Bachman deprived me of my tonsils. During my brief sentence of torture in the southwest second-floor bedroom of that infirmary, I saw Ethyl E. Walker, superintendent of the place, for the first and only time. I thereafter carefully avoided her premises by at least one block whenever I cycled in the vicinity. Before coming to Estherville, Miss Walker had been superintendent of a military hospital at Danville, Ill.

Dr. Anderson, preferring his own hospital, started one in 1900 close to the business area and later moved it to North Eighth Street. In 1924 Dr. R. C. Coleman built a thirty-five–bed, three-story brick structure there after purchasing the Anderson property. He used a frame building that Dr. Anderson erected in 1916 as a dormitory for nurses who received training. Dr. C. E. Birney operated his own hospital on Central Avenue, and Dr. M. T. Morton later built a clinic-hospital east of the square on North Seventh Street.

On the afternoon of May 13, 1909, my father was apparently acting as babysitter, when the west window of his law office, which overlooked the Rock Island depot a block and a half away, put us on the fifty-yard line for one of the town's many magnificent fires. The volunteer fire department offered as much opposition as it could muster but ultimately conceded defeat. It was a splendid fire. And if it had not occurred, there is no telling how long the Rock Island would have put up with its frame building. As it was, before another year went by, the railroad had constructed a handsome new brick depot, poured $26,000 into the economy, and favorably impressed passengers who looked upon the station through their train windows.

Father did not always provide an exciting fire to witness when Maude attended a tea party and stuck her husband with minding the kid. But I usually enjoyed myself on such occasions by rubber-stamping and scribbling over all the paper I found around loose. Mother protested lightly of the grime I got on my hands from father's stamp pads and from my manufacture of carbon copies by use of his letterpress. This machine was also effective in flattening fingers. Father was his own secretary, law clerk, and stenographer. He produced his pleadings, wills, contracts, leases, and other legal documents on a "blind" Remington typewriter. The type bars on that model struck the paper from below the platen, and thus the typist could not see what was being written. Only by lifting the carriage could the operator discover (sometimes to his surprise) what he had typed. Father used only two fingers to work the Remington as he put his legal thoughts on paper. In later years, after he had hired a stenographer and equipped her with a more sophisticated machine, I inherited the Remington. I found it an interesting but baffling contraption. It is now peacefully interred in the Emmet County historical museum, along with butter churns, spinning wheels, and other relics.

Estherville's growth from 1900 to 1910 was negligible. But from a population of 1,475 in 1890, the town grew to 3,237 inhabitants by 1900. In 1910 the city count was 3,404. County population decreased slightly during the first decade—from 9,936 to 9,836. Railroad division-point employment and improved transportation facilities had provided growth in the last decade of the previous century, although the most dramatic increase of county population had occurred during the period of rapid settlement from 1860 to 1870, when the county's growth was from 105 to 1,392.

The need for a better post office was such that in 1911 the federal government invested $65,000 in stone, terrazzo, oak lumber, brass fittings, and other materials for a building.[2] I. N. Salyers was the contractor. An unplanned dividend of the improvement was a monument to Fort Defiance placed in the park across the street from the new post office. A stone column rejected by inspectors because it had been damaged in shipment became an imposing monolith, capped by a sphere of stone. The pillar stands on a massive square of granite in a patch of grass, an island surrounded by asphalt. Four Civil War cannon stood guard around the monument until World War II, when they were turned over to the Boy Scouts and were melted down to defeat Hitler and the Japanese. A fountain, near which grandfather and I ate pears, was part of the memorial provided by members of the DAR chapter, but a new courthouse with parking lot stands where I liked to watch tadpoles in the fountain.

When Alex Johnston and Guy Gardner built a new hotel in 1912 at the southeast corner of the square, they called it the Gardston, giving themselves shares in the name, for which Elsie Horswell won a prize. This new three-story building was the most imposing structure of its day and became favorite lodging for traveling salesmen and other worthy transients. The Western Union located its telegraph office there and George Bale's pharmacy occupied the corner space, handy for Bromo Seltzer and aspirin. Fire had de-

Fort Defiance monument in park, built about 1912.

stroyed the old Lincoln House in 1904, when the whole Coon block burned.

Much more durable than Estherville buildings was Mack J. Groves. He survived political defeat, fires, bank failure, depression, and sometimes scalding newspaper attack. Smooth shaven, round faced, and of rosy boyish complexion, Mack attired himself differently from anyone else in the town. His trademark was a wide-brimmed, soft felt, tan hat of uncreased crown. I seldom saw him without it, whether at a huge farm south of Swan Lake that he liked to call his ranch or on the occasional visit he made to the bank in which he owned a controlling interest. He also owned the Farmers State Mutual Hail Insurance Company, a business he and Fred G. Parsons conducted in an office over the apparel and dry-goods store of L. M. Christensen, the town's most successful merchant, who weathered a fire, bank failure, depression, and chain-store competition. Now on North Sixth Street, the store is bigger than ever.

Like numerous other downtown buildings, the Christensen store building belonged to Groves. His office, extending over half of the wide store building, included a room at the back that was his private domain. There he presided over a vast table piled high with mail, some of it opened and some of it not. If there was any order to it, only Parsons, second in command, had any clue. In the front room Parsons sat at another large table, which was more orderly than Mack's, for it was up to Parsons to get things done. Parsons's early training had been as secretary to the Rock Island division superintendent. Along the west wall of the main office was a tall, two-door safe crammed with deeds, bonds, bank share certificates, abstracts of title, leases, insurance policies, hail insurance company records, ledgers, journals, correspondence, and guardianship and trust papers. Mack was acquisitive, even of pieces of paper.

He and his wife, Marietta, whom I never saw in his office, both drew salaries from the insurance company, as had brother George. Their generous pay drew criticism on occasion from the state insurance department. Besides hail insurance profits, Groves received substantial income from store building and upstairs office rentals, extensive farmlands, bonds, and bank investments. He was regarded as the richest man in town. Despite adversity, hard times, bank failures, and other economic mishaps, his estate was inventoried at a little over a million dollars when he died April 19, 1953.

Gardston Hotel.

It included 2,900 acres of land valued at $493,000, 11 buildings in town worth $356,000, stocks of $78,000, life insurance of $57,000, and other items including 3 residences and 6 vacant lots. Mack never got around to writing the will he kept telling father he intended to draw.

Administrators of his estate distributed $985,000 to thirty-six heirs in all, including $600,000 to Mrs. Groves. The estate was administered jointly by Mrs. Groves and by Clyde Sanborn, to whom Groves had given assistance after the death in 1913 of Clyde's father, Ed Sanborn, who with Groves had started the hail insurance company in 1898. Income from the estate helped defray $209,000 of administration costs and $217,000 of death taxes. Groves had by the time of his death disposed of some of his property to pay his bank stock assessments when the Iowa Savings closed and later when the Farmers Savings of Wallingford, last of Emmet County's bank failures, threw in the sponge.

Many townsmen blamed Groves for all the community's economic ills because he controlled many store buildings in the best locations. But when he passed on to his reward, nothing much changed, although some of the merchants acquired their own buildings when they were auctioned off by the administrators. His tombstone in Oak Hill is the most impressive rock in the cemetery.

Childless, Mack and Marietta lived in a house on Central Avenue big enough for a family of ten or fifteen, but it suited their lifestyle for two. For one thing, there was ample shelf room for Mack's books, many of them carefully selected to suit his taste — including political biography. A law graduate at the University of Iowa, Groves taught school briefly, worked for an insurance company, and then practiced law four years in Iowa City and from 1901 to 1919 in Estherville. In 1906 Groves ran for the state legislature on the Democratic ticket against my father. He lost, despite a flamboyant campaign that featured a special train to win voters of Armstrong and the rest of the east end of the county, where more Democrats lived than in Estherville.

With 120 loyal supporters on board, Mayor Groves's special train departed from the Rock Island station at 6:30 Saturday evening, shortly before election day, making stops at Gruver and Maple Hill to greet voters. At Armstrong the town band welcomed the Groves entourage with appropriate tunes to put voters in a Democratic frame of mind. Ringsted Danes, who normally voted strong for the Democratic ticket, were on hand. At the Armstrong opera house the Estherville mayor delivered what J. J. Reardon in the next week's Estherville *Democrat* described as "a great speech." The special train and its passengers departed the eastern precincts for home at midnight. But editor Reardon had to report a week later that, although Mr. Groves had "put up a stirring fight," the results were adverse: 775 to 1,028.

Groves retired as mayor the next spring, when Dr. W. P. Galloway was elected, but Mack had served two terms, from 1903 to

Mack Groves's house at Ninth and Central streets where the new Catholic Church is located.

1907, and he was again mayor from 1915 to 1919. He was interested in and worked toward developing municipal electric, water, and gas plants. He also was elected to the school board, of which he was a member from 1917 to 1920. During his tenure, no schoolteacher dared be reported as attending a dance or playing cards. Fortunately for his peace of mind it was not yet fashionable for women to smoke cigarettes and drink whiskey.

Groves was not timid in raising the rents on his various store buildings and offices. But there was occasion when he tore up a bundle of rent checks of a renter in distress. He delighted in tipping his barber a dollar bill. Groves generously supported charities and causes he favored, and he enjoyed being solicited for gifts by persons he liked coming to see him in his office. He liked to scribble all over the face of a check made payable to some pet charity, leaving barely discernible the information needed for the bank to be sure what sum to pay out. He wrote these messages, often on checks sent by mail, to reinforce his approval of a cause rather than bothering to write a letter. But the bank never issued a complaint about this odd practice; after all, he owned the bank.

Marietta was more careful, particularly after Mack's death, when she somehow could not understand that she was wealthy and had no need to skimp. Indeed Mack's death spread wealth among many relatives but there was plenty left for his widow. Upon her death, the executor, after probate expense, paid inheritance taxes on assets that included $146,000 of buildings in town, $267,000 in cash, $85,000 of bank stock, $217,000 of United States bonds, and the hail insurance company stock, which sold for $20,500 to Leo and Francis Fitzgibbons, lawyers for both Groves estates. Marietta was down to her last $783,000 — after probate expense — when she died.

Although Mack was content to find his recreation at the farm, Marietta liked to travel, often with her sister, Ethyl Walker, the hospital woman. The two of them saw America first, and then in an auto that Marietta took with her by steamship, they made a grand tour of Europe. Foreigners could look out for themselves as best they could in escaping fenders of the machine she piloted fearlessly and according to her own driving theories across the European continent.

One of Mrs. Groves's enjoyments was a cottage on the south shore of Spirit Lake. Whether or not it was modern depended on the point of view. With an inventor's pride, Marietta once pointed out to me the funnels in the floor of each bedroom that enabled a guest to avoid the necessity of retiring to the outdoor privy to meet a call of nature in the middle of the night.

While Mack admiringly gazed at steers feeding on his ranch, Marietta found her own pleasures at the card table, on the lake shore, sightseeing, or painting china, which she fired in her kiln on the third floor. Fred Parsons ran the insurance company, collected Mack's rents, and served as a liaison officer between Groves and Lloyd Stockdale, who tended the bank. Mack surrounded himself with people who could help build his little empire while he thought big.

Our Neighborhood Was Rarely Dull

MY first educational experiences were learning to build sand castles, to cut out paper dolls, to mold objects out of clay, and otherwise to amuse myself at Longfellow school in Des Moines. We lived on Pennsylvania Avenue, near University Avenue, while my father pondered legal niceties as assistant to Attorney General George Cosson. Father had been a serious candidate for attorney general in 1910 but decided not to run against Cosson, who apparently rewarded him with a consolation prize after being elected.

In addition to the exercise I received on a long walk to school, I was permitted to gather eggs in a henhouse father built in our backyard. I also watered oat sprouts in the basement that were part of the poultry nutritional program. This operation helped keep father from longing too much for some sort of a farm atmosphere, in which he felt most comfortable.

Although I enjoyed the daily visits down Pennsylvania Avenue of an ice cream wagon, which announced its presence by a tinkle bell, Des Moines life held as little attraction for me as it did for the rest of the family. However, I was to miss the long sticks of licorice from the little neighborhood store on University when we moved back to Estherville in the spring of 1912, not many months after going to Des Moines. My baby brother, Robert, was sickly and so was my mother. The Des Moines climate got blamed for their illnesses, and perhaps not unjustly. The town was heated and powered by soft coal that enveloped the capitol city in irritating smoke. A severe case of whooping cough had done baby brother no good, either.

The home we moved back to in Estherville had been built by father on North Eighth Street when he and mother were married in 1902. The roof was so steep it could split a raindrop. Behind it was a chicken coop and a privy that was soon replaced by more modern

*First home of Maude and
Nelson Lee, on North
Eighth Street.*

facilities in an upstairs dormer that carpenters fashioned. A neighbor described the roof dormer, built for a bathroom, as a wart.

For soft water we depended on rain that fell on the roof and was conveyed into galvanized steel gutters and through downspouting into a lined cistern. In the earlier days, the cistern water was pumped by hand; when the electric age arrived, an automatic piston pump did the work. The cistern collected not only soft water but also whatever else happened to collect on the roof. An iceman who made a regular route supplied our household refrigeration. He brought a chunk of ice carried over his back with a pair of tongs to replenish the icebox daily. A placard in the front window informed him what size lump the housewife needed to keep her perishables cool.

When we got back to Estherville, I felt put down because my Longfellow education in paper dolls did not qualify me for second grade. Of course it didn't. That was a good thing, for otherwise I would have missed the experience of first grade in a pleasant room at Lincoln school. Sunbeams produced all hues of the rainbow as they played on brilliant prisms hung at the window. That is all I remember about first grade.

What I remember about second grade was a handsome bandage Dr. Bachman contrived to hold in my brains after I stooped on our back screened-in porch and split my scalp as I raised my head against the edge of an unfriendly two-by-four. No other second-grader was privileged to wear such magnificent headgear. Every kid in the room was green-eyed with envy. Third grade was memorable because a big bully who had regularly repeated all the grades opened a long pocketknife in a threatening manner when Miss Peterson reproved him.

At the time I was learning to ride a bicycle, the city government apparently permitted such traffic on sidewalks. My first ride turned out badly. Not having yet learned that a cyclist should look where he wants to go, not where he doesn't want to go, I riveted my eyes ahead of me on the seat of Pat Heaton's pants. Suddenly Mr. Heaton, an elderly gentleman, found himself astride the front wheel of my bicycle. His gracious understanding of my embarrassing error endeared him to me for life.

Fred Robinson, then assistant postmaster, lived in a snug cottage up on North Sixth Street, where I fetched milk in a pail for our family use. In summer I rode my bike on these evening excursions to supply us with fresh Jersey milk, which I often saw Mrs. Robinson strain through a white cloth. The cow was tethered close to my kite-flying haunt on a vacant lot. There were few houses in the neighborhood beside Tom Sunde's when I took my homemade kites there to fly them from the high ground.

So far as I was concerned, sidewalks were not only for bicycling but also for roller-skating. I must have logged enough miles on skates to girdle the equator three or four times. A marble player, I prized glassies, steelies, aggies, carnelias, and other beautiful vari-colored collector's items. We often played "chaser" on the way to school and gambled for clay commies when we got there.

Worth Schloeman and "Squeak" Kilgore, two older boys, owned the patents on my kite designs and other things I made, such as revolvers and weathervanes carved out of pine. Powered by rubber bands, the guns fired navy-bean ammunition. This artillery was replaced somewhat later by homemade slingshots and still later by an air gun that shot BB's. Worth, who lived next door, owned an Indian motorcyle, supplanted in time by a racing car, which became the death of him on an Indiana racetrack. "Squeak," like his pal Worth, owned a motorcycle — a Harley Davidson, I think. Later he became associated with his father, Charlie, in the K & K Hardware Store. But nobody ever seemed to call him Verne, as his mother had planned.

I remember racing through *Tom Swift* books purchased by my grandmother. I also read *Boy's Life* and *Popular Mechanics,* as well as books intended to improve my mind. I experimented endlessly, making gadgets illustrated in *Mechanics.* Only strong willpower enabled me to resist filling out coupons for free trials of bicycles, horns, and other tempting merchandise.

By the time I reached fifth grade, with no repetitions, I had to ask for frequent excursions to the boys' privy in the basement. Maria Pingrey, one of Amos's daughters, questioned my need for these trips to the latrine, but of course she could not be sure. Superintendent Sunderlin prevented irreversible injury to my kidneys when he transferred me from Lincoln school and banished me to Miss Kraft's room at the centrally located Washington building. Washington was constructed originally for the high school but had subsequently become a grade and junior high building.

Transfer from Lincoln deprived me of the robust games of pom-pom-pullaway that took place in the school yard while we watched the Human Fly in action. Easily the meanest kid at Lincoln, he was regularly indicted by his teacher for one crime or another and locked up in the principal's office, in a front, second-story room. While the principal taught her class, the mean kid, whose name might have been Munson, climbed out the window and entertained the rest of us at recess time by climbing along ledges in the brickwork. He sometimes ventured out far enough that he could peek into another window, further compounding his crimes by amusing and distracting pupils passing through the hall. If Munson was his name, he wasn't one of the family of "Pop" Munson, whose Crystal Springs Bottling Works quenched the thirst of young Estherville with all the known flavors, including my favorite, which was cream soda.

After school the Human Fly acted in the capacity of matchmaker in arranging pugilistics between us boys. Donald Pro, who turned out to be a competent bricklayer and later a tough proponent of full-value real estate as a member of the board of assessment and review, was my ally in frequent fistfights on the way home from school. We developed an effective strategy of alternating rearguard action for mutual protection. My friend Joe Pullen's style was so unorthodox it had no logical defense. He simply waved his arms in such a menacing fashion that everyone was reluctant to wade

Maude Lee.   *Judge Nelson Lee.*

through the human windmill. Our school route took us past the yard of widow Strong, who accused all Lincoln school inmates who came her way of teasing her fox terrier. I don't know that we did, but it is possible that Mrs. Strong's violent annoyance could have encouraged our baiting her dog. It was Mrs. Strong's bank account, not her terrier, that would make the front pages about a decade later.

The redheaded Miss Kraft, into whose fifth grade I was sentenced, must have enforced the least discipline of any teacher in the Estherville school system — or any system. I had no problem with her in arranging frequent visits to the dank, smelly latrine; the more pupils missing from the schoolroom, the simpler Miss Kraft's management problem became. She committed habitual offenders such as John and Clarence Golla (known by most members of the class as the Goolie kids) to disciplinary exile in the supply room off the back south corner of the room.

Actually, commitment to that cell had its advantages. While serving time in the cubbyhole, a culprit enjoyed an excellent view of the athletic field, where sometimes the high school football team engaged in rough practice. Also, the supply room was more peaceful and orderly than the classroom, in which somebody was always being whacked over the hand with a ruler for one misdemeanor or another. Even the smells of the toilet room were welcome relief from fifth-grade bedlam.

I might well have become a second Palmer and a leading prac-

titioner of his penmanship skills if Neva Hayden, my pretty seat-
mate across the aisle, hadn't written my slants, concentric ovals and
other noble writing-lesson flourishes. We easily smuggled this contraband between us because Miss Kraft was eternally busy with her
ruler. I always thought Palmer method writing was characterless,
although I admit it was reasonably legible when accomplished by
those more talented than I. No one ever accused my penmanship of
being attractive, or even legible. In junior high, Miss Marie Sorum,
who later became county superintendent of schools, sharpened my
arithmetic, if not my handwriting. It was wistful little Rachel
Amundson who won my heart. We exchanged amorous, lacy valen-
tines and affectionate glances as we marched from one class to another.

Junior high didn't impress me much otherwise, except for a
memorable observance of Arbor Day on the school front lawn. As
we junior high scholars gathered around a sapling that was in the
process of being planted, Bill Deming made a speech in behalf of
forestation. Upon concluding his long-forgotten words, he then said
solemnly: "We shall now put the trees around the dirt." This impressed me as good comedy and made me always remember Arbor
Day. As an adult I was to help plant hundreds of trees, perhaps inspired by Bill Deming's speech.

The George Lyon yard, on the way to Washington school, held
the interest of all the boys and girls in our part of town. A half block
of neatly manicured turf surrounded the red brick Lyon home of
wide veranda, Victorian bric-a-brac, and green-roofed turrets. A
three-foot wrought-iron fence invited passersby to stay where they
belonged. At the rear of the lot was a barn in which Virginia Lyon's
pony and her red pony wagon were housed. Near the corner in the
lot was a fountain, where sprays of water played in the breeze. We
resisted wading in the pool by resolute self-control. We were also
tempted to hurdle the fence and explore the yard. We did this only
if it appeared that the Lyon family was safely absent.

Once in a while an inept hurdler caught the seat of his pants on
a picket. We ruined scores of pencils and rulers by using them to
make a clicking noise as we rubbed them past the pickets. My pals
and I often discussed how wealthy we thought the Lyons must be to
support such opulence. One chap thought maybe old man Lyon
must have been worth at least $10,000. But that seemed modest to

another, who guessed he probably had $100,000 in the bank. All the estimates could have been conservative.

A wisp of a man, George Lyon had been secretary and general manager of the Northern Lumber Company since it was organized in 1892. The Northern, together with the Lehigh Sewer Pipe & Tile Company near Fort Dodge, of which he had been secretary and treasurer since it was organized in 1908, made a fortune for him and for James J. Spaulding of Sioux City. Lyon could afford a mansion, a pony, a red cart, a fountain, and a wrought-iron fence. And also long Havana cigars. In winter he wore a long fur coat that scarcely cleared the sidewalk as he lurched through snowdrifts on his way to the office. On his way, he would often stop at George Bale's drugstore for a Bromo Seltzer, especially on mornings after poker parties at the Northern's general office. W. C. Fields never portrayed anything more artistic than Lyon's slight figure pitted against the rigors of an Estherville snowstorm.

George Lyon became a legend after a trip he once made to Chicago, where he purchased a mahogany dining room table that he was sure would please Cora and perhaps make her less unenthusiastic about the weekly poker sessions. Not all went as planned. When a drayman delivered Lyon's surprise gift at the front door, George was at hand to escort his donation, along with a smile, to his spouse. The drayman, however, soon nodded knowingly to his employer. A slight hitch had developed, he said. The table was significantly wider than the doorway. George suggested various alternate postures in which the table might be insinuated into the house. They took measurements. They made calculations. The drayman and his helper stretched their muscles. But, no way. Excusing himself, Lyon marched down the steps and back to the pony yard, returning with an axe. Telling the teamsters to step aside, he delivered a mortal blow, splitting the center of the table with a well-aimed shot that seemed to muster strength beyond his means. He ordered the teamsters to finish the work and to deliver the polished firewood to the barn. The Lyons could eat on the furniture they already had. Thus George Lyon made his reputation as a no-nonsense person. How he comported himself upon losing a hand at poker I never learned.

Directly across Seventh Street from where Virginia Lyon's pony munched oats lived Jay and Annie Johnston and Annie's father,

Robert Barklie Callwell, whom the neighbors referred to as Old
Man Callwell. He was a civil engineer, who surveyed the first rail
line into Estherville. An Orangeman, born in Belfast, Callwell was
sometimes referred to as "The General"; he bequeathed to his
daughter much of his strength of opinion. His domain in the Johnston household was a spacious second-story, southwest bedroom,
which looked west upon the street and the Lyon menage. Through
the south window, his view of the A. O. Peterson home was unob-
structed; he had ruthlessly tucked away Annie's fancy lace curtains.
Callwell, who retired early each evening, regarded it as an unneces-
sary formality to draw the blinds of his windows as he stripped to
don his nightshirt. This oddity gave our neighborhood a certain
amount of character and interest but chronic annoyance to the Petersons.

A. O. Peterson may have thought that as a respected member
of the community — in his career he had not only retailed hardware
but was also a long-suffering volunteer fireman who had served four
terms as mayor, occupied the city clerk's office, and managed the
Chamber of Commerce — he might be entitled to sit with his family
at dinner without the embarrassment of front seats at a disgraceful
spectacle in General Callwell's bedroom. Although reluctant to
cause any problem among the neighbors, Mr. Peterson finally proposed to Annie that she discuss with her father the matter of his
failure to draw the shades. That she agreed to do. In short order she
relayed to A. O. her father's reply: "Tell them," he told Annie, "if
they don't like what they see to pull their own shades." That settled
the matter. Now the matter of privacy was all up to the Peterson
household, which included daughter Lucile, long the city's librarian, and son Russell, a classmate of mine, who for many years was
to superintend the city's public works. Nobody, but nobody, pushed
the general around.

I was grateful to him, though. When he came from Ireland, he
brought along plants that produced the finest rhubarb of the neighborhood. Annie shared the roots with mother, and, when she broke
up her home, wife Everyld and I transplanted them to our yard.
Succulent, delicious, tinted rhubarb pie was a Maude Lee specialty,
as it is Everyld's, as well. But we omit gooseberry pie, also one of
father's favorites.

Annie, like the general, had a mind of her own. By not always limiting herself to objective reporting, she could make any narrative interesting. One night she also made news. On a bitter cold Tuesday night in December 1925, Jay and Annie locked their drug and jewelry store at 11 P.M., after a busy evening of serving Christmas shoppers, and drove home in their Packard sedan. After parking the auto in the family garage at the extreme back of the large Johnston yard, they were walking toward the house when two men accosted them. "Stick 'em up," one of them commanded, believing that the jeweler had brought precious gems home with him. Jay responded by striking one of them with his fist, the newspaper later reported. Annie screamed—in such good voice that the neighbors, including Emmet County's Scottish sheriff, Thomas Nivison, heard her a half block away. As the sheriff and a passerby ran toward the group, the thugs jumped in their car and sped off.

At this point, versions of the story differ. According to the *Democrat*, the sheriff approached the Johnston home but hesitated to shoot because he couldn't be sure of whom he would hit. He shot twice at the car as it drove off. According to the other version, which I much prefer, the sheriff fired his revolver twice through the bedroom window, explaining later, "I'd've got 'em if I'd had ma puntz on." The fact is, though, two of Tom's bullets did hit the car, as the prisoners related in court three years later when they were apprehended. They pleaded guilty and were sentenced.

Tom's thick accent made him an interesting person but not one loved by the bootleggers who flourished during his time. During summer before the Johnston episode he, Mayor Lilley, and deputies liberated fifty-two gallons of booze when they smelled out a hideaway in the hayloft of a farm near Wallingford. I have to this day a pearl-handled revolver that Tom gave father one time after he had taken it away from some badman.

Tom's office was decorated with several noteworthy works of art that had deeply impressed me years before. These were classic cartoons of common motif—bathroom subjects. The sketches depicted unsophisticated users trying to comprehend the intended purposes of modern plumbing fixtures then not long in common use in Estherville homes. I recall one drawing of a confused bather sitting in a tub and holding a parasol over his head to ward off a torrent of water from the overhead shower. Another depicted a dopey-looking character standing in the stool of a water closet pulling on

the chain that hung from an overhead tank, obviously irritated because the shower declined to function. Perhaps the one who hung
these sketches and an immature schoolboy were the only viewers
who regarded this bathroom art as uproariously funny.

For entertainment, my boyhood companions and I depended
little upon spectator amusement, although occasionally we found
our way to see a Fatty Arbuckle or a Ben Turpin comedy at the
King Theater. Mainly we devised our own entertainment. Although
we all enjoyed skiing, I'm sure that none of us developed the skills of
youngsters who now zoom down Estherville's well-appointed Holiday Mountain, which overlooks the south bayou, a favorite ice-
skating pond of my day. We skied down bluffs west of the river and
also down Squier's hill, which was a tricky run. The skier had to remember to duck his head just before swooshing under a barbed wire
fence.

One of the few regrets of my boyhood was the lack of a good
pair of skates. I was too bashful to ask for a pair of shoe skates and
too careful of my meager earnings to buy a pair. I skated on hand-
me-downs that clamped on my shoes. The Johnson Shoe Repair
made a fortune off my father replacing heels and soles I tore off my
shoes. Numberless times I spilled onto the ice when one skate or the
other ripped loose from its moorings. The school administration
sought to cooperate in providing for winter sports by flooding the
old athletic field west of the high school. But invariably an unseasonable thaw filled the basements of neighbors' houses with the
water from our rink. I can't remember ever playing a game of
hockey or using a puck; we played shinny. A crushed condensed
milk tin can served as a puck. Churches and other groups organized
bobsled parties but I was shy and avoided them. I learned to like
girls somewhat later.

When it was decided I would attend Camp Foster on the shore
of East Okoboji with other Boy Scouts of the area, my father fashioned a trunk out of a wooden packing box. He fastened a lid on it
with hinges at one side and a hasp with a padlock on the other. At
each end he bored two holes and into these attached rope handles.
Even Northwest Air Lines couldn't have destroyed that substantial
piece of luggage. In it I packed my worldly possessions for two weeks
of broadening. A group of us scouts boarded a Rock Island passenger train to Orleans, all of fifteen miles away, where we disem-

barked and carried our trunks a few hundred yards to the end of the lake. That's where the fun began.

The steamer *Des Moines* picked us up at the dock for the voyage through a drawbridge at the town of Spirit Lake and then through the winding lake to Camp Foster. Somehow I found myself elbow to elbow with the skipper. He served as captain, quartermaster, chief engineer, and purser. When we had passed the drawbridge, the captain said he needed someone to guide the vessel while he collected fares from the passengers. He couldn't miss me as a likely candidate for the appointment, because I was virtually glued to him. Indeed I would be happy to take the wheel. "Just keep the prow on that barn roof you see over there," he directed. "I'll give you another sighting when we go 'round the point." How could anyone possibly strike it as rich as I did? And let it be said that helmsman Lee avoided all shoals, reeds, docks, fishing boats, driftwood, and other impedimenta. At Camp Foster my dream ended.

After my euphoria of piloting the *Des Moines,* everything that followed was anticlimactic. The camp food was acceptable but washing our tin dishes in swill proved unappetizing. I enjoyed group singing around a campfire, the baseball and volley ball games, and a rowing contest. I was an experienced oarsman. But the swimming instructor found me a lost cause; I seemed to have the buoyancy of lead sinkers. Somehow I managed to stay afloat long enough to win points needed to receive a coveted bronze button but I decided I was no fish, just as in time I determined that birds are best suited for flying.

Two weeks at camp were adequate for my camping career. As life went on, I became increasingly enthusiastic about rough outdoor life when experienced inside a tightly screened porch fitted with upholstered furniture. It was my son Bob, when old enough to know better and despite extensive educational advantages, who became addicted to backpacking in the wilderness, eating campfire grub, and sleeping on the ground in a tent with rabid skunks and poisonous snakes while matching wits with wood ticks at the risk of a painful death from Rocky Mountain spotted fever.

Ray Dauber, who lived on the next street, incited the envy of me and every other boy who knew him. He owned a long pole with which he developed unbelievable skills. He could invade any yard he chose, vaulting over fences and hedges into forbidden places, and could leap back out of danger in seconds. When Dauber reached high school he became a star. All of us boys caught the vaulting fever, but no one could rival the powerful Dauber. I never heard of his getting into mischief, but it must have required some- one of his superb physique to help loft a wagon high in a tree near the school yard one Halloween.

Roy Nelson, who like Dauber lived on Sixth Street, was an- other pal of mine. We enjoyed reading Tarzan stories in the loft of his father's barn, where we learned something about biology. It was there that Roy's cat delivered her kittens. We formed a small, select club, the eligible members of which were entitled to full reading privileges and other amusements such as card playing and watching the cats.

I enjoyed several sources of income but none of them produced riches. I mowed the neighbors' lawns and shoveled their sidewalks. Dr. Bachman, our family physician, who lived across the street, was one of my clients. I mowed his grass despite my unhappiness with his frequent orders to my parents that they should dose me with cal- alactose and castor oil for whatever ailed me. The potency of this heroic treatment fell somewhere between gunpowder and TNT.

Because of these ministrations, or despite them, I survived boy- hood. Since castor oil was invariably spiked into orange juice, it was ten years after abstaining from castor oil before I could drink a glass of plain orange juice without gagging. Upon the good doctor's recommendation, our family consumed gallons of cascara to com- bat constipation. I looked more favorably upon yard customers who didn't pollute me with castor oil and cascara.

On one occasion, when I had apparently been exposed to some sort of noxious disease, my mother hung a lump of asafetida around my neck. The malodorous stink given off by that oriental resin was sure to ward off any plague or person sensitive to putrefaction. Dr. Bachman was probably not responsible for my wearing the foul- smelling necklace made from the gum of a plant so fetid that it was named asaFETIDa.

Although our family was invaded by measles, whooping cough, World War I influenza, and chicken pox, it was never necessary to hang a yellow pest placard on the door to warn whomever it might concern that the house was infected by a communicable disease. When the Clinites, next door, were quarantined for diphtheria, the neighbors and friends left food offerings at the back door, careful to escape a safe distance from the banished derelicts when they opened the door. Young Frederick developed a nasty mastoiditis that destroyed much of his hearing. Those were days before merciful wonder drugs had been discovered.

Mother was a talented meat and pastry cook, who created sweet or sour milk pancakes, waffles, bread, muffins, cinnamon rolls, plum dumplings, and every known flavor of pie—all served in portions worthy of the appetites of threshers. In building a fortune for General Mills by keeping our bin filled with Gold Medal flour, our family may have neglected a good balance of fresh fruits and vegetables.

My appetite was stimulated not only by trimming the grass of the doctor but by serving as handyman for Dr. J. I. Clinite, Wesley Robb, L. M. Christensen, and Walter Crowell. Dr. Clinite, our dentist, was my favorite customer. For one thing, he didn't sentence me to castor oil, and for another he paid me to launder his black Hudson Super-Six coupe oftener than needed. My father encouraged me to husband the meager earnings from neighborhood employment by committing them to a savings account.

Weeding the family garden permanently prejudiced me against vegetables, particularly string beans, radishes, and green onions. I never could figure out why the weeds grew faster than the vegetables, which had to be babied and pampered. When I worked for the neighbors they paid me in cash. I received my garden pay eating string beans. Besides that, Amos Pingrey brought in better-looking truck than grew on our 20-foot-square farm. And I figured if I kept at truck farming I would get as stooped over as the elderly Mr. Pingrey. Father greatly respected him as a pioneer farmer and an exceptionally bright schoolteacher, as was daughter Lucy, my Latin teacher.

Because my mother thought I ought to learn to play the piano, Mrs. Jay Dunham, whose husband was a locomotive engineer, came to our house every Saturday morning to hear if she could notice any improvement in my thumping. She sat sternly at my left elbow as I clumsily ran the scales and played simple ditties on our Everett upright piano. Florence Morse, daughter of one of the railroad dispatchers, was the next one to try to make a musician of me. She was better looking and taught me to play "Narcissus."

Then came Nora Marie Harker. Her father coined a mint of money selling International Harvester implements and parts, and lumber. Marie was a product of the New England Conservatory of Music and was a disciple of Mary Baker Eddy. Nobody in her recitals could play louder than I. After I had thundered through a Chopin "Polonaise," the audience, composed of suffering parents, applauded respectfully when they were sure I was finished with the performance. Miss Harker also taught me the rudiments of harmony, which I enjoyed more than trying to read notes.

I later prostituted my slight harmony skills in my college years by improvising catchy tunes of the Roaring Twenties. My buddies and I, equipped with a mandolin, drum, horn, and Steinway, observed the Sabbath and certain other occasions with jam sessions. Miss Harker recognized in my curly-haired little brother more talent than she could discover in me. Mother also took piano lessons from the prim little Miss Harker, who firmly believed in perfection.

Threshing rigs were powered by steam engines that resembled railroad locomotives. A long, wide leather belt, with one twist in it, took power off the steam engine pulley and conveyed it to the grain separator, which was placed several yards away. A threshing crew included not only the neighborhood men, who were members of the "run," but also their wives, who prepared vast kettles and pans of victuals to stoke their hungry husbands. The crew gathered the shocked oats or barley in the field, hauling away the tied bundles on wagon racks drawn by teams of powerful horses. Pitching the bundles into the mouth of the threshing machine was easier and more fun than hoisting them with a pitchfork into the wagon in the field. Chaff and straw blew high into the air from the machine to form a huge stack, while the threshed grain spouted into wagon boxes. These wagons hauled the grain to a terminal in town or to the farmer's own overhead granary. I tried my hand a few times at pitching bundles when Bill Hageman threshed his oats. It was the hardest work I ever did; at Mrs. Hageman's dinner table I ate disgracefully.

Dr. Clinite later gave up his practice to manage a Flying Circus when his wife's brothers, the Donaldsons of Milford, came back from World War I aviation and, after doing some barnstorming, began putting on airshows. The idea flopped because there was no way to restrict viewers to those buying tickets. Everybody could see the aerial spectaculars for free.

Threshing crew at the Jens Christensen farm, about 1914.

Dr. Clinite, my best source of income, taught me to drive at a tender age. After he drove me down to his dental office one noon, he told me to drive the Hudson back. I don't know if he was unaware I had never piloted a car before, and I didn't tell him. A proud moment of my life was steering the Hudson up Seventh Street and into the Clinite driveway, neatly missing both the house and wall of the porte cochere. By warding off disaster I pleased my mother, who always expected the worst to happen, and my father. He was prone to all sorts of little auto misadventures and was disbelieving that I hadn't collided with something. He never quite got himself out of the horse-and-buggy era and into the motor age.

We never did own a Model T Ford or any other car that had to be wound up with a crank. It was a good thing, or father would have fractured one or both of his arms for sure. Not that he was awkward—in fact, he was quite well coordinated. As a boy he played baseball, before mitts and gloves came into vogue in Estherville, and he could repeatedly lift sacks of flour as high as he could reach when he worked in Einer Sondrol's grocery store while going to school. Father just didn't get along easily and peacefully with automobiles.

Our first car was a Dodge touring model that the literature glowingly described as equal to the punishment of a trip through Death Valley. That was good enough recommendation for father, and I agreed. I remember that the car had seven narrow isinglass windows that provided the only viewing access to the rear.

One time when father brought home a load of shrubbery from the George nursery at Graettinger and drove into his driveway, he forgot that the bushes protruded through the open back door of his car. The awful noise Maude heard was Nels's Death Valley Dodge scraping the brick house along the full length of our built-in buffet.

Another time he lost a front door of his Hudson Super Six coach while pushing it into the garage after he and I had washed it. The door broke off when he carelessly got his arm between the car door and the garage. The arm escaped damage. The Hudson was perpetually thirsty, seeming to consume as much water as gasoline. Whenever the Hudson faltered, my mother, who knew even less about autos than my father, invariably suggested that the machine was probably out of water. The Super Six chewed up numberless fan belts, which often came apart at inopportune times on lonely stretches of highway remote from a service station.

My mother regarded father as a dangerous man at the wheel. But she also was accustomed to horse-and-buggy tempo. One time while driving north on Sixth Street, he stepped the Hudson up to forty miles an hour. He suggested it might be discreet not to relate this foolishness to Maude. But he took pride on our annual trip to Des Moines that we needed only two hours to reach a country schoolhouse south of Algona, sixty miles from home. We always stopped there to use the two outdoor privies. On the Des Moines jaunt, we invariably had to bring out the side curtains and button them on to keep us dry. It always rained. Our route was identified by markings on telephone poles that pointed out the Lincoln Highway, the AYP, the Daniel Boone trail, and other competing traveled ways. Whenever the telephone company replaced a key marked pole at a highway intersection, we were in trouble: to turn or not to turn. Muddy roads sent my nervous mother into spasms of fear. But we always made it without disaster.

The four-cylinder Dodge packed lots of power; none of that nonsense of having to back up a hill as some of our friends did, after they learned that reverse gear was more powerful than forward low.

Early cars with gravity-fed gas tanks located under the front seat encountered trouble on hills so steep that the gas wouldn't feed into the carburetor. That wasn't a problem with our Dodge. Let it be said that although father was not the handiest automobilist I ever rode with he did master the art of coordinating feet, hands, and mind to shift gears on a hill. Father was so conservative in turning corners that now and then, when he approached a turn faster than intended, he feared upsetting the machine and steered into the road ditch. Continuing off the road a few yards, he watched for a gentle slope and guided the car back on the road without changing the expression on his face. But he scared hell out of his passengers.

One of his lawyer friends, Byron Coon, always made it a practice to back clear down and start over again in low gear at the bottom of a steep hill. Charlie Barber — yes, the same Charlie Barber who helped dig up the meteorite that fell in 1879 — was a conservative motorist disinclined to trust either his skills or his brakes. He built doors at both ends of his garage, which had access from the street and also at the rear down an alley. Charlie was known to make as many as three runs at it before coaxing his Buick to settle down in such position that he could close the doors both fore and aft. One time he ran into a bull on one of his more awkward motoring experiences. When Charlie got his car stopped, it was atop the bull, which bellowed discontent and regained freedom only when a garage tow truck summoned from Estherville lifted the car back on its wheels.

Conservative George Letchford, who lived two blocks down the street from us, was for a brief time the Hudson automobile dealer. He led interested prospects to his garage and told them that they could feast their eyes on his sedan through the side window. He didn't intend to have dirty-fingered customers smudge up his Super Six. His agency did not flourish. George was never a hand to have too many things going on at one time. While he was operating a grocery store, the Masons urged him to take an office in the lodge. But he declined. "By the time I remember all the cost and selling prices in my store, there just isn't room in my brain to learn the ritual work too," he told them.

In 1914, the year father built a brick house on a Seventh Street lot, where his parents and he had lived previously, Uncle Lewis came to visit us. Our family was spending a two-week vacation on

*New Lee home on
Seventh Street.*

the south shore of Spirit Lake when father's uncle arrived from Wisconsin. Not finding the family at home in Estherville he got back on the train, rode to the station at Spirit Lake, and walked over to the cottage two or three miles away. Then he walked back, bought a bathing suit, donned it at the cottage, and dived off the end of the dock. Not bad for a man of seventy. His outdoor life in the Wisconsin pineries had kept him young; he never missed two or three dips a day at the lake. It was my lot to sleep with him, snoring and all. Uncle Lewis, who I learned many years later while in Voss, Norway, was christened as Lars, liked us so much that he went back to Wisconsin, packed his trunk, and came to stay. A fatal tumble down stairs eleven years later terminated his visit.

Uncle Lewis's partiality to the Democratic party added yeast to discussion in our progressive Republican home. Debates were frequent. He plagued my mother when she was scrubbing and waxing the kitchen floor and forbade him to walk over it. "I'll step lightly," he would compromise. When at dinner my mother invited him to have a second piece of apple pie, his answer would likely be, "Too much of your pie, Maude, is just enough." He rarely turned down a second wedge of anything. An old-time fiddler for barn dances in Wisconsin in early days, he often tuned up and entertained us with "Irish Washerwoman" and other melodies. He spent most of his time reading and studying French, which he wanted to add to the Norwegian and German he spoke.

Assigning himself the post of chief engineer, he pretended he was back in the pineries as he monitored gauges on our hot water heating plant and kept vigil on the faucets, toilets, cistern pump, and other mechanical nuisances. Our living room might be filled with guests when Uncle Lewis would command father's undivided attention: "Nels, that twaletta is leaking again." The guests were not supposed to know he was referring to our temperamental water closet. My mother's already red face got still more crimson. She embarrassed easily.

Uncle Lewis had no patience with Minnie Swartz, who assisted mother with cooking and housecleaning. Minnie tried to excuse Kaiser Wilhelm's army for its invasion of Belgium and France. He mimicked her broken English and caused several embarrassing incidents. Minnie, who had been in America only a short time, felt she still owed some loyalty to the fatherland.

In winter our eleven-year houseguest insulated himself with two of everything—and topped them off with a coat made of bearskin, buffalo hide, or some other furbearing animal. He was a formidable, furry snowplow as he struck off in stormy weather for the square. Whenever he was tempted to invest in shares of stock of some newly organized Estherville concern, he always asked my father's advice. But he rarely followed it. He had little resistance to such ventures as Norman and Max Maine's Hardwood Milling Company and their piano factory, H. D. Hinsch's Purity Yeast factory, the Silver Fox Farm, and other such unseasoned investments.

Conversation at our dinner table was usually lively and now and then got off to an uncertain beginning if my father allowed Maude's beef roast to cool while he honed and steeled the carving knife. She thought a knife might be more appropriately sharpened before the guests seated themselves. The range of dinner conversation subjects was almost limitless, and our meal might be spiced, if the pièce de résistance happened to be fowl, with his anecdote about Judge Cook. The temperamental judge, while carving, wrestled with an uncooperative goose that slid onto the tablecloth and ultimately onto the floor. The judge then kicked the misbehaving fowl through the screen door. The moral of this story seemed to be that, despite my father's tribulations in dealing with what Maude had put before him, he was by no means as impatient and violent as Judge Cook.

Father also enjoyed telling about a lawyer representing an insurance company in court who, in defending a personal injury case, sought to prove there was nothing unusual about a person developing a numb scalp. He told the jury that he himself, even though he had never been run down by a two-ton truck, possessed no feeling in his skull. Having fortified his cranium with injections of novocain, the lawyer became a human pin cushion during his argument to the jury as he stuck one pin after another in his head to reinforce each point in his brief. We never learned who won the case.

For one Christmas dinner mother planned to serve a fat goose brought to her by "a generous lady from the country." But we never got to eat it. Father sent it back to the country when he discovered that the donor was involved in a lawsuit coming up before him in district court. He was fussy about such things.

Diners at our table were a captive audience as Father enumerated how many jackknives he lost on the prairie as he herded during his boyhood. One of his favorite reminiscences was how he and his friend Peter Peterson, misunderstanding Mr. Peterson's wishes, set fire to a haystack in the farmyard. Good luck saved the township from devastation. Through numberless other tales told and retold, my mother listened in good humor—so long as Nels didn't delay serving the victuals while they were hot. Sometimes in summer we listened to music during the meal as Sam Blacketer, who lived a half block away on Sixth Street, practiced on his ocarina. He played bells, and fiddled, too. Father was unenthusiastic about the ocarina music, which he said did nothing to aid his digestion.

Father took pride in the house blueprinted in Jim Cox's architectural office, which he built of brick and mortar. Ample John Pro was the mason. His son, Donald, who developed into a better bricklayer than I, joined me in constructing miniature buildings of our own from mortar and chips of brick left from each day's work. That was more fun than my assignment as cleanup, a duty I performed reluctantly each evening, when I gathered shavings, sawdust, and scraps of wood to tidy up the premises. Father was particularly proud of the five-coat inside finishing job done by the painter, Tom Leiren. When Mother disposed of the house more than fifty years later, the oak woodwork was bright as ever, although her immaculate housekeeping was partly responsible for its preservation.

Leiren was the Tom of Tom & Jerry, as Knut Gronstal and his brother-in-law were known after they painted a steel bridge built over the Des Moines River two miles north of town near the old Amos A. Pingrey farm. Tom & Jerry's paint and varnish store turned into one of the town's most spectacular fires for the year 1914 because it contained all the combustibles required for a first-rate blaze. As I recall it, Harry Toll's livery barn and a three-story business building across the street went up in smoke at the same time. During that fire Ed Stockdale and Jack Strube rushed up to their second-floor offices to save what valuables they could. When they safely reached the street, they found that what they had rescued were stacks of posters that had been delivered by the printer to advertise an Elks show.

The *Opera House Reporter,* which published news of the theatrical community, attracted national circulation. James S. Cox, an architect who designed the Lough Opera House, and much later the high school building, the Gardston Hotel, Graaf's theater, and many other buildings and houses, including father's, started the *Reporter* in 1898. He was joined in the venture by his brother Jesse, a widely known figure among actors and producers because of his

Shop for theatrical newspaper, Opera House Reporter.

studio, which painted scenery for theaters from coast to coast. He invented and patented a type of backdrop scenery that could be rolled up and stored. It was sold all over the world.

The *Reporter,* of which L. C. Zelleno became editor, was one of a kind. It was published in the town until 1917, when Zelleno took it to Des Moines. It was the *Variety* of its day. Theater personalities depended on it for news of the world in which they revolved. After the Opera House burned, the lot remained vacant until in 1917 the Elks Lodge, with a membership of 500, built a new home on the space. The talented Jesse, whose skills included playing the horn and who for years led the town band, decorated the new Elks quarters with artistic, original artwork that glorified the antlered creatures of the wild from whom Elks took their name. The building was a disappointment to aquatic members, however, because in some sort of oversight the basement swimming pool was built too low to drain into the sewer outlet. Much later, modern pumps and more funding got the pool in operation, but my swimming suffered neglect.

Although I then had no taste for tobacco, Richard Hogett's cigar factory next door to the Elks held my interest. I was fascinated by the twenty-two women who rolled tobacco into neatly wrapped stogies. While working in our basement on some toy-building project, I occasionally smoked grapevine root, which must be about the foulest smoke anyone could breathe. Later, when I went to college, I began polluting my lungs with cigarette smoke and experimented briefly with chewing Beech Nut tobacco. A few of the boys in high school smoked some, but most of them indulged only experimentally.

On my first visit home from Chicago after my freshman year in college, I went into George Bale's drugstore and asked for a package of Chesterfields. "Oh, no," said Mr. Bale. "You're exactly the same age as William and I know you're not yet 21." He lost the sale but not my respect. His son Bill was then a student at the University of Iowa. We were friends while in high school, and also later when he opened a law office and served as county attorney.

Bill was a talented athlete whose misfortune it was to acquire chronic heart disease, which cut his legal career short. He and Willis Gruwell were two fast high school backfield men who also starred in track and basketball. Along with Ray Dauber, they were the nu-

Hogett Cigar Factory. From left: Joe Danielson, Dick Hogett, Charles Butler, Dorothy Steele, Ella Steele, Mrs. Hogett, Mrs. Charles Baker, Fred Maloy.

cleus of great teams. Dauber was himself a one-man track team. He vaulted, high jumped, broad jumped, hurdled, put the shot, hurled the discus, and, flatfooted, ran whatever sprint or relay race the coach needed him for. Bill Bale was capable of playful pranks, but nothing as entertaining as the brilliant mischief invented by a fellow whose name I think was Torbet, son of the Methodist preacher.

The night before Torbet's father was to utter reverential remarks one morning at the high school opening assembly, his son planted a Big Ben alarm clock in one of the ceiling light fixtures. He timed it to awaken students in the midst of preacher Torbet's remarks. It was a highly successful program innovation deeply appreciated by those not sitting on the platform. Principal Pearl Bemis of course held a different view. I don't remember Torbet's punishment, but it was short of pillory or burning at the stake.

I discovered that the high school Hesperian Literary Society had little to do with literature or much else of intense interest to me. When I progressed to solid geometry, I was over my head, and although I enjoyed Latin grammar and reading Caesar's *Commentaries*, I found Cicero insufferable. What I did like the most was mechanical drawing, plane geometry, English composition taught by Clara Brees, and writing the *Pepper,* particularly when I took the copy to the printer and helped Ed Sillge make up the paper. Oratorical contests I found frightening, but because I like arguments I debated. John Lytle was the coach.

My high school senior English teacher, Dorothy Latchem, did her best to make her students relish gems of Chaucer and other of her favorite poets, but my taste in literature ran to prose and I was not one of her pets. In fact, one day I fell asleep in class. She punished me by allowing me to snore well into the next batch of seniors that filed in. She gave me the lowest marks of my high school experience, which probably proved she wasn't as easily deceived as the other teachers.

Miss Latchem was as enthusiastic about music as she was about Chaucer. She played the organ at the Methodist Church for forty years, played and taught piano, and wrote poetry. When she retired from teaching English in 1935, she married Chris Gronstal, a painter son of Jerry. After Chris died in 1952, she lived on in meager circumstances for another ten years. One day she drove up to the site of the community's first settlement at Emmet Grove and there at the bridge drowned her loneliness.

As an athlete I was a washout, but I did cure my flat-footedness by running the 220 and 440 — at my own deliberate pace. The coaches regarded me as fourth-rate material. Golf was not recognized as a reputable school sport at that time and there was no team for many years to come. Coach Sauerman was relatively safe when he generously offered me a "letter" for my sweater if I could sink enough putts to win the state tournament, which I did not do.

If "foot-and-a-half" had been a scheduled event I might have come closer to winning an *E.* Each morning and noon we played foot-and-a-half, which was a sophisticated form of leapfrog in which tall kids like me enjoyed some advantage. The game involved making a wild leap, after a variety of hops and skips, over the rump of whatever player was the stooped-over goat who had upset the previous goat.

At the last minute before a graduation party, I steeled myself to ask a girl by the name of Hazel for a date. Those were the most difficult words I had ever tried to get out. She just eyed me and walked off.

I tried lodge life at an early age as my friends and I, high school juniors and seniors, became charter members of the Charles Keeler chapter of DeMolay. I think I might have been the first senior deacon, or held some such office. F. M. Jones was the Masonic "Dad," responsible for the conduct of our lodge. He directed us in reciting the ritual and comporting ourselves, watching, I suppose, to see that we acted as responsible youths rather than as an outlaw gang. Although I have been a member of the Elks for more than half a century, lodge meetings somehow never caught my fancy. Somewhere in an old trunk is my purple DeMolay cap, trimmed in gold braid.

War Days
and Happier Times

NO ONE who had ever visited Frank Carpenter's printshop could have been surprised when in 1915 the *Democrat* reported that the Estherville post office, over which Carp was presiding as postmaster, had been judged by inspectors to be the cleanest in the whole state of Iowa. Carpenter was an appointee of President Woodrow Wilson, for whom the *Democrat* repeatedly expressed undying loyalty and high esteem. James W. Ghoslin edited the paper and managed it for a time while Carp ran the post office — from 1914 to 1922. Roscoe Allison succeeded Ghoslin. Later, Carpenter sold the paper to W. C. and G. C. Fancher, who were still operating it when voters elected Warren Harding as president, and Carpenter, a Democrat, had to turn his thoughts back to newspapering. During his absence as editor the paper continued to support Democrats, including Mack Groves and other cronies of the editor-turned-postmaster.

Town commerce began looking up at the end of 1914, when Roy Buckingham opened the Estherville Wholesale Grocer Company, a branch of the Fort Dodge Grocer Company. Roy rivaled Mack Groves as the town's best barbershop customer. He perhaps rated second only to George Lyon as a consumer of cigars. Roy's gait was as self-assured as it was long. He soon became one of the town's leading figures. In 1918 the Grocer Company finally finished a three-story building it needed. Retailers from a wide territory came to see the special displays of food at the plant and be guests at a festive dinner served in the new Elks home, which had been completed only in February.

The suffragettes, who tested their wings at meetings in 1916, were consulted on their opinions a year later, when 800 petitioners asked the city council to take over the independent Estherville Gas Company, which had barely gotten started before becoming financially distressed. The council at first rejected the petition because it lacked female signatures. Mayor Groves and the council had become conscious of woman's suffrage; they wanted to get the housewife's point of view on a matter that involved fuel to bake, fry, broil, and stew the aldermen's victuals. By an overwhelming majority the taxpayers voted to bond themselves $11,000 to get the gas system going. The city completed the works and continued to operate the plant until 1940, when Northern Natural Gas bought the system and operated it as Peoples Natural Gas Company. In 1917 any kind of gas was welcome to housewives. It was better than coal or wood.

Electricity was also available in abundance. Two years before, the city had switched from steam-powered to diesel-powered generators. With indoor plumbing conveniences, electricity rather than kerosene lamps to read by, and gas for the kitchen ranges, the housewife was having it better. But while women's opinions were being consulted about cookstoves, the climate was not yet favorable to equal rights across the board.

However, there were some champions of suffrage, and one of them was William Jennings Bryan, who in 1915 resigned as secretary of state in disagreement with President Wilson's views on the European war after a U-boat sank the *Lusitania*. When Bryan spoke on the Estherville chautauqua platform a year after he resigned, he chose a four-point subject: woman suffrage, liquor, war, and peace. The *Democrat* reported after the program that he spellbound his audience of 3,500 members. There was no hint that inclusion of "liquor" in his topic was tailored to suit Estherville thirst. He was probably unaware that, just before Mayor B. B. Anderson turned the mayor's chair over to Mack Groves, officers spilled 181 gallons of drinkable refreshments that his raiders had seized in Jay Johnston's drugstore and elsewhere around town. And besides, Mayor Anderson posted a $175 reward to anyone helping to dry up the town by identifying liquor law violators. Strong drink was therefore a timely topic for chautauqua platform rhetoric when Bryan came to town. Although President Wilson's view had prevailed over Bryan's, and he successfully campaigned in 1916 on the theme that he had kept the country out of war, it would not be long before the European war was very much an American conflict as well.

Only a month before young men of the community began

offering their services as soldiers in World War I, a group of hardy basketball players settled a grudge against Emmetsburg, the town's arch athletic foe. To ensure neutrality for a game that aroused intense emotions, town basketball teams of the two communities agreed to play each other on the Spirit Lake high school floor. Red Egan of Des Moines came up to officiate the encounter. George Booth, Hans Robb, John Murray, Ralph Potter, John Webb of Spirit Lake, and Ed Madison of Goldfield rode to Spirit Lake the night before the game and rested together at a hotel to assure their maximum effort next day. A. J. Flaucher was the coach. Both towns brought brass bands, which along with the spectators rode to the supergame in twelve coaches of a special train. The outcome by no means ended the combative spirit of the two towns, but a 53–23 trouncing over Emmetsburg sent Estherville enlistees off to training camp the next month in an ebullient victory mood.

Fifty-three Estherville men, cheered by a throng of about 2,000 townspeople who gathered at the Rock Island station, departed for camp as volunteers for military duty, just eight days after the United States on April 6, 1917, declared war against Germany. Among the first thirty-six men to respond to a call of arms was Maurice Doyle, the town's first casualty in action on the western front. An estimated 4,000 persons attended a flag-raising ceremony for enlistees entering military service. At farewells and banquets, Estherville sent a steady flow of volunteers and draftees to camp. Cheers and tears mingled at the partings. By June 6 the draft board had registered 1,284 young men between twenty-one and thirty years of age. On September 5 the board's members—J. J. Klopp, Tom Nivison, and Dr. M. E. Wilson—began calling the first numbers drawn for service. A militia company organized to hold drills on the home front, while on the Washington front L. L. Bingham's brother Walter, a distinguished Swan Lake son, took leave of his teaching duties at Carnegie Tech to apply his psychology skills in deploying United States Army personnel.

By the end of the summer the home front was feverishly trying to assist the soldiers, sailors, and aviators who with little training soon became engaged in action on the seas, in the trenches, and in the air. Kinfolk and friends of the servicemen tried to make the war more bearable by giving time and money to supply needs for the American Red Cross. During the first four months, Red Cross women knitted 87 sweaters and 180 scarves, sewed 225 "bed shirts," 187 "nightingales," 60 pairs of leggings, 678 handkerchiefs, and produced scores of other items, including vast numbers of bandages. It was only the beginning of their production. In a single drive, the Emmet County Red Cross chapter collected $10,000 in cash. It auctioned off gift items, staged benefit performances, and employed other schemes to raise money for support of the fighters. The YMCA in one drive raised $6,000. Late in 1918 the community gave $40,000 for United War Work—the YMCA, the YWCA, the KC, and Jewish Welfare. Ethyl Walker went first to Washington and then soon to England to take charge of nursing wounded soldiers. When news was received at Christmas time from Norfolk that Leo Duffy of Armstrong was a naval casualty, Emmet County people became starkly aware of the grimness of the conflict.

In four Liberty Loan and one Victory Loan drive, Emmet County residents bought $2.65 million of government securities, including War Savings Stamps. (See War Loans in Emmet County in Appendix.) The county's quota was $2.43 million. Mack Groves bought more bonds than anyone else—$10,000 worth. Many of the subscribers purchased bonds bearing 3½ percent to 4¾ percent interest—with money they didn't have.[1] They had to borrow it, at 6 percent, 7 percent, or 8 percent interest. In some instances it meant downright hardship. Some purchasers had to make payments on bonds a few days before they could collect bank savings interest.[2] Coming in rapid succession, the drives soaked up credit and savings, to a large extent before the money had actually been accumulated.[3] The first Emmet drive, conducted by W. G. Saunders, was subscribed only about 20 percent. Ralph Miller of the First National Bank conducted the second, also undersubscribed, raising less than 80 percent of the quota. The experience was typical of most rural Iowa counties, whose population was 41 percent foreign origin. German-origin population made up 40 percent, Scandinavian-origin 20 percent, and Irish-origin 10 percent.[4]

Under pressure from the comptroller of the currency, banks hesitated to be stigmatized for failing to subscribe their quotas or neglecting to cooperate in making bond loans to their customers. The third and fourth loan drives developed more steam. The Treasury also helped the drives by raising the interest rate and shortening maturities of the new issues. County loan committees in

Iowa conducted kangaroo and loyalty courts, directed at pro-German individuals, using strong-arm methods of soliciting. Individuals appeared by request before quota committees and were told what was expected of them. Bankers bore the cost of local bond-selling expenses.[5]

John P. Kirby, president of the First National Bank, acted as chairman of the Emmet Liberty Loan committee for the third, fourth, and fifth drives, sparing no punches in seeking to oversubscribe them and push Emmet over the total quotas for the war. But tough methods left long-lasting scars on the community. Strong-arm tactics, described by the *Iowa Homestead* as a "Reign of Terror," and by the *New Republic* as "Borrowing with a Club," were commonplace in the state. As reaction set in, however, the United States Treasury warned C. H. McNider, head of the Iowa campaign, against use of force.[6]

Vacating its temporary wooden quarters, the Kirby bank moved into its new, magnificent home in April 1918, just after the third loan drive got under way. The loan committee erected a yellow "slacker board" directly across the street from the bank in the corner of the square. Individuals who purchased fewer bonds than demanded by the committee quota found their names prominently printed on the yellow board. Indignation ran high, and the high-handed sales methods erupted into newspaper controversy. The *Democrat* made comment about the "slackers" only after the *Enterprise* criticized its competitor for lack of patriotism in not castigating the "slackers" in print. Then the *Democrat* fired a salvo.

Two of the names displayed on the yellow board were brothers, sons of Sever Lee, on whose farm north of Estherville the main portion of the 1879 meteorite fell. The *Democrat* took notice in print of the seamy proceedings only when its own loyalty was questioned in *Enterprise* print. The *Democrat* then published a broadside blast at the *Enterprise* in big type in the center of page one. In one prominent column, the *Democrat* estimated that the two farmers named on the yellow board had a net worth of about $15,000. They had purchased $1,100 worth of bonds. In a second column, the *Democrat* displayed the estimated net worth of George Allen and his son Kirt of the *Enterprise* as $46,000. They had bought $1,000 worth of bonds, the paper said. "Now who are the slackers?" the *Democrat* asked in print big enough to be read across the room.

Two years after the war the Lee brothers sued members of the bond drive committee and editor Allen of the *Enterprise* for $40,000 injury to their character and reputation and for subjecting them to "ridicule, scorn, hatred, and contempt." But they collected no damages. A district court petit jury found that the committee had "acted in good faith, without malice or intent to injure in prosecuting a public duty."

Among other names the bond committee posted on the board in the square was that of a German family who became famous in World War II, when Dwight D. Eisenhower became supreme commander and later president of the United States. Even though loyal to America, Germans were suspect of being unsympathetic to the war effort. Many of those of German origin had to prove their Americanism. I recall one exciting evening when a parade headed up North Sixth Street toward the censured family's home. The fire truck drew a crowd, and red flares from the railroad provided an eerie setting. The crowd was not unruly, though somewhat menacing, I thought. No bodily injury came of the incident.

In June 1918 the community conducted memorial services for John W. Brawford, missing in action when the *Cyclops,* a navy collier, left the West Indies and was never heard from afterward. On every Memorial Day hence, J. S. Brawford paused as the procession crossed the river toward Oak Hill Cemetery to drop a wreath in the river in memory of his son for whom the Estherville VFW named its post. In July news arrived that Maurice Doyle had suffered mortal wounds. When after the war an Estherville American Legion Post organized, it was named for him, the first Estherville soldier killed in action.

The Maurice Doyle Post organized a drum and bugle corps that performed often at public parades. Along with its Auxiliary, the Legion in peace soon busied itself assisting the disabled and helping to rehabilitate veterans. At the next general election, Emmet County selected as county recorder veteran Ray Kennedy, who had lost a leg in the war. A granite marker, erected in 1939 by the Service Star Legion's war mothers, memorialized the debt owed the 612 men of the community who had served America in the war.

Among the many Estherville men who suffered serious wounds and were decorated was Emmanuel Stavros, injured the day after his comrade, Doyle, was killed. The war department awarded

Stavros the Service Cross, Oak Leaf Cluster, Purple Heart, and Silver Star. Many years later and long after my father's death, Emmanuel told me how nervous and excited he was when he applied for citizenship upon return from service. As he heard father from the bench question several applicants for naturalization about their knowledge of government, Emmanuel, a native of Crete, realized he was sure to flunk. Finally, it came his turn to appear before the stern-looking district court judge for questioning. "Are you the Emmanuel Stavros who served your country in the war?" the judge asked, while reading Emmanuel's war record. The little Greek remembered replying timidly, "Yes, your honor." Then the judge looked up, smiled, and said "Citizenship granted." "It was the happiest moment of my life," claimed the plucky fellow, who impressed everyone who knew him as afraid of nothing—except his meager knowledge of the history of his adopted country. Emmanuel started in Estherville shining shoes and cleaning hats at Bob Penn's barber shop, then at the Johnson Shoe Repair Shop. After learning the repair trade he at one time or another resoled most of Estherville's inhabitants and reared a family he was entitled to be proud of. A son, George, worked hard and loyally for his father and became a Phoenix physician. Emmanuel fenced in an area back of his boot-shop where with tender and loving care he created a beautiful flower garden.

During the war, farmers grew wheat whether they wanted to or not. Emmet's quota was 1,000 bushels, although the county grew primarily corn and oats, not wheat. Farmers plowed up their pastures and meadows to grow row crops at the insistence of the government to help feed Europe. The country went on daylight savings time to save fuel. Boosters of the bond drive and other war causes made four-minute talks at theaters before the flickers began. Readers pored over the pages of Arthur Empe's *Over the Top*, available at bookstores and at the public library. The local newspapers printed column upon column of letters from men in army camps and particularly from men overseas. Jim Ghoslin, who had edited the *Democrat* for a while, was soon writing letters to the paper from camp and then from France, beginning in July 1918, as a member of the Sixtieth Engineers. Relatives mailed hundreds of packages to the soldiers, hoping to make them more comfortable and less homesick.

I don't know how much I sold of the $227,000 in War Savings

Stamps purchased during one Emmet County drive, but I was one of the town's most pestiferous of all Boy Scout salesmen. We were called the gleaners of the loan campaign, working the town to sell low-cost 15-cent and $5 investments in the war. I much preferred this activity over trying to qualify for second-class scout status, which involved learning how to bake a potato on a campfire. I did labor to learn the Morse code. Keeping my dots and dashes straight kept me awake nights.

Telegraphers who could rattle a Morse key always amazed my slow wits. Other scouts were more proficient than I in wigwag signaling and other uses of the code, which I always thought had its limitations as a means of handy communication. Scoutmaster Bob Knight must have despaired of me as a scout, except when it came to selling War Savings Stamps. I earned so many clusters there wasn't room for them on my shirt. The neighbors and others I annoyed must have been relieved when the Huns threw in the towel, if for no other reason than to get shed of the kid who became a War Savings Stamp pest. They were happy, too, because the influenza epidemic that quarantined the town and laid low civilians as well as servicemen had abated.

Before the war ended, the town lost its First Lady; in March 1918, Esther Ridley died. The pioneer who in 1857 journeyed by ox team with her husband to settle a new town in virgin country surrendered to the struggle for life. In her eighty-six years she had seen a community settle, grow, and survive Indians, blizzards, prairie fires, locusts, and hardship. If she had lived a few more months, she could have helped welcome home young men from the war. Some, of course, never did return. Their graves were marked by white crosses. Others came back minus limbs or with other serious injuries. But there was little restraint in expressing gratitude for those spared. The *Democrat* described Armistice Day as bedlam. Ten thousand people crowded the town to parade, build bonfires, and become delirious with joy. The homecoming would have to wait until June, when the celebrating started all over again.

The war aroused intense interest in flying machines. Returning airmen utilized skills they had learned on the western front. Barnstorming by former war pilots became popular. They sold air rides, usually at $15 for a 15-minute spin. An Esthervillean by the name of W. P. Helinzky and his son Joseph built a biplane from blueprints they obtained, but I never learned if the machine ever became airborne. The first plane to touch down at the community had landed in 1915 in Lough's pasture in southwest Estherville. Curious lookers gathered there to inspect the open-cockpit ship piloted by a daredevil who entertained spectators with a program of wing walking, parachute jumping, and other rash acts that were more exciting than the balloon ascensions then common at fairs and carnivals. Some of the foolhardy paid dearly. Captain Adair's parachute never opened after he jumped out of a plane above near-by Milford at 4,000 feet altitude.

Barnstormers drew attention to the desirability of an airport, which was thirteen years in materializing. John Murray and Colonel Art Hanson were among the returning war pilots who barnstormed the country. Murray liked flying so well he went to work for United Airlines and flew countless airline trips across the continent during his career. The Donaldson brothers of Milford—Orville, Grant, and Flavius—were daring flyers who apparently inherited their father's love for speed and excitement. The elder Donaldson died in an accident at the Spirit Lake fairgrounds while racing an Emden. Flyer Selby Broms suffered critical facial burns in a crash.

Not until 1928 did the city of Estherville get around to pro-viding an airfield. On a sixty-five–acre patch of ground in southeast Estherville known as Legion Field, enthusiasts built a hangar and sponsored a rally. The *Des Moines Register & Tribune* sent Charley Gatchet in his "Good News" Fairchild plane, in which I took my first plane ride, along with Chief of Police Herb Nourse and two bankers—Irv Hall and Fred Parsons. Lieutenant Homer Munson, one of Pop Munson's boys, piloted an army plane that took part in the air festival. Munson later became a colonel and the personal pilot of General George Marshall.

Democrat subscribers were soon reading "Ravings of a Radio Bug" after Frank Carpenter turned over the postmastership in 1922 to Fred Robinson. Carp had become fascinated with listening to the faint radio signals that could be heard by those patient enough to listen. There were few radio sets in town besides Carpenter's and George Gruwell's Atwater Kent outfit in his garage on Central Avenue. Fans gathered evenings at both places hoping to catch snatches of programs from the Drake Hotel in Chicago or powerful KDKA. Only rarely was reception at all clear. Every week the *Democrat* front-page radio column reported what Carp had heard and what luck other fans were having. He related radio gossip he picked up at the evening sessions in his office. Another *Democrat* innovation was the use of cartoons drawn by photographer Art Erickson, who signed his drawings Arteric.

With the war out of the way and the country returning to "normalcy," as President Harding put it, Estherville thoughts turned to improvements. Getting streets out of the mud was one of them. Early in 1919 Groves, Carpenter, and others began calling for paved streets, and by April, shortly after B. B. Anderson defeated Groves for mayor, the *Democrat* assured readers that the city would pave its streets by the next year. The promise was kept. By 1960 the town had built nineteen miles of paved streets. Today every street in the city is hard-surfaced.

Maude, as other housewives, was sorely tried when the asphalters moved into town and her kids began tracking black goo on her kitchen linoleum, oak floors, and carpets. but it was needed progress. Youngsters enjoyed watching as workmen spread steaming asphalt from curb to curb. The most important functionary of the paving outfit piloted a huge steamroller to smooth and mix and pack it. I thought I might enjoy a vocation as a steamroller operator. But when the telephone company began installing cables to replace bare wire on poles, I thought that was glamorous employment, too. I collected scraps of brass wire dropped by the linemen and pieced them together for use in my basement inventions.

While holding court throughout the Fourteenth Judicial District, father became infected with the golf virus, which was to affect both his life and mine. Upon adjourning an afternoon session of court in those county seats that supported courses, lawyers would often entice him to join them for a game of golf, a sport to which he had been a total stranger. Estherville had no links. At Spencer and Algona, such fellows as Frank Cook and Jesse Bonar lent him clubs and coaxed him to try his hand. He quickly fell in love with the game.

When in the autumn of 1920 a group of men met to organize a club in Estherville, father was ready to be asked for a membership. Fred White, president of the Northern Lumber Company, was named to head the organization. Although I never saw George Lyon on the course, he joined White in giving the Northern's full support to the venture. Grainman Ed Stockdale, banker C. D.

Tedrow, lawyer J. W. Morse, Dr. G. G. Griffith, Ford dealer N. P. Walker, wholesale grocer Roy Buckingham, and shoeman G. H. Raife were officers and directors. Most of these men never played much golf. Father not only became interested in developing the local course but played the game at every opportunity the rest of his life. It was on the golf course that he was stricken with angina pains in 1952, the year before he died, at 80. A year after the course opened, John Greig, James Rainey, and father selected trees and saw that they were planted.

Thirty-five years later several of us, including Greig and Paul Pearson, began a program of planting hundreds of trees, many of them green ash and silver maple. When the course was started in 1921, there were no trees except those in the wooded, hilly area along School Section Creek, which proved to be the club's most effective hazard. Hundreds of balls have been washed downstream while golfers played the eighth and ninth holes. The earliest games were played over only five fairways, because the north forty acres of the course had been in corn the previous year and were newly seeded to bluegrass. Father, Frank Woods, and I played many games together, as golf supplanted our fishing expeditions up the river and in Angler's Bay of Spirit Lake.

We spent a good share of our time looking for sliced balls that sailed across the highway into George Frank's hog pasture. George was tolerant of our trespassing because he held the job of trimming the fairway grass with a three-gang mower drawn by his team of horses.

Because there was no professional to instruct the club's members in how to play the game, each beginner, except Mort Anderson, developed his own peculiar grip, stance, and swing—if "swing" was the right word for our awkward motions. Mort had played for a few years on other courses and was more proficient than the rest of us. His brother, George, used only a brassie and even putted with it. He did better than most of the players because of good natural ability. B. B. Anderson tended the grain elevator, leaving golf to his two sons.

I insisted upon holding the club cross-handed, but father's more orthodox view of a good grip fortunately prevailed. The only player I know who played cross-handed beat me in a game about fifty years later, but he looked pretty awkward. Both the players and the course improved as the club watered and beautified the premises. Even comfortable clubhouse facilities were added. Much later the Mack Petersons seeded part of their farm southeast of Estherville and built a fee course that became a popular place to play. Back in 1921 we teed up the ball on mounds of sand, a supply of which was provided at each tee along with a bucket of water with which to moisten it into a lump on which to place the ball. Father and I built the divided boxes at the teeing grounds for holding the pails of water and sand. The only building on the grounds was a machine shed, later converted into the first clubhouse. Frank Carpenter lent me his .22 rifle so that I might slow down the gopher population.

In addition to annual editions of the circuses it sponsored, the Elks Lodge entertained the community with minstrel and musical comedy shows. Entertainment also included an annual home-talent show organized by some woman who seemed to just happen along. She both recruited talent and directed the production. These events provided an outlet for those who liked to act, dance, and sing. The director usually brought her own supply of costumes, scenery, script, and other needs. She usually encountered little difficulty persuading budding talent to take the stage.

Silent movies became less silent in the twenties when the Grand Theater installed a pipe organ, on which Laura Angel produced storm, love, chase, war, and music of other moods keyed to the film's episodes. On Laura's day off brother Bob gladly substituted. He especially enjoyed playing the organ for sing-a-longs. The audience watched a bouncing ball and words for the music projected on the screen as the organist provided accompaniment. When Robert worked the regular shift, he earned a welcome $25 a week. Organ music was much superior to Henry Graaf's mechanical orchestra, but about the time Bob was getting himself professionally trained in Chicago to be a big-city theater organist, the invention of talking pictures unobligingly changed his projected career.

A strike of Rock Island shop workers in 1922 crippled town payrolls. When the strike was finally broken by a federal injunction that prevented a lockout, many workers did not go back to work. Although the financial loss was most severe to the strikers themselves, impact was felt throughout the community, for the railroad was a chief source of its income. Work at the rip track and in the car shops steadily declined from the time of the strike. In 1931 the railroad transferred the division superintendent to Cedar Rapids and discontinued its two good passenger trains, Nos. 419 and 420. In 1937, amid loud Estherville objection, the dispatcher's office was transferred also. Frank Martin, long a trainmaster and then division assistant superintendent, retired. Locomotives that could make longer runs without being serviced permitted the railroad to economize by consolidating facilities.

Estherville nonetheless continued to be a point at which enginemen and trainmen changed crews and made their runs. The first diesel locomotive arrived in 1949, and the roundhouse and its turntable gave way to a diesel shed. The coal chute, which was loaded with fuel by running coal gondolas up a long ramp, was no longer needed to service steam locomotives. The landmark was razed. Steam engines were junked or put on display in museums. Upon the death of Bill Hunt, long a R.I. trainman, Emmet County's historical museum will inherit his vast collection of switch keys, lanterns, switch locks, conductor and brakeman insignia, timetables, ticket blanks, a depot stove, a station semaphore, railroad spikes, chunks of rail, and still other items Hunt has collected from his own railroading experiences and during his vacation visits to railroads all across the land.

H. H. Tosdal, a tall, gaunt Norwegian who wore a fur cap even when the weather did not seem to require it, was the town's early-day photographer. He operated a studio on Main Street that depended largely on illumination from the sun through a glass roof. He photographed my playmates and me in a scene that somehow survived through the years to a family scrapbook. Tosdal gave up photography for more lucrative storekeeping, acquiring several business buildings and the status of capitalist. The Tosdals' son Harry became one of Estherville's distinguished sons. A professor of marketing at Harvard School of Business, he wrote several texts, edited the Harvard Business Review, traveled extensively, and taught at the University of Lausanne, Switzerland.

The Ku Klux Klan threw some life into the twenties by claiming to enlist about 600 members. That notorious movement reached its local zenith in a parade led by the town band, all marchers appropriately nightgowned for the occasion. A cross was burned on a west-side hill. For a time, meetings were held in a lodge hall, but the movement was short-lived and largely escaped the notice of the community. For some reason I have no personal recollection of the local KKK. Newspaper files yield little help.

For almost as long as I can remember, Estherville's grocery stores were somewhat out of the ordinary. My mother preferred to buy Richelieu brand canned goods from Fred Kilgore, and she trusted him to send her fruits and vegetables of reliable freshness and quality. We usually bought meats from Bill Oehrlein, who regularly cut me a 35¢ slice of sirloin steak for our family of four. I stopped after school at his shop, in which fresh sawdust had been spread on the floor. Ralph, his son, was a good distance runner in high school. He helped his father and continued the business.

Myhre & Jeglum was perhaps the oldest and one of the best patronized firms in town then. But when in 1916 Sconberg & Kilgore moved their grocery and hardware store to new, modern quarters at the corner of Sixth Street and First Avenue North (then

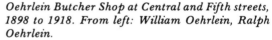

Oehrlein Butcher Shop at Central and Fifth streets, 1898 to 1918. From left: William Oehrlein, Ralph Oehrlein.

called Main Street), they had by far the most elegant store building. It now houses the Emmet County State Bank in completely refurbished quarters. One of the town's grocery operators, Fred Ehlers, was an innovator who later served as mayor for twelve consecutive years and in the legislature for one term.

Charlie Norby was one of the first grocers to emphasize price, which became increasingly important to householders during and after the war. Norby was the victim of one of Estherville's many disastrous fires when he imprudently rushed into his burning building to save something he valued. He was overcome by smoke and perished. The *Democrat* described the loss as a $50,000 fire, which destroyed and damaged much Central Avenue property.

Dan Howard made competitors wince when he began publishing regular weekly newspaper ads that featured low cash-and-carry prices at his Cut-Rate Grocery. His brother, Jay, after resigning from the Northern Lumber Company, joined him in the store, and later became a councilman. Arnold Mouritsen came to Estherville from Ringsted to open a spotless meat department in the store. The Howards built a success that meant downfall to less competitive stores, including the A & P.

Helping at the Howard store was an old-timer by the name of George Rugtiv. Like father, the Nau brothers, and many others in the community, Rugtiv was a son of Norway. Knute Nau loved to prime some unsuspecting customer he happened to see in the Howard store and ask Rugtiv how to spell his name. The Howards, Mouritsen, and Norseman Elwin Bringle of the produce department would then prepare to hold their sides in laughter. "Why, I spell my name R-u-ee-tee-i-wee," George would oblige the jokesters. The Howard Cut-Rate cash-and-carry at holiday time did a lively business in lutefisk, an item that the Norwegian trade savored; it made them nostalgic for fjords of the homeland.

There was sharp disagreement among some in the community as to whether fish that had been soaked in lye was fit to eat. However, ladies of Immanuel Lutheran Church in the Ryan Lake neighborhood knew the secrets of freshening and cooking lutefisk and preparing lefsa and other Norse fare. Esthervilleans— Norwegians, Irish, German, Danish, and Yankee—devoured and relished these delicacies in huge quantities.

Butcher Mouritsen later bought the Howard store and expanded it successfully into a much larger market. As stores such as Fareway, Red Owl, Super Valu, and Hy-Vee moved in, Estherville became an increasingly active grocery outlet. They succeeded Myhre & Jeglum and Sconberg & Kilgore, who had followed Einer Sondrol, Henry Graaf, and Percy Fullenwider in provisioning the pantries.

Mack Groves's brother George described himself as a broker willing to buy or sell anything. Mostly he dressed faddishly and wore a diamond stickpin in his tie and a diamond ring on his finger — until a low-lifer came along in 1926 and robbed him of his gems. When the thief was found a month later in Duluth, justice was done. George owned a pool hall, which he frequented but I'm sure rarely tended. He fancied fine horses and liked to watch the races, but more often he played cards. George's husky, throaty voice always got attention in any group. At one time he was listed as superintendent of the Hail Insurance Company, but I'm not sure what duties, if any, he performed.

In 1924 Estherville brought college opportunity home by establishing a junior college, which much later mushroomed and grew into Iowa Lakes Community College. During World War II the junior college developed an active pilot training program. In 1964 it built the Rotunda building at a cost of $400,000 of which $213,000 was subscribed locally as matching funds for federal assistance. From a modest beginning of 26 students who matriculated the first year of operation, enrollment climbed to 160 graduates in the '68 class. An Estherville Junior College Foundation gave substantial and continuing assistance to the local two-year college. When in 1967 the school became Iowa Lakes Community College, as a part of the Iowa public school program, expansion came rapidly.

The college now serves five counties of Area III with a wide variety of programs that include liberal arts and sciences, nursing, career-option courses, preprofessional training, vocational and technical programs, college transfer courses, adult and continuing education, evening classes, and a variety of special-need educational offerings. It now occupies huge, modern, one-story $1.3 million buildings of classrooms, library, offices, and student center in east Estherville. It also maintains a center at nearby Emmetsburg for the vocational and technical training. Enrollment at Iowa

Lakes, fully accredited by the North Central Association of Colleges and Schools, is now about 1,800 students.

Recognizing that their future was closely identifed with farm prosperity, Estherville business and professional men joined in subscribing $25,000 to build a modern building for the Estherville Cooperative Creamery. Oscar Fagre finished the building in 1925. The next year the creamery paid its patrons $82,000, which farmers found helpful in meeting their expenses not easily covered from the sale of grain at declining farm commodity prices. The creamery pumped income into the community, eventually growing into big-figure business as it added retail milk and cream marketing and milk drying to its butter-making business. P. E. (Polly) Frettem managed the creamery when it underwent its big expansion program. Farmers needed the checks they received from the sale of milk, cream, and eggs to bolster farm income when financial disaster struck the community in the twenties.

During this postwar era, robberies plagued the sheriff and the police. Nothing was safe. Burglars robbed the post office, banks, service stations, stores — even poker players. The Middlewest was undergoing a severe transition from wartime to peacetime economy: a difficult period of deflation and, finally, liquidation.

When All the Banks Failed

DURING the summer after finishing high school, I clerked at the Iowa Savings Bank, where I also posted one of the bank's two checking-account records. This was eons before the advent of dual posting machines and the age of electronic bookkeeping. It was 1923 when Emmet County's banks began collapsing. It has never been established, however, that my services had any direct effect in bankrupting the town's financial institutions, even though my posting of the books yielded generous and frequent errors. These mistakes were invariably remedied by the talented Frank Crumb, a wizard with debits and credits. For the small price of a black cigar

Iowa Savings Bank on East Lincoln Street, about 1918.

from Charlie Robinson's drugstore two doors away, I bribed Frank to discover the transpositions and other errata that marred my performance. To this day I have lost none of my special knack, handily transposing bookkeeping entries, telephone numbers, zip codes, golf scores, typed words—anything.

When I was not occupied at bookkeeping, I stood at the till of one of the "windows," guarded by an ornate brass cage, to receive the attention of those who wandered into the bank. Sometimes my till balanced and then sometimes it didn't. It was Hank Long who always came to my rescue by putting the till back in balance. Banking, obviously, was not my forte; there were too many flaws in my ability for me to make a career of finance.

The most interesting member of the bank's cast of characters was Jim Ghoslin, who had edited the *Democrat* for Carpenter for a time before serving with the army engineers on the western front. He always kept a loaded revolver in the center drawer of his desk, which faced the vault. One of Jim's responsibilities as an assistant cashier was to minimize bank expenses, and he took the duty seriously. He was particularly annoyed by employees who forgot to turn out the light in the vault. Once, when the light was left on, Jim impulsively seized his revolver and shot out the bulb. What Ghoslin didn't think of was that only a thin plastered partition separated the bank's vault from the customers' safe deposit repository directly in line with Ghoslin's line of fire. Fortunately, there were no customers there that morning. One of the fascinations of my summer employment was the prospect that Ghoslin might one day shoot a bandit, a customer, or even another light bulb. When the bank failed two years later, I still had $9.36 of my savings left that I'd forgotten about.

What amazed me as a green youth of eighteen, though ignorant of the ways of finance, was the lack of prosperity that seemed self-evident as farmers paid off loans of amounts such as $6,000 or $8,000, only to sign new notes for almost the same amounts a few days later. It seemed to me they were on a treadmill as they fattened pigs and calves for market. The customers' assets did not appear to be growing, and in fact they weren't. Although I was not aware of it, trouble was on the way for the banks, their shareholders, depositors, and borrowers. The Emmet delinquent tax list occupied four full pages of the *Democrat* in the fall of 1922. The economic barometer was falling fast.

The Great American Depression did not start in 1929, when the stock market crashed. The depression began in the early twenties, when farmers no longer were feeding vast armies and the impoverished, hungry civilians of Europe. In 1918, with the war in progress, corn was worth $1.23 a bushel on December 1. A year later a bushel brought $1.17, but by 1920 was worth only 47¢ and in 1921 brought only 30¢. The other leading cash crop in Emmet County was oats, worth 64¢ in 1918 and 1919, only 36¢ in 1920, and semiworthless at 23¢ in 1921.[1] And cheap feed meant cheap livestock prices. The Great Depression did not start on Wall Street; it spawned in Emmet County, for one place, as farm deflation spread to the equipment industry, to the financial centers, and finally general business.

As farm commodity prices plummeted, the land itself declined in value. When commodity prices farmers received were higher, the price of Emmet County farmland soared to $250 and $325 an acre. But as the soldiers sailed home and European battlefields were returned to the growing of crops, Iowa farmland was no longer in sharp demand or able to support the debt on it. Crops at depressed commodity prices did not justify inflated land values. Not only had insurance companies lent generously on land purchases during the war boom, but many farms had also been encumbered by second-mortgage loans, held by previous owners, speculators—even banks.

Many of those persons who purchased Liberty and Victory bonds during the war obtained the money to buy them by borrowing from their bankers. When the war ended and commodity prices collapsed, bond purchasers soon found themselves needing to cash the securities so they could pay off the notes they had given bearing approximately double the interest return of the bonds bought. And they could liquidate the bonds only at a loss, for the securities were market bonds that fluctuated in price with supply and demand. As investors cashed their bonds, the supply greatly exceeded demand. Bonds that patriotic investors had bought at par, often with borrowed funds, became worth as little as 82¢ to 95¢ on the dollar in May 1920, depending on the particular interest rates and maturity dates of the issue.[2] Those who had no other funds with which to pay off the loans, and needing all the capital they could raise to continue their farm and business operations, had little choice but to sell their bonds at a sacrifice. Such sales of course further depressed bond prices on into 1921, when most of the issues sold at between

85¢ and 90¢ on the dollar. The bond market strengthened in 1922 and on into 1923 and 1924, but by then distressed owners had already liquidated their holdings. It was too late to help those forced by circumstances to cash their bonds at losses.

In 1923 Estherville's five banks held deposits of roughly $4 million; the smallest bank, the Estherville State, held $500,000. The largest, the Iowa Savings, had $1.2 million. Estherville State didn't make it through the summer for lack of cash. Overloaned and overborrowed from central banks, which had rediscounted some of its notes, the bank's assets could not be liquidated to meet customers' demands. It closed its doors in July 1923. The receiver found loans of $629,500, along with $60,000 in foreclosed real estate. The deposits were only $506,000, while the bank owed notes and rediscounted paper of $122,000. Estherville State was not the only Emmet County bank that had overloaned, overborrowed, and given credit to borrowers beyond their capabilities to repay, but it was the weakest Estherville bank. G. Zeeman had been president until 1914, A. D. Root was vice-president, and Zeeman's son-in-law, Andrew Smith, was cashier. Probably the most liberal and lenient in its loan policies, the bank was consequently the most vulnerable. Zeeman, partner with H. S. Greig in the grain business, had with Smith come to Estherville from South Dakota. They were among the town's respected citizens. I was awed by a large silvery sphere in the center of Zeeman's spacious flower garden north of his showy home. He died two years before the bank crashed. Smith, never to recover from the shock of what happened, ultimately took his own life.

Under Iowa law, stockholders not only lost their capital investment but were obliged to pay an assessment equal to the shares they owned in the bank. The Zeeman shares were $26,000 and Andrew Smith's $2,000. The examiner in charge and his attorney, acting in behalf of the superintendent of banking, sold property, foreclosed mortgages, and collected notes given by borrowers and other receivables so that dividends could be paid to depositors. Ralph Oehrlein bought the bank building for $12,000. In addition to payment made on preferential deposits of public bodies, the bank paid general depositors a total of 29.3 percent in three dividends, starting in July 1925. The last was paid at the end of 1927, when the receiver made his final report.[3]

Estherville State Bank,
about 1900. From left:
James Espeset, Howard
Espeset, Howard Graves.

Irreversible economic forces that obliged "the bank with the chimes" to close did not abate. All the Estherville banks, as well as their affiliate banks throughout the county, were overextended and in some instances undercapitalized. The largest of the Estherville financial institutions, the Iowa Savings, had at the beginning of 1923 loaned out $1.4 million and in addition had taken over $73,900 in foreclosed real estate. These assets, many of which were by no means liquid, exceeded the bank's deposits of $1.2 million. Moreover, the bank owed central banks $211,300, including rediscounted notes. In the next year and a half, the payables, which had been borrowed to keep the bank open, increased to $278,000. In another six months they stood at $392,000.

Not because the bank was in a good enough cash position to pay off borrowed money but because of pressure from the central banking system, the Iowa Savings managed to scale down its debt to $207,000. The shrinking of credit was one of the many factors that triggered failure, or at least the timing of it. By May 1925 the Iowa Savings had collected its notes down from $1.4 million to $909,000, even after paying down customers' deposits from $1.2 million to $795,000. Overdrafts climbed from $700 in 1925 to $6,300, and the notes it had to foreclose became frozen assets in the form of real

estate, carried on the books at $92,000. The short cash position
threatened to become even worse as the city council and county
board of supervisors demanded that the public deposits be substan-
tially reduced, despite the fact that such funds were by law guaranteed by the state and were preferentially treated in liquidation.
These public actions, encouraged or even inspired by friends and
supporters of the other banks, further eroded depositor confidence
in not only the Iowa Savings but the other banks as well. This increased demand for cash at a time when bank assets sorely lacked liquidity.

When the Iowa Savings finally closed its doors November 24,
1925, its deposits had been heavily drained by withdrawals. The
general depositors received two dividends. They totaled 14.7 percent when the final report of the receiver was filed at the end of
June 1930.[4] Mack Groves, the leading stockholder and president of
the bank, promptly paid his stock assessment of $30,000, which was
in addition to the loss of his original investment and a deposit of
$27,000. Iowa Savings shareholders paid all but $660 of the bank's
$50,000 capital stock assessment, making the bank unique in that
respect.

When it closed, the Iowa Savings had survived by three months
an incident that scandalized the community and was the ugliest episode of the animosity engendered between partisans and officers of
Mack Groves's Iowa Savings and John P. Kirby's First National and
Provident Savings banks. George K. (Kirt) Allen, who referred to
himself as junior editor of the *Estherville Enterprise* and who had
practiced some law, undertook to assist Mrs. S. B. Strong, a widow,
in cashing her deposit in the Iowa Savings. Her intention was to
transfer her money to the First National Bank, where Allen and the
Enterprise did business. When Allen appeared at the bank with
Mrs. Strong to make her withdrawal, they were met by an outraged
Mack Groves, who pulled Allen's hair, grabbed him by the shirt,
and, according to Allen's *Enterprise* account of the proceedings,
threatened to kill the editor if he continued meddling.

Other accounts of the episode were milder. The *Vindicator &
Republican* described the incident as an effort to gain an advantage
in Allen's personal grudge against the president of the bank
(Groves) and "to embarrass the Iowa Savings Bank by withdrawal of
the woman's deposits." The *V & R* called Allen's act "audacious"

and "outrageous." I was employed during the time of the Allen-Strong-Groves confrontation at the *V & R* office, where for two summers I substituted for Adelaide Nichols in writing and editing the newspaper while she took extended vacations. As I recall, however, it was George Nichols who wrote about the bank episode. Although Groves was by no means backward or reticent of manner, he was hardly the alley-fighting type that Allen portrayed in his three-column, bannered story of the affair. Mrs. Strong was permitted to withdraw her deposit, but the Groves bank was not outflanked.

Enoch H. Hanson, friendly to the Iowa Savings and to Mack Groves, had taken office the previous January as treasurer of Emmet County. He had replaced World War I veteran Leo Brawford, a friend of the Kirby banks. Inasmuch as the board of supervisors had at that time not yet begun to interfere in the treasurer's prerogative of designating depositories, Hanson could have transferred much of the county's money from the First National to the Iowa Savings to give it a fairer share of the public funds, but he refrained from doing so to prevent creating a critical cash problem at the Kirby bank. Hanson, however, readily agreed to drawing a check on the First National for the amount of Mrs. Strong's $9,850 account. So Mrs. Strong took $9,850 out of the Iowa Savings and the county treasurer put it back in the Iowa Savings by transferring public funds. The score remained the same. But the incident further infuriated the two factions. It led to arguments at city hall and with the board of supervisors, some of the officials insisting that deposits in the Groves bank should be reduced. It was proposed to transfer funds of such considerable sum that the Iowa Savings position could easily become critical, which is what happened. But depositor confidence in all banks continued to decline, and they all failed.

The First National Bank, along with its companion bank, the Provident Trust, which operated in the same building with basically the same officers, survived the Iowa Savings by only two months and six days. The two Kirby banks in Estherville and also the sister banks at Huntington, Dolliver, and Gruver locked up on January 30, 1926. At the beginning of 1923, the First National, with deposits of $580,000, had loaned $987,000. Instead of a conservative ratio of loans to deposits, the loans were close to double the deposits. Vastly overloaned, this bank owed $380,000 to other banks and

First National Bank at Sixth and Lincoln streets, torn down in 1917.

before it closed the deposits had been drawn to $410,000. The bank reduced its loans to $638,000, but central banking pressures squeezed down payables to $72,000, which depleted the cash and precipitated closing.

The First National was able to discount its notes directly to the Federal Reserve Bank, but as Robert Knight, who handled the rediscounting of paper, recalled recently, the bank had to supply considerable collateral in addition to the rediscounted notes. Of course the collateral notes could not be liquidated to supply more cash. The bank paid out 46.2 percent to general depositors.[5]

It was apparent that the First National had been able to reduce its loans as much as it did by transfer of frozen assets to its sister bank, the Provident Trust, which operated under less stringent examination by reason of its state, rather than federal, charter. In May 1925 the Provident Trust held $323,000 of real estate that had been foreclosed. Somehow the bank whittled this down by the end of the year to $237,000, but this was at the expense of liquidity it seriously needed. Less than a month before it closed, the bank's deposits had shrunk by half in two years, to only $453,000. Upon liquidation, general depositors received two dividends that amounted in all to only 16.3 percent.[6]

Unable to pay his bank assessment, John Kirby took bankruptcy. A short time later he became the local Ford Motor Company dealer, taking in his son Don, the former cashier of the bank with him. Kirby told the *V & R* that overloaning to customers so they could buy Liberty bonds during World War I was the reason for the bank's failure. When Einer Sondrol died in 1916, his estate was the largest ever probated in Emmet County. Believing bank stocks to be an ultraconservative investment, Sondrol had invested his earnings in stocks of the Kirby banks. When the banks closed, the stocks became worthless and subject to 100 percent assessment as well.

The First Trust & Savings Bank survived the longest. Frank H. Rhodes and his brother Will were more conservative than the others, but they were undercapitalized. With only $45,000 of capital and surplus, the Rhodes bank at the beginning of 1923 held $837,000 in deposits. These withdrew in two years to only $780,000. The bank was unlike all the others in town in that it owed no money to central banks and it had rediscounted no paper. In the two-year period to 1925 it reduced loans from $778,000 to $606,000, but in the meantime it carried $78,000 of nonbank real estate that obviously represented frozen assets. Its overdrafts had mounted from none to $1,700, and it began listing its banking house on the books at $30,000 rather than nothing. These indicators revealed the pinch that closed the bank's doors in November 1926. It had survived the Iowa Savings by just a year. The depositor payout was the second best of all five banks—43.9 percent.[7]

In one last convulsive action growing out of bank failure, suit was brought in January 1927 against officers of the Iowa Savings Bank on charges that the bank had made false statements of its condition and that it was known to be insolvent when a customer made his final deposit. The day before the bank closed its doors on December 24, 1925, George W. Bale, a drugstore owner, deposited $211.35. It was a complaint based on the Bale deposit filed by accountant E. B. Rayner of Rayner & Company of Minneapolis that led to the arrest of Mack J. Groves, Fred G. Parsons, Lloyd E. Stockdale, and James Ghoslin, who were officers of the bank. By law, the complaint should have been filed in the nearest justice-of-the-peace court, presided over by Gus Peterson, but it was taken instead to Justice B. E. West. After my father as attorney for the bankers objected to West's jurisdiction, the justice transferred the case to Mayor John C. Lilley, a friend of the Kirby adversaries. When the Ghoslin case finally got to Peterson's court, he dismissed it after what the *Democrat* described as a stormy session.

After the cases landed in district court, Judge James Deland dismissed all of them. As had Peterson, he held they had no validity. But that was not the end. A small group of unhappy citizens sought suspension of County Attorney Oscar N. Refsell for failure to assist in the Rayner case and for neglecting to indict Iowa Savings officers. A short time later District Court Judge D. F. Coyle dismissed that case as well.

The banks became insolvent gradually. At what point keeping them open became hopeless was a judgment call. All the officers in the banks had been inept to a degree and all were also victims of circumstance. But through it all none was found to be a crook.

After Ralph Miller departed from the First National, he became a highly successful banker at Algona; Robert Knight from the same bank would become a key figure in a new Estherville bank and later its cashier and then president; Lloyd Stockdale departed the Iowa Savings to operate his own insurance and loan agency; Sever Egertson of the Estherville State became a federal bank examiner; from the First Trust, C. D. Tedrow became a banker at Princeton, Illinois; Edwin Rhodes went with a Jesse Jones bank in Texas; Perce Pullen went to a West Coast bank; and A. A. Herrick from the First National practiced law in Des Moines and became a district judge.

Upon paying his Iowa Savings stock assessment of $30,000, the unsinkable Mack Groves proceeded to organize a new bank, the Iowa Trust & Savings, which is one of the two banks that serve the community today. Groves was not a stockholder, although he unquestionably supplied the funds to buy the controlling shares issued to Fred G. Parsons, his right-hand man. To Groves's inconvenience, Parsons pre-deceased him in 1949. The question of who owned the bank stock and what the settlement should be was still not completely resolved before Mack's death in 1953.

The new bank's capital and surplus of $60,000 was supplied by about twenty-five stockholders, who elected lumberman L. J. Bennett as president, Fred Parsons as vice-president, and Henry J. Long as assistant cashier. Later Irv F. Hall, who had been examiner-in-charge in receivership proceedings for both the Estherville State and the Iowa Savings, was named as cashier. For $35,000 the bank acquired the imposing building the First National Bank constructed during World War I at a cost of $80,000. When the newly organized Groves bank moved into the splendid structure, across the street from the old Iowa Savings, stockholders contributed $20 a share to write down the investment to $25,000. The Iowa Trust opened for business January 6, 1927, a little more than a month after the city suffered its last bank failure.

Meanwhile business was served by a Clearance Association organized by Hugh S. Greig, a grain merchant operating elevators at Estherville and many towns on the Rock Island railroad, who supplied a capital of $35,000 to start it. Among supporters of the operation was Alfred Rhodes, a lawyer, who became a highly successful Chevrolet and Buick dealer of the city. James Rainey was named as manager of the association, which served as a stopgap in the vacuum created by the loss of all the banks. It dissolved as soon as the new bank began operation. Before the year was out, in December 1927, a second bank, the Emmet County State Bank, opened its doors with capital and surplus of $60,000. The first officers were Henry W. Mahlum, president; Neil H. McKerral, vice-president; and Wayne C. Currell, who became the controlling figure and owner of the bank, as vice-president and cashier. Both McKerral and Currell lived originally at Traer, Currell coming to Estherville from Manchester. Currell became president in a relatively short time.

Depositors did not lose just money, they lost assets as well. Land that had sold at $300 or more before deflation became worth only $50 or $60. Corn at 30¢ a bushel and oats at 23¢ a bushel didn't support $300 land. Consequently, farmers could not pay their taxes, the interest on their debts, and the amortized payments on their farmland loans. Paper profits of the speculators evaporated, and farms reverted to the earlier owners in a chain of transactions that reversed their earlier sales. Lucky were those not caught with deficiency judgments. Many were glad to take their losses if they could step away from further liability. The low commodity and livestock prices not only punished farmers but destroyed the values on which bankers had based their loans to farmers.

Insurance companies that had made loans on farmland became the unwilling owners of much Emmet County soil as they foreclosed on farmers and other landowners unable to pay interest and taxes. Many insurance company representatives made offers as attractive as they felt they could to avoid taking over ownership. Second mortgages on almost any security became worthless in the liquidation process brought on by collapse of commodity and land prices and failure of banks. Not only farmers but also business and professional men who had speculated, expecting land prices to go higher and higher, lost the capital they had invested. They were unable to hang on to their investments long enough for the far-off day when farmland would be worth not just $300 an acre but eight times that much, or more.

As examiners in charge of liquidating banks for the department of banking began unraveling affairs of the Estherville State Bank and subsequently the others in the community, they faced many trying situations. In some instances it was ruled that a customer could offset notes he owed with deposits he held, but in other cases the loan paper signatures were different from ownership of deposits and consequently not eligible for offsetting credit. This caused hardship and led to lawsuits to test validity of the position taken by the banking department. The district court then had to decide who was right. Adverse decisions ruling that customers had to pay their notes while losing their deposits broke many hearts. They received some of their deposits, of course, as examiners liquidated assets from 14.7 percent to 46.2 percent.

Throughout the receiverships, Frank Carpenter in the *Democrat* encouraged depositors in a hope they would eventually get all their money. But it was not to be. As a director of the Iowa Savings, Carpenter knew some loans would not and could not be paid. And then of course there was the huge expense of the receivership in collecting loans, keeping books, and paying out depositor dividends.

Some unfortunate depositors exaggerated their losses, overreacted, and oversympathized with themselves. The psychology of failure was worse than the small amounts that some customers lost in the banks. Defeatism stunted and marred the careers of many victims. Twenty years after the failure of the State Bank, a trades-man working at my home lamented that he had "lost everything in the bank failure." My curiosity caused me to search the court record, in which I found that indeed he had suffered a loss. But it was less than $300. He had resigned himself to failure, lacking the energy and spunk to start anew. He failed to recognize the loss for the really inconsequential sum it was in comparison with the prospects for profit that lay ahead.

Clothiers, among the most devastated of those affected, found themselves stocked with garments for which there were no purchasers who had any money. By the time the economy began to improve, their clothing stocks were hopelessly out of style. Merchants' notes were as worthless as those of many farmers. With no credit to buy fresh merchandise, many storekeepers became insolvent and humiliated.

In two instances they started the autos in their garages with the doors tightly closed. Carbon monoxide ended their grief but not that of their families. A hardware merchant, a clothier, and a druggist who shot himself were all victims of the economic disaster that ruined their lives. Respected, community-minded, generous merchants were not only despondent — they felt disgraced.

One Estherville merchant found just the right timing to open a grocery store, the same summer that the state superintendent of banking locked up the Estherville State Bank and the county moved into painful deflation. While established merchants were struggling to liquidate their stocks of merchandise dearly bought, George Lyman opened a neighborhood store on North Sixth Street, just as the price of sugar plummeted from $30 a 100 pounds to $5 a 100. This sugar jolt, along with depressed prices of canned goods and other staples, stripped the Estherville Wholesale Grocer Company of its working capital as it sold off inventory at a fraction of cost. Retail grocers suffered along with the wholesalers. But Lyman built a store and stocked it just as the bottom fell out of the market for farmers and storekeepers alike. "I sold canned goods by the case, and good-paying customers who lived near my new store began patronizing me generously," George told me recently when I visited him at the Good Samaritan Center, a few months after he celebrated his centennial birthday.

His timing was perfect in selling his farm in 1920, before the deflation. He then entered business with a stock of goods bought at depressed prices three years later. He was shrewd, lucky, or both. When I knocked at his door in the Center to interview him, George was just getting his underwear buttoned and was about to get into a shirt and a pair of trousers. "I like to dress myself," he explained. Upon adding a sleeveless vest, he moved off the edge of the bed and seated himself in an armchair. "Glad to see you," he greeted, "we were late with my bath this morning." We soon fell into a relaxed conversation about old times, including two of the city's infernos that had made indelible impressions upon his keen memory. It was the story of his first job, though, that I relished.

After starting to work for Henry Graaf in his grocery store, George was about eighteen when he accidentally set off a Fourth of July fireworks display in the store's front window. The head of a match flew off into the fireworks as he was lighting a gas lamp. The store didn't burn down but the eruption produced a spectacular show, as Roman candles and skyrockets shot across the street into the square. Graaf didn't fire him then, but did so about two years after moving his store a block down the street, where he later started a confectionery. When Lyman had worked for him about four years, Graaf gave sudden notice as he opened the store one morning that he could no longer afford to pay the wages of the young man who delivered his groceries. George accepted the fact and left.

"I went right up the street to where Percy Fullenwider had opened a grocery in the building vacated by Henry," said Lyman. "I asked Percy if he could use a boy, and he said to me 'How much do you want?' I said 'I don't want anything; I want a job. If I can't increase your business you don't need me.' He asked me if I minded going on the delivery wagon and I said 'That's exactly what I want.' Percy then said he'd pay me $7 a week. So I hitched up the team and started taking orders from all my old customers. Of course I told them they'd be getting their groceries from another store, but they said that was all right; they'd stick with me." George said the Fullenwider store soon had the cream of the Graaf trade, and Percy began raising him $1 a week, until he became affluent at $11. Within a year he became Fullenwider's partner. Graaf's offer to take the eager young man back on his delivery wagon came too late.

First in partnership with Fullenwider and then with other partners, Lyman made money. After selling the store to Thompson & Sweet, Lyman converted his capital from groceries to land. "I got the farm fever," he explained. He farmed successfully during a profitable era, raising purebred cattle and horses with the guidance of George Murray and growing field crops. Then he opportunely converted land back into groceries. A downtown grocer who questioned the wisdom of Lyman's starting a neighborhood store did not discourage or derail him. "I told him he did business downtown, where nobody lived, and I would open a store near the customers." George was ahead of his time—years before the days of proliferating neighborhood shopping centers. I decided as I sat listening to the centenarian that he was not just lucky. Shrewd in his timing of when to sell an operation and when to buy one, he also knew the secret of all business success: convenient and courteous service to the customers.

As for those who held only modest deposits in the failed banks, some investors lost more money in the Drake Estate swindle. Gullibly persuaded by smooth-talking slickers, many persons who needed to conserve their pennies convinced themselves they were descendants of Sir Francis Drake and would inherit a vast bundle of gold if they would keep supplying funds to pay the fees of lawyers who were supposedly about to close the lush Drake Estate and share the wealth. A bank receivership dividend of 14.7 percent was a better investment return than the Drake Estate.

Within a year after opening, the two new Estherville banks had received deposits of about $1.6 million between them; within another year deposits had grown to about $1 million each. Confidence in banks was returning. Fifty years after the two new banks opened for business they, together with the First Federal Savings & Loan Association—operated by lawyer Ed Rosendahl and his sons, Fritz and Jim—were custodians of $98.2 million of community money in checking and savings deposits.

Not only had investor confidence been restored, but prosperity, expansion, and inflation made depositor totals of $4 million in 1923 seem insignificant. The capital alone of the two banks in 1977 was $5.8 million, more than total deposits in the twenties. After the 1920 debacle bankers became conservative and sought to keep their loans at 40 percent of deposits. Gradually policies were liberalized to 50 percent, then 60 percent, and at the end of 1977 Estherville's two banks held loans of $46.7 million. This was 72.6 percent of the banks' $64.3 million in deposits.

Such a ratio is conservative enough, perhaps, in view of only $1.6 million of borrowed funds. And yet some thoughtful persons in observing the inflated price of land at $2,500 an acre, expensive farm machinery costing farmers $50,000 or $60,000, and high-priced cattle on feed in the lots—all financed by generous loans—were advising caution. Could history be repeating itself, despite federal deposit insurance and regardless of other economic insulating factors that might make a panic or a severe depression unlikely?

Estherville businessmen and the farmers of their trade area who were starting anew after the banks all closed could not dream that things could go so right with them as they did—eventually. But meantime, before lasting prosperity was to return, there came the Great Depression, which for Estherville was a second shock wave. The farm-state deflation in the twenties that broke banks and their depositors set in motion the underlying causes of the depression, triggered in the East by the 1929 stock market crash. Esthervilleans would again have to suffer through a trying period of adversity.

The Newspaper Game

TWICE a day Murray Hale delivered mail at our house in a large leather pouch strapped over his shoulder. He always walked to make the morning delivery. He stopped to chat a minute, if father was home, to ask him if he had caught any walleyed pike and to express his envy of the Pfluger fishing reel father had purchased not long before he became addicted to golf. Hale never forgave him for his apostasy. On the light afternoon postal delivery, Hale rode his bicycle. His patrons then received the special service of a whistle from his pursed lips when he had mail in the pouch for them. The housewife was usually on the front steps by the time Hale had dismounted from his bike and approached the house.

Murray was such a familiar person to just about everyone on his route that when his twin son Merle was fatally injured by an automobile that ran him down in 1921 the loss to Hale's patrons was like that of one in the family. Henry, the other son, distinguished himself as a physician, teacher, and researcher in aerospace physiology. Only Mr. Beasley in the Blondie and Dagwood comic strip rivals Murray Hale in mailman color.

After I left in the autumn of 1923 for the Chicago Midway to attend liberal arts college, Hale added a special service at our house. The one time he puckered his lips for a whistle on the morning delivery was if he had a letter from the University campus from Maude's son. Alerted by Murray's distinctive whistle, she would be waiting for him at least as far as the front door. If the Chicago missive were a penny postal card, he would have digested the principal news in it and be ready to brief mother on it.

I was never able to send home tidings that I had aced all my courses, inspired the dean to words of praise, or earned an invitation to Phi Beta Kappa membership. The closest I came, though, to outright censure was when the *Chicago Tribune* published a story I had written about a turbulent session of campus women on whether national sororities should replace the U. of C.'s women's clubs. A friend who was present at the confrontation with the dean had leaked the story that angered Dean Ernest Hatch Wilkins. I felt sorry about that because I liked him, not only because he was a fine scholar of romance languages and a hard-working dean but for a personal reason as well.

I had been on the campus only a few weeks as a freshman when on my way after lunch to Bartlett gym Dean Wilkins approached. He stopped me, a total stranger to him, and asked where I was bound. I told him to the gym for P-T. "Here," he said, "are two tickets for the opera *Siegfried.* Find a friend and hurry along to the Great Northern Theater so you don't miss the overture. You'll get more out of it than gym class." I hurried. Although I thought the acting of the San Carlos opera company somewhat stupid, the music was heavenly. Wagner and I became lifelong companions.

In my sophomore year, thanks to my sterling qualifications as a journalist — and because I was a nephew of the city editor — I landed the part-time job of *Chicago Tribune* campus correspondent — successor to Charlie Parker, bound for Rush medical campus. This employment paid about half my college expenses. Other students on the campus who gleaned news for the Chicago newspapers were Howard Mayer of the *American,* who later went to the West Coast to become a Hearst executive; Cliff Utley of the *News,* who became a radio commentator; and Seymour Berkson, who became managing editor of INS and publisher of the *New York Journal-American.* George Morgenstern, who wrote a funny column for the *Daily Maroon,* became editorial writer for the *Chicago Tribune.* The *Tribune*'s campus correspondent became an obscure country editor in Esther's town.

The *Tribune* job, along with my writing and editing chores on the campus *Daily Maroon,* consumed as much interest and time as my classes and study. Books were often neglected as I stayed up half the night at the printer's shop putting the *Maroon* to bed or went chasing off on some noncampus *Tribune* assignment. I lived not far from the Hyde Park police station and a hospital patronized by shotup hoodlums that reporters hoped might "talk." I was convenient to covering the Del Prado Hotel fire and some of the precincts where Mayor William Hale Thompson and other politicians campaigned. Understandably, nonscholastic experiences competed with classes for my attention: long before I had set my sights on preparing to run Frank Carpenter's newspaper some day.

Frank O'Hara and James Weber Linn, who instructed me in newswriting and in English composition, encouraged me as I sought to build some sort of foundation in political science, history, sociology, and other smarts. Rich sources of knowledge could be mined in campus classrooms and from interviews. For the *Tribune* and the *Maroon* I gained access to such giants as H. H. Newman and Fay-Cooper Cole, who taught courses I took, along with James Breasted, Julius Stieglitz, A. A. Michelson, Harvey Lemon, and a number of other greats who made news.

Michelson's unveiling of a laboratory to measure the speed of light drew a distinguished audience. In a pasture in South Chicago, Michelson, the first American to win a Nobel prize, chased beams of light around a four-sided, vacuum-sealed tunnel equipped with mirrors at the corners. He measured the speed of light at 186,282 miles a second. Both ace reporter Philip Kingsley and I reported the event for the *Tribune;* for some reason the editor chose Kingsley's version of the historic moment.

In the autumn of 1926, starting my fourth year at the Midway, I received a letter from father suggesting I go out to Gibbs Sanitarium to visit Carpenter, who was a patient there. Carp had been receiving heroic treatments at the hospital after his health failed him the summer before. When in July he published a front-page story in the *Democrat* describing the injury of scores of people in an assault at the corner of Sixth Street and Central Avenue, his friends realized that the editor suffered from a serious mental disorder. Father and Uncle Robert, together with Carpenter's two brothers and his sister, made arrangements for his care at Gibbs under the direction of a promising physician who had received special training in Europe for the treatment of the disease. When I visited him, he had regained his sanity, talked normally about many subjects, and seemed headed for full recovery.

But a few days later, in November, he contracted pneumonia and, in his weakened condition from the high fever to which he had been subjected, he lost his fight to survive. Carpenter, who learned the printing trade from Peter Johnston, had always published an interesting newspaper because he energetically filled it with news, concentrating on personal items. The *Democrat* also reflected his neatness and order, free from typographical blemishes. His style of making every story a single paragraph no matter how many column inches long was unique, but his paper nonetheless won a *Register & Tribune* trophy for the best front page. He was a careful, conscientious newspaperman.

George Wilson, a locomotive engineer, helped keep ends tied at the newspaper while Carpenter was ill, and he continued to do so after Carp died. Rachel Hawthorne came to Estherville from the *Mason City Globe-Gazette* to write the paper and put it together. When I arrived home after the spring quarter of 1927, the *Democrat* was definitely on the market, needing a buyer. One in particular was eager to take over. Father traded the Carpenter family a house and lot for it, and on the first of August I was in the newspaper business.

Neither father nor I had thought anything about the need for working capital to operate this new venture of mine — purchased with money borrowed from dad — until Friday, the day before George Vedder and Harry Conners in the printshop and Ruby Hemmingson in the little front office would be expecting paychecks. What would I do? When I told father of the fix I was in, he asked if there were some accounts receivable of a size I might collect quickly. Could be. I picked out two, each of several hundred dollars.

"There is probably some dispute about the two bills," father guessed. "Why don't you go to those two merchants and ask them if they claim some sort of an adjustment. If they name a figure you think is reasonable, then say 'All right, make me out a check for the difference.'" That's exactly what I did. Each of the two storekeepers said he was entitled to a credit. Thus Herman Oransky and Ed Strube supplied me with the only working capital I needed.

I think Ruby more than earned her salary of $8 a week. She wrote social items, accepted subscription payments (if any), posted books such as they were, and read galley proofs. Vedder, who ran the four-year-old Intertype C, and Conners, the printer, drew $25 a week, as I recall. The payroll was light, but business had also been light in Carpenter's absence.

Conners was a tramp printer of excellent ability, but he had itchy feet. Although he roomed at the old Crawford Hotel, he regularly carted cans of soup and other food to the "jungles" at the south railroad bridge, where the hoboes camped. Only a week or so after I acquired the paper, Conners didn't show for work one morning. Without giving notice, he had moved on. But every year afterward he revisited the shop to spin yarns about where he had traveled, where he had been employed, and what his experiences had been as an unpaying passenger on freight trains of America. Unlike most tramp printers who came along, many of whom satisfied their thirst for booze by drinking worked-over "canned heat" and denatured alcohol, Conners did not drink at all. When a few years later he visited the shop, he was minus a leg. He had made a miscalculation while departing a moving freight train. But his spirit was undampened.

Faye Warner, who with his brother, K. D., owned the *Emmetsburg Reporter*, came up to help me out when Conners left abruptly. This assistance was largely out of friendship to George Vedder, who for a short time before the Warners took over had been a partner in the *Reporter* with Clifford Mayne, after his father L. H. Mayne, turned it over to them to publish. George's memories of the *Reporter* were indistinct, but he had not forgotten the time when press day rolled around and the partners had neglected to "kill" the old forms and put together a new issue. "We decided," George told me, "that the previous paper had been such an unqualified success we ought to repeat the issue." So they did. George's publishing career was brief but he was an excellent operator of our Intertype. He worked long and faithfully until in 1954 he suffered a heart attack that ended his life at 61.

Warner, an ex-marine, was a fan of Gene Tunney, also a marine. One day when he and Vedder were together in the washroom—a thin, wood-framed enclosure—I heard a fearful commotion. I concluded that the two men were fighting, although that seemed unlikely. Rushing out to the back room I discovered that Faye with his bare fists was demonstrating against the wood partition the damaging punches that made Tunney a prizefight champion. Warner's fists were sorry to look at. Whenever the two printers were tardy getting back to the shop from the noon hour recess or in returning to work for one of the night sessions we often needed to get the paper out, I always knew where to look for them. They would be in John Martyr's building next door, where "Pop" Ellis and his two boys, Sid and Tommy, ran the Hawkeye Cafe.

Arguments about prizefights and baseball games made it a

lively spa, where refreshments of most any kind were not frowned upon. The Ellises were Jack Dempsey partisans and devout St. Louis Cardinal communicants. Warner was a Tunney supporter and both he and Vedder believed a New York Yankee could do no wrong. And in those days they rarely did. Before the fourth game of the 1928 series got under way, the Ellises came into my office at the noon hour. Having lost money to my printers for three straight games, they wanted to know if I cared to cover their bet on the Yanks. I said I guessed that I did. "Those two printers of yours are not going to get one more dollar of our money on this series," Sid vowed. They didn't, either. I was the beneficiary, as New York made it four straight.

One day a printer of much resourcefulness came in and said he wanted to quit at the *Enterprise* and go to work for me. Since the one thing I was shortest of was a printer, the conversation was short. I don't know how many years it was in all, but Bill Mason worked as a compositor in the shop for a long time. However, George Vedder and I were disgusted with him one morning when Mason shut off the press motor, hung up his apron, and announced that he was going to take time out for breakfast. We had worked through the night but needed to print only a few more papers when Mason's appetite, which was considerable, could be curbed no longer. Contending with an ancient Campbell cylinder press that produced newspapers at a pace of a snail and an attached Omaha folder that mangled papers tried the patience of everyone in the shop.

Static electricity in the pressroom during winter months, when the shop's hot-air furnace removed every drop of humidity from the room, drove us to distraction. Like rheumatism, there seemed to be no sure cure for the static electricity created when dry newsprint paper was fed through the press. The lack of humidity made the sheets of paper unruly. They misbehaved in the press. Sometimes the static was so bad that the sheets acted like magnets, and if lifted against the wall, could cling there as tightly as though pasted. When the newspaper consisted of more than eight pages, I fed the insert into the Omaha folder. Vedder operated the Mustang mailer, addressing newspapers on galleys of type that contained the names of subscribers and their addresses.

One day upon entering our washroom after helping to make

up the paper, I discovered a full-grown, well-fed rat nibbling on a sack of dry paste that we used to mix the adhesive for single wrapping out-of-town newspapers. I called for Mason to come quickly into the washroom, which he did. When he saw what I was looking at he grabbed a mop and I reached for a broom, as we went to work on the rat. Although we won the contest against the outpointed rat, it was not until we had made a number of hearty swipes at the creature. These strokes resounded noisily against the thin walls. Not sure whether he should try to settle the argument Mason and I appeared to be having or whether he ought to summon the police, Vedder did neither. Moments later Mason and I came out, wearing smiles worthy of soccer partisans. Mason proudly carried the trophy by its tail.

Shortly before the *Democrat* became the *Estherville News*, when the young Republican took over and renamed the paper, one of the Lees' old Eighth Street neighbors defeated John Lilley for mayor. M. H. Schloeman took over city hall in the spring of '27 with a margin of thirty-four precious votes. The friends of Mack Groves had garnered many of the Schloeman votes, for they knew Lilley to be a "Kirby man." Kirby was no longer a banker and was broke, but the hatred generated during the fight for deposits of public funds lingered. The Kirt Allen and Widow Strong episode, and the Rayner attempt to put Groves and other officers of the Iowa Savings Bank in jail were fresh memories. It had long been the practice of the competing banks to seek election of city, school, and county treasurers so they could gain a lion's share of the public's deposits. Nothing unusual, therefore, that Fred Parsons, a Groves lieutenant, would be active at election time seeking to get the "friendly" vote out for mayor and treasurer. He solicited absentee votes of shut-ins and cripples who could not make it to the polls.

A rather droll fellow, inclined to sarcastic humor, Fred, several years after the Schloeman-Lilley contest, told me what happened when he had solicited the support of a woman whose name was on his "friendly" list and to whom he had taken an absentee ballot. In those days absentee votes could be cast on the same day as the election. It was before Iowa's complicated, foolproof absentee-voting procedure was enacted. After Fred entered the woman's home, he stood where he could observe what happened as she took her ballot to one side of the room and held it up against the wall. She proceeded to commit heresy by marking an "x" in front of the name of John Lilley. Benedict Arnold had done nothing worse than that.

However, long-standing infighting against the Kirby crowd had prepared Fred to expect any sort of reverse. "Can you beat what that woman did?" he asked me. "She knew darned well I was there working for Schloeman and she deliberately double-crossed me," Fred stormed. I said, "Well, Fred, what did you do?" That's what he wanted me to say. "I'll tell you what I did. I sealed up her vote in an envelope, addressed it to the city clerk, and took it down to the Rock Island depot. When passenger train 420 to Chicago started moving out of the station, I dropped it into the U.S. mail car letter slot. I'm sure it got to Estherville — eventually."

Unlike probably any other team so good it had difficulty finding opponents, the Estherville All-Stars were a football outfit that never held a practice. The only scrimmage was against some luckless other team; no point in the All-Stars maiming each other. When in 1928 the team had whipped everything in sight except Valley Junction, now called West Des Moines, the thing to do was to seek a game with that team. Like Estherville, it was a railroad town. Ernie Johnson, who with Wally Berg's financial stewardship managed the team, went to the capital city both to scout one of Valley Junction's games and to complete arrangements for what came to be billed as a contest for the semipro championship of Iowa.

Ernie took with him on the trip an elaborately muscled man by the name of George Deck, a wrestler. As the two men entered the Valley Junction dressing room after the game they had scouted, the All-Stars' manager made sure that each member of the team received one of Deck's bone-crushing handshakes. This was by way of warning the opposition of what it might expect from Estherville supermen. Arrangements were completed; the game was on.

Announcement by Hugh Dempsey, a blithe spirit, that he would drive a thirteen-coach special Rock Island train chartered for Estherville's invasion of Valley Junction caused some reservation upon the part of those who knew Dempsey. There were many curves, bridges, and stretches of doubtful track between Estherville and environs of the capital city. Sunday arrived, the coaches were filled, and as Dempsey had promised, he opened the throttle and gave 613 football players and watchers an unforgettable ride. The

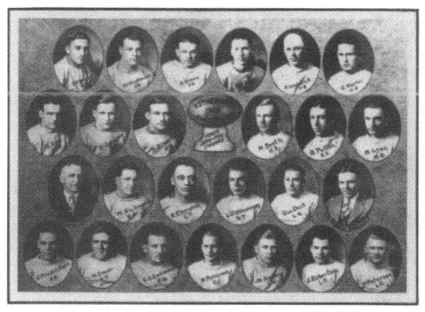

Estherville 1928 All-Stars football team, Iowa semi-pro champs.

passengers included fans from Spirit Lake, Emmetsburg, and other outlying precincts. Upon arrival at Des Moines the Maurice Doyle Drum and Bugle Corps tuned up and paraded through downtown streets, a few miles from the field where the main action soon took place.

My account of the historic game that day, when I was wearing my sports department hat, was detailed. It included a report of all the key plays and others besides. But my rereading of it recently on microfilm revealed that the story omitted one memorable incident. That was when Irv (Baldy) Ellerston went into the game to relieve a tired lineman. Before kneeling down to defend the line, Ellerston called out to no one in particular and to all the gladiators in general, in a voice easily heard as far away as the side lines, "What bastard in here is giving you the most trouble?"

The Estherville line was formidable no matter who happened to be playing in it. For one there was Cliff Fredericksen, an ex-sailor from Ringsted who one time after he became sheriff of Emmet

County threw editor Kirt Allen of the *Enterprise* through the door of the Gardston Hotel coffee shop without bothering to open the door. Cliff played right end. Glen Johnson, a semipro prizefighter, was one of the quarterbacks. George Deck wasn't handy, but giants are useful and he saw some action. Merle Moller, a policeman, was not easily pushed around by anybody, especially when he wore a cop's badge or played left guard. Russell Peterson was a dependable and durable center. Monk Omer, Wally Richmond, Lawrence Ullensvang, and Albert Dick were nice enough guys—out of uniform.

Sid Ellis was a reckless quarterback and about as elusive as Fran Tarkenton. Max Lynn, whose Estherville high school gridders won thirty consecutive victories, lent his brain as well as his person to the squad but was somewhat light for All-Star roughhouse play. Gordon Meeter was an exceptionally fleet back. Merritt Brown and K. V. Stephenson were strong fullbacks. Gene Rost was a quarterback and Keith Albertson and Max Soeth were backfield players who saw action. As Jack North, *a Des Moines Register & Tribune* sportswriter, summed it up: "Whenever an Estherville player was taken out of the game, a bigger and tougher guy came in." North refereed the game.

Justice prevailed. The All-Stars slugged out a 7-3 conquest over the most rugged talent the southern half of the state could recruit, and the Estherville troops headed home. On the joyride back to Estherville, the rooters counted what winnings they hadn't spent in the big city while refreshing, nourishing, and appropriately congratulating themselves after the mayhem. Some of the exhausted celebrants dozed as best they could amid the confusion. Arriving at the Estherville station about five o'clock in the morning, the heroes and their followers received greetings from the town band, a huge gathering of people, and the fire department.

The fire fighters had been racing a truck with full siren up and down the street at that obscene hour. "Where's the fire?" a drowsy fellow called from his front porch. "We haven't started it yet," yelled the happy fire-eater from the back running board of the red truck. Shortly the bonfire got under way. By then few in town were still asleep.

Recently I stopped at Ellerston's back door and asked him if I might visit a few minutes about the old All-Star days. Shirtless, he welcomed me to come in and we then sat at his breakfast table in the kitchen, chatting about the past. I said, "Irv, do I remember right about that Valley Junction game?" recalling to him what I remembered his saying when he was sent into the game. "I 'spect you do," he replied. "You see, Ernie sort of expected me to take care of the tough ones. Do you remember the time we played the White Line Transfer outfit here at home?" he asked. I said I didn't.

"Well, before that game when we were suiting up, down in the Gardston Hotel barbershop, which we used as a dressing room, Jim White was there. He asked me if I'd like a drink, and I said I guessed that would be all right. Then he drove me out to the fairgrounds where we played our games. When we got there, Ernie spotted me, apparently figuring that I might have been drinking a lot, which I hadn't. He said he wanted me to come up to the other end of the field, where the visiting team was running signals. 'You see that fella there?' Ernie asked me. I said I could see him all right. 'Well, I want you to play against him no matter what he plays. If he plays end then you play end. If he plays tackle then you play tackle. If he plays guard then you play guard. You stay with him.' I said all right, I would. I pretty soon caught on to the fact that my man was the meanest guy on the squad, and I got some kidding by the rest of our fellows about what kind of an afternoon I was in for. He was an ornery cuss."

At that point I said to Irv, "How did you get along?" Ellerston, his expansive chest exposed under his BVD's, grinned. "You know," he laughed, "it wasn't until the third quarter was almost over that I could get that mean sonofabitch outta there." Irv was eighty-four years old that warm July morning when we talked about old times.

Hugh Dempsey not only held the job of training and supervising locomotive engineers—and hauling All-Stars—but also wore the hat of division director of Rock Island athletics. He recruited the likeliest available track and field talent to send against other division teams of the railroad. Only two points short of the system championship the year before, Dempsey fielded a stellar outfit in August 1929 to represent the Dakota division for the annual event at Topeka.

This time the margin of victory was more impressive than two points; Estherville won by sixty-five. Merle Moller, who could handle drunks and football opponents, could also heave the shot

125 feet. John Warrington and Leon Blake were standouts. Blake, married to the daughter of William Moore, a dining car steward, received a gold medal from Senator Capper. He ran the 220 and was clocked in 10.2 seconds for the 100-yard dash.

Sports fans of the town showed major interest in football, baseball, basketball, and track. Boxing and wrestling matches had been going on since 1910, when promoters staged bouts in the old armory building on South Sixth Street. Such athletes as Ralph Parcaut were matched against Ben Reeves, a powerful auctioneer who then lived at Graettinger. Andrew McAndrews, Glen Johnson, Everett Strong, Glen Milligan, and Frankie Soultis were other performers.

The wrestler I enjoyed watching was the mighty Lars Larson, a farmer who lived near Superior, a few miles away. He usually challenged whichever wrestler came along with the street carnivals, usually held on the main street. On such occasions slickers fleeced the local dart throwers and pin-wheel spinners of their money. Lars was so powerful he didn't even use a jack for his car; he just carried a block of wood that he shoved under the axle whenever he blew a tire. Father sold him our Death Valley Dodge when father bought a Hudson coach from Matt Donovan.

One morning in June 1929 five bandits brandishing a machine gun held up the Emmet County State Bank, a year and a half after it opened. The bank's quarters at the time were across the street south from the Gardston Hotel. While gunmen stood outside the bank holding off all who came their way, the others scooped up about $2,000 in cash and took $3,500 in bonds from Mart Whelan. Police and the sheriff lost the trail of the robbers, although they searched for them in an airplane, armed with a high-powered rifle. Robberies and holdups were common throughout the decade but the bank loot was the biggest local haul.

Joe and Art Steele stirred excitement as the town's leading bootleggers. They were crafty operators, rarely caught with any alcohol, although federal operatives once shot up Jay Steele's auto while he was on a liquor run. They planted their booze at carefully platted spots along country roads beside designated fence posts. These were revealed to customers after they had paid cash in advance to one of the bootleggers.

In August of the same year that outlaws robbed the bank, the

Steeles' luck ran out and they were netted by the sheriff, who sent them to jail. Taking the matter of gaining freedom in their own hands, the Steeles broke jail. Then they were in more trouble than the bootleg evidence against them. When restored to jail, they received penitentiary sentences—for jail breaking.

Of the Steeles involved in the booze trade that went on in Estherville in the Roaring Twenties, Joe was the most experienced in jail. While housed in the Estherville lockup on one occasion, he boasted to Policeman Merle Moller that he had been a guest in jails from the East Coast to the West Coast and from Canada to the Gulf but had yet to meet a sheriff he couldn't whip. Moller promptly went to the police station office, picked up the phone, and called his old buddy on the All-Star football team, who at that time was the sheriff. Moller told him what Joe Steele had said. "I'll be right down," Cliff Fredericksen promised. In a few minutes the sheriff was there. "Let me in the jail, and lock the door," he told Moller. It was then that Joe Steele met a sheriff who could whip him. Fredericksen was fearless.

Nobody I heard of went blind from drinking the alcohol peddled illicitly in Estherville, but it was a fear that customers of bootleg liquor always had in mind as they sampled a fresh batch of hootch. Many drinkers of bootleg booze made a practice of igniting a bottle capful to see if it made a blue flame. If it did, this was regarded as some assurance it would unlikely cause the imbiber to go blind—at least immediately.

The town started 1930 auspiciously by voting in February to build a needed new city hall. The next month baseball enthusiasts raised $782 to repair the fence and grandstand at the ball park, and prepared to field a team in the southern Minnesota league. The Eagles claimed my Sundays from then on as I kept box scores and reported baseball successes and disappointments. George Tomer, a big, awkward-looking fellow who I think came from Perry, managed the team and played first base. Dan Howard, Herb Drey, O. J. Spande, Ernie Johnson, Clint Smith, Homer Denham, and Spike Blakey were the main plotters, worriers, fund raisers, and Monday morning strategists.

Otto Wold, who had apparently pitched some baseball many years before, was a Walter Mitty who saw himself as whatever hurler took the mound. On Otto Wold Day this most enthusiastic of

all Eagles went to the rubber and threw a few pitches, to the delight
of his patronizing cronies, who loved to spoof him but hesitated to
offend him. Jerry Wegs, a catcher, and Shanty Dolan, a shortstop,
were among the Eagles who stayed in Estherville after the Eagles
disbanded in a few years. They won 40 of the first 65 games they
played; 90 of 109. Their success was partly the cause of the league's
disintegrating. Unlike the Eagles, some of the teams in the circuit
languished.

The 1930 census takers counted 500 more souls than in the
1925 tally. Only 60 short of 5,000. In June the county voted to bond
itself for $770,000 to pave its primary highways crossing north-
south and east-west through Estherville. A state primary road now
crosses the county north-south through Armstrong and Ringsted in
the eastern side of the county. In addition, the county has built 155
miles of hard-surfaced farm-to-market roads and has graveled all
the others. Congressman L. J. Dickinson came to town in
September 1930 to speak at the dedication of a handsome new
junior–high school building named for Teddy Roosevelt. At the
fairgrounds in southeast Estherville, aviation enthusiasts provided
three new hangars and improved the runway at the airport, which
had been dedicated in 1929.

For me, 1930 was a year made memorable by Robert Tyre
Jones. I watched him win the U.S. Open at Interlachen Golf Club
in Edina, Minnesota. Jim White invited me to join him, his father,
and two Spencer men—a lawyer, Morgan Cornwall, and Franklin
Floete, who like White was a lumberman. Only a few miles out of
Estherville, Mr. White, sitting with Cornwall and Floete in the back
seat, called to Jim, who was driving. Jim's father, president of the
Northern Lumber Company, was dignified, handsome, and polite.
He seemed somewhat out of character as he asked Jim, "What did
you bring to drink, James?" Jim, a product of Shattuck and Yale
and as well mannered as his father, replied that he had brought
nothing at all. Fred persisted. "Oh, I'm sure you did. What did you
bring along?" Again Jim protested that his leather grip, resting on
the back floor where the jump seats had been folded away, held
nothing whatever to drink.

At that point Fred pulled the grip toward him, opened it, and
jerked out a quart of whiskey. "I was sure you wouldn't disappoint

us," triumphed the distinguished-looking Fred. Completely baffled at the moment, Jim soon sensed what had happened. Susan, Jim's mother, was the daughter of James J. Spalding of Sioux City, who became wealthy in Northern Lumber Company and other lumber interests and from Lehigh Sewer Pipe and Tile Company profits. Just how rich Mrs. White was nobody knew. But it was no secret that she aimed to protect husband Fred against whatever evils might beset him, while her Jimmy enjoyed freer rein. He was entitled to special treatment if for no other reason than the perpetual pain he endured after a hideous sinus operation performed years before in St. Paul. Fred had calculated shrewdly that stowing whiskey he obtained for the trip in Jim's grip was safer strategy than risking search and seizure of his own baggage.

If all the golfers who claim they witnessed Bobby Jones skip a ball across the water on the ninth fairway at Edina were gathered in one place, they would populate a fair-sized city. I was there, I saw, and I was awed by the Jones magic touch. Jock Hutchinson, past his prime and merely enjoying himself, provided relief comedy as he and Jones played the back nine on the last round. Bobby's patience must have been tried as Hutchinson played ante over the sand bunkers on one hole to score a ripe eight as Jones concentrated to finish his round and win the tournament. He was on his way to the only grand slam in history.

Don McGiffin, publisher of the *Fairfield Ledger* and owner also of the *Shenandoah Sentinel,* had hoped to buy the *Estherville Vindicator & Republican* from the Nichols family so that we might consolidate the two papers and publish daily. But Nichols and his daughter Adelaide could not decide they wanted to part with the *V & R.* By 1930 I was tired of running a weekly. The town ought to have a daily newspaper and I was the one to publish it, I thought. So I proposed to Don when we met in the spring at the Iowa Press Association meeting that he put up in cash the same amount I had paid with father's gracious loan for the *Democrat.* We would use the capital to buy two more typesetting machines, a web-perfecting flatbed press capable of speedier production, and other needed items. He readily agreed.

On arriving home, father and I negotiated with the Iowa Trust & Savings Bank to build a structure for a new plant just west of the bank on Central Avenue along the alley. By the first of October the building was ready and we moved in. Pat Hurlbut, who had an unbelievable capacity for whiskey, came up from Liberty, Missouri, to install a QQ model Duplex flatbed press he had dismantled and brought up from Pawhuska, Oklahoma. Pat held his ulcers in check by his own prescription of coating his stomach with cream before each drinking bout.

On October 6 the Associated Press teletype was humming; Mason, Vedder, Mike Korts, and Curt somebody were feverishly setting and assembling type; Lee was systematically losing his mind. Press deadline came, and then it went. Delays and more delays. Not a single schedule was kept, and the shadows lengthened. Some of my best friends, unlike others who had forecast a quick and humane end of my folly, were waiting at the windows and crowding in to witness the first daily paper come off the press.

Our tardy performance not only vexed me; it injured my pride. Eight schoolboys waiting to deliver their first papers wiggled, shouted, and scrapped, just beyond the immediate press area. Even Tony, the little Mexican boy who wanted to sell single copies on the streets, was waiting. Hurlbut had not got around to making a dummy pressrun and so he had no idea of how the Duplex would perform. Meantime, I worried whether in overlubrication of his person he had put all the parts back the way they were before he dismantled them. Finally Earl Briar, whose experience I soon learned had been limited, started the motor. The web of paper started through the press. But it didn't get far before tearing to shreds.

The web was rethreaded over this roller, under that one, beneath the printing cylinder, under this, over that, and finally into the folder. Another start; and another loud report as the paper ripped under tension. Another threading. Another start. Another failure. Adjustments. More of them. And profanity, despite the sober, God-fearing audience that had come to share our history — not to hear obscene pressroom talk. At 8 P.M. the press began to turn out printed pages of our "afternoon" newspaper. Eight blood-drenched pages.

That first issue related how Jimmy Foxx's home run disappointed the Cardinals. The British and the French were investigating the crash of the R-101 dirigible. Zeppelin Commander Eckener would explore the North Pole. President Hoover told

American Legionnaires that peace never seemed more assured, but in an adjoining column a Gold Star mother warned members of the Estherville Legion Auxiliary they must keep war memories alive. The chairman of the state conservation board promised that the road in Fort Defiance Park would be improved. The bank receiver advertised the coming sale of the remaining assets of the Iowa Savings at public auction. The J. A. Cummings Rexall store was selling linseed oil for $1.30 a gallon and H. N. Jensen & Sons agreed to coarse grind grain at 8¢ a hundred pounds. According to a Cut-Rate Grocery ad, housewives could buy two tall cans of Alaska pink salmon for 23¢ and a pound of Swift's Premium sliced bacon for 39¢. Why, of course the paper was worth waiting for—even until late "afternoon." The editor promised himself to do better about deadlines and early delivery.

Before the move into the new building for daily publication, George Phillips, a young journalism graduate, had begun helping me with the news department. He moved into advertising when the daily started, but he soon left to go back to college for advanced training. He accumulated more degrees and wound up in Brookings, South Dakota, running the journalism school. Merchants were not breaking our doors down to buy our white space. They needed to be coaxed, lovingly.

For my understaffed news department, I was fortunate in recruiting hidden talent I found in a dress shop around the corner. Dorothy Gruwell, who married Glenn Story, came to work for us, developing skills quickly. She utilized her liberal arts education at the University of Iowa more gainfully than by selling women's apparel. She was a sister of my high school companion, Bill. Her

Dorothy Story.

father, George Gruwell, had once been an owner and publisher of the *Vindicator.* Dorothy's service to the *News* was long, faithful, and competent. Her husband as a young man was one of the valued clerks at the Sconberg & Kilgore store and, eventually, upon returning from service in World War II, became city clerk. I found his account of an experience at the doctor's office one of the more amusing incidents I had heard.

Troubled with a persistent sore throat, Glenn visited the office of Dr. C. E. Birney, who enjoyed a large practice of medicine. He also owned the store and building that filled his prescriptions and the hospital where he performed surgery on his patients. He was one of the few physicians in our town who saved money and invested it wisely. The doctor firmly believed in the value of placebos, always readily available from his small black bag. His pink pills cured the imaginary ills of many patients.

When Story went to consult him about a raw gullet, the redheaded doctor peered into the patient's mouth and quickly announced the verdict. "You need to have your tonsils removed," he told Glenn. "But I don't have any tonsils, doctor," protested the patient, "they've already been removed." Dr. Birney frowned and asked, "What darned fool did the job?" The trap snapped shut. "You did, doctor." Glenn vowed that the incident happened just that way. Whether it did or didn't, more than one youngster's tonsils were inexpertly snipped off by early practitioners. I was one of those kids.

Despite the numberless cooking schools our newspaper sponsored annually, starting in the winter of 1931, and despite exposure to my mother's cooking techniques, Everyld regards me as the most underprivileged person in the kitchen she has ever encountered. The cooking schools were fashionable events with some social standing. Photographs prove they were attended by the town's best cooks—Marietta Groves, Katherine Kirby, Bessie Greig, Mary Rainey, Elizabeth Birney, Nettie Tedrow, Hattie Rhodes—and hundreds of others. Handsome prizes awarded at drawings for door prizes among the 800 or more at each session may have aided attendance. The ladies all smiled as Harold Sorenson blinded them with flashbulbs to film them for the next day's paper. Home economists from leading universities employed for these instructive occasions showered our subscribers with useful kitchen facts. But nothing rubbed off on me.

The spring of '31 unfolded on one of the town's most lively municipal elections, at which Mart Whelan defeated M. H. Schloeman for mayor. Whelan was about as acceptable to the Groves crowd as John Lilley, whom Schloeman had defeated four years before. A distinguished-looking man, Whelan dressed immaculately and in summer always wore a straw sailor hat. He had been prominent in community affairs for a long time. He was a conservative (standpatter) Republican and had been vice-president of John Kirby's First National Bank until it collapsed. After his election as mayor he made Lilley his chief of police.

What most voters who marked their ballots in 1931 had forgotten or never knew was that Whelan had been appointed sheriff of the county forty-nine years before. In 1886 he and his deputy, Thomas Storhow, stirred the community with their courage by tracking down and capturing two horse thieves who had hidden themselves and their stolen horses near Raleigh station. But a few old-timers remembered those days and gave their votes to Mart. Some people erroneously called him Mark, but his given name was Martin, as it is chiseled in stone at Oakhill Cemetery.

Although the mayoralty race got out a share of the vote, the most heat was generated in the election of councilmen. Charles Kilgore, a colorful hardware merchant, and Hans Gaarde, a conservative and wealthy land-owning Dane, ran for the council because they disapproved the extravagant notions of the incumbents. How Estherville should economically procure an adequate, safe supply of drinking water was at issue. The old council had been accused of willingness to spend the taxpayers' money loosely for filtration facilities and engineering services seen by the insurgents as unneeded and wasteful.

The voters elected Kilgore, Gaarde, Rube Green, merchant George Shadle, and M. C. Petersen to guide the city's destiny for the next two years, but the *Estherville Enterprise* was unhappy with the outcome. It had supported the incumbent council, the members of which were well respected in the community but simply victims of the water issue. Although the losers soon forgot and forgave, editor Kirt Allen did not. And his *Enterprise* not long after found an issue with which he could assail those who had unhorsed his friends in the council chamber. The city government had purchased some supplies from alderman Kilgore's K & K Hardware Store, and the *Enterprise* thought that smelled bad.

Charlie Kilgore didn't think so, and Charlie's customers knew he was not bashful about speaking his mind. Unlike many merchants, who soaped their patrons with mishmash talk, Charlie drew trade by telling customers, including farmers, what he thought of them. He lectured daily as his customers sat in a row like blackbirds on the store-long counter beneath bins of nuts, bolts, clamps, springs, hooks, eyes, and thousands of other hardware items. A long ladder supported by rollers on the counter and by a track near the ceiling enabled Charlie, Squeak, and Leon Pratt to reach the remotest bin on the wall with ease.

Charlie had friends. He inspired confidence because he told his own version of the way it was. When reelection time came along, he fired both barrels at Allen and his *Enterprise*. Itemizing every item the city had purchased at his store, including six snow shovels, he told what his markup was on every purchase. And believing that a good defense calls also for a potent offense, he printed a broadside in which he recalled history of twenty years before when the Allen family sold a site for the town's first water storage standpipe atop Gobbler's knob for the sum of $1,250.

Charlie fumed that a sheriff's jury would have been insane to appraise the patch of ground for more than $250. It could not have been sold at any time, fretted Kilgore, for any other purpose for more than $150. The more Charlie thought about it, the more worthless he thought the place was, and so he concluded, "If put at auction today it would not bring $50." If anybody had overcharged someone it was the Allens, Charlie thought. The voters turned out in numbers to have their say.

I was in my office election evening receiving returns from the various precincts when Charlie came in. "What's it look like?" he wanted to know. "Well," I told him, "it's a sure thing that the voters are going to have to put up with your looting for another two years." Charlie admitted he was not surprised, but he had worried, he said. "Are you sure about the result?" he wanted to know. "Positive," I assured him. With that he wanted to know if he could borrow a line to make a telephone call. "Of course," I told him, "help yourself." After waiting for the operator to ring the number he wanted, he clacked his teeth. Then he boomed into the mouthpiece, "Kirt, this is Charlie Kilgore. Say, Kirt, I understand that you feel like the new bride." Then after a dramatic pause, he added, "sore, but satisfied."

Charlie and his brother, Fred, a groceryman, had tried partnership at one time but they were utterly unsuited to each other as partners, although both of them were scrupulously honest. Hans Sconberg fitted with Fred better as a hardware partner; Charlie went his own way to join Henry Klocow in a different location, becoming the K & K. I got to know Charlie best after he went on the council, perhaps because it brought us in closer touch.

Whenever I went into his store he invited me up a narrow, steep flight of stairs to a tiny office at mezzanine level to talk about city affairs, in which he took a keen and continuing interest. The top of his rolltop desk was littered with empty Fasteeth bottles. Although he apparently consumed the product in amazing quantities, it did not deprive him of his characteristic speech. The clanking of his false teeth gave emphasis and conviction to anything he had to say, which was never equivocal. Charlie's daily audience of counter sitters included numerous railroaders who liked his plain talk. Before entering the hardware business he had been a Rock Island division locomotive engineer. One time, in a reflective mood of candor, Charlie admitted, "You know, Deemer, it really is a lot of fun to spend the taxpayers' money."

On almost the very day that the J. S. McLaughlin Company finished paving No. 9 highway east and west across the county through Estherville, the achievement was marred by one of the few events of its kind that ever took place in the community. Less than two months after Deputy William G. Gordon took over the sheriff's office from F. M. Brown, he received a complaint of gambling at the Otto Buysman pool hall in Gruver. Transient paving workers usually gathered for entertainment there, which was almost the center of the stretch of highway they were grading and surfacing.

Gordon and his deputy, fullback Merritt Brown, went to Gruver and entered the Buysman quarters, where the proprietor was standing guard over a poker game. As Gordon started to enter the room, he was greeted by a .38 caliber slug. The *Daily News* issued daily bulletins until his recovery was certain. The event dampened joy over the smooth new road just laid across the prairie, which had earlier been swampy and frequently impassable. Now

Esthervilleans could fill their tanks with 16¢ gas (a gasoline war was in progress) and have a good time joy riding.

The pavers not only built a needed highway but they bequeathed to the Estherville Golf & Country Club long lengths of pipe they had used during the pouring of the slab. Golfers frequently acknowledged silent thanks to the J. S. McLaughlin Company for supplying the pipe used to construct water lines that only recently were supplanted by an automated tee, fairway, and greens watering system.

Eleven-Cent Corn,
108-Degree Heat,
and a Twister

LITTLE wonder that Emmet County voters deserted their Republican ways in November 1932 to help put Franklin D. Roosevelt in the White House, hoping he might straighten out the economics that plagued the country. Even so, the Roosevelt margin in Emmet was only 297 votes.

The weather was unfriendly as the year opened. Heavy snows snarled highway traffic and tied up railroad trains when high winds whipped through the county. A rash of break-ins, shoplifting, daylight robberies and nighttime safecrackings, petty thievery, even purse snatching set new police records as men lost employment and incomes dropped. After state agents made a haul of 189 gallons of bootleg liquor, 187 gallons of it quickly disappeared from a courthouse basement vault where officers stored it. Thieves were stealing everything: potatoes, chickens, cigarettes, coal off railroad cars, harness, gold from dental offices, liquor—everything. Hard times were upon the whole community.

Unemployed and underemployed families lacked the money to buy food, even at ridiculous prices. Howard's Cut-Rate was selling five pounds of cornmeal for 12¢, salted mackerel at 22¢ a pound, bacon at 17¢, and veal steak for 8¢ a pound. The K & K Hardware sold barn paint for 85¢ a gallon, a wash tub for 63¢. At any price, merchandise clung to the shelves. George W. Shadle had closed his store in the autumn of 1931, and another established women's wear store, Herman Oransky's, soon folded.

Farmers and their wives could spend little money when local grain elevators offered only 10¢ a bushel for oats and 11¢ to 14¢ for corn (depending upon grade). Average prices at Iowa elevators De-

cember 1, 1929, were 70¢ a bushel for corn, but the price dropped
to 58¢ in 1930, then to 35¢ in 1931, and hit bottom at 12¢ a bushel
in 1932. Oats prices followed the same pattern: 39¢, to 28¢, to 21¢
and finally down to 10¢ a bushel in 1932.[1] The farmwife who
depended on chicken-and-egg money for her immediate cash needs
found that she could sell her chickens for only 6¢ to 9¢ a pound and
her eggs for only 14¢ to 23¢, depending on grade. Buyers paid 18¢
for cream. Poultry, egg, and dairy checks didn't go far at those
prices.

Bill Foshier and Ben Burns busied themselves crying sales of
farmers who were no longer solvent and able to continue farming
and were forced to auction off their equipment and livestock. When
Foshier died in 1961 at ninety-three years of age, he had cried 6,000
sales over a sixty-year period. Most of these occurred during hard
times.

The board of supervisors reduced the salaries of courthouse
deputies, and the city hall followed suit by cutting the rates for electricity by 10 percent. Councilmen noted that Estherville was spending an alarming $26 a day just to keep the city hall open, so they
found a way to reduce those expenses 22½ percent. The home
economists urged housewives to use more cereal to make food pennies go further. The Red Cross brought in 150 barrels of flour. Wel-
fare workers distributed 190 food baskets to needy families.

The *Daily News* employed numerous columns of front-page
space soliciting cash donations for Christmastime, when Mack
Groves invariably sent over a check to cover whatever the goal defi-
cit turned out to be. "Make it anonymous," he always scribbled on
the face of the check.

Farmers of the community encountered adversities other than
the grain and produce markets. Winter's cruel cold was followed by
sweltering heat that registered temperatures during one week that
ranged from 97° to 100°. Some farmers suffered severe hail damage. They were invaded by army worms. Supporters of the Farmers
Holiday Movement tried to blockade roads in an effort to bolster
prices by withholding supply, but that didn't help. The only good
news in the town newspaper in the election year of 1932 was that a
new Thorpe Brothers well could pump 1,400 gallons of pure water
per minute. But of course water isn't nutritious.

At Graettinger Jake Spies, who owned several thousand acres

of land, took credit on share rent payments due from his tenants, allowing them 50¢ a bushel for their corn. That was better than 11¢ or 14¢ a bushel for the tenant farmers, while the trade made Spies even wealthier. He and his son Adolph arranged for cheap, temporary, pole-type constructed cribs on the home place close to Graettinger where they stored thousands of bushels of car corn. Two or three years later they shelled, delivered, and sold it at the elevator for 75¢ to $1.00 or more a bushel. Spies got back his cost and a rattling good profit besides.

Not only did farmers find themselves insolvent and forced to hold auction sales of their livestock and machinery, but many lost the land they lived on. The newspaper published many columns of legal notices of foreclosure. Business was stagnant, which meant that advertising space went begging. The *Daily News* went behind every month. By summer it owed the Butler Paper Company for five carloads of newsprint. Just before the Democratic convention in July, the credit manager of Butler called me from Chicago, asking what I intended to do about the debt for paper I had piled up. Like many other newspapers, the *News* had used the paper company as its banker. Unlike the bank, the paper company charged no interest.

It looked like a prudent idea for me to go to Chicago and discuss this little matter of five carloads of paper I hadn't paid for. Also the time was just right to attend the Democratic National Convention. Having witnessed the nomination of Herbert Hoover four years before in Kansas City, I felt I ought to have a look at what appeared to be a sure thing for FDR. There was still a third Chicago attraction: the Century of Progress World's Fair on the lake front. Francis Shadle, employed as a bookkeeper for John Greig, had no interest in becoming involved in my credit problem with the paper company but he did like the idea of seeing the fair and the convention. Greig, who had succeeded his father, Hugh, in the grain business, thought he could spare Francis for a few days. So the trip was on.

Francis said he would drive his Ford. That suited me. We intended to drive all night to save hotel expense, but his auto developed a vicious malady a hundred miles from home that took hours to repair. That's how it happened we spent the remnant of the night in the cell of a fifth-rate Clinton hotel recommended by an unfor-

given policeman. Arriving in Chicago the next morning, Francis
found free lodging at the Northwestern chapter of Sigma Chi and I
bedded down for free at the Midway Phi Delt house. We accepted
some free meals and foraged for the others. But of convention tickets we had none. Even the friendly *Tribune* claimed to be completely out of supply. Optimistically, we took an L train out to the
stadium anyway.

Having just resigned from the Associated Press because I could
no longer afford its teletype service, I managed to get the attention
of the manager of the United Press by waving frantically through
the window and talking sign language. My pressure point was the
fact I had just subscribed for UP pony telephone service to replace
the teletype wire. The blond-haired man, whose name might have
been McCabe, said he had no tickets, but I was not used to defeat so
I persisted. What other ideas did he have besides no tickets? After
thinking a moment or so, he said to wait. He would be back in a few
minutes.

He brought back two copy-boy badges used as credentials by
runners going in and out of the stadium on various errands. "Put
these on your hats, fellows, turn up the front brims, and try to look
like gum-chewing, don't-give-a-damn copy boys. And if you don't
give those badges back to me pronto I'll have you arrested and
shot."

No problem. We were soon inside the UP room on the main
floor receiving the rest of our instructions. If we loitered on the
main floor we would soon be tossed out, he said. Due to a peculiar
arrangement, each toilet room was shared by two floors. "Go to the
rest room," he ordered, "then when no one is looking, climb over
the low wall and presto you walk out a ramp and have access to the
next floor above. Repeat the procedure and finally you are up in
the stadium where you can negotiate." Beautiful. The final lap was
to the gallery, to which a friendly policeman escorted us up an outside fire escape after I had cordially shaken his hand with a dollar
bill in my palm. Under the ceiling of the stadium we saw and heard
history being made.

I looked forward to my confrontation with the credit manager
of the Butler Company with little pleasure. But like some of my surgical experiences, the anticipation was worse than the operation. A
fellow with a Polish name listened patiently to everything I had to
say about how I came to favor his company with so much debt. I

also told him business could be no worse; it had to get better. Moreover, I persuaded him I was much more worried about the huge account than he was. And, finally, I proposed a regular schedule of frequent payments that would possibly balance the account sometime before the second coming. We parted amiably.

Shortly after Francis and I arrived home in Estherville, I received in the mail a copy of Gene Fowler's delightful book, *Timberline*, the story of the *Denver Post*. A note enclosed with the book from the Butler credit manager said he hoped I would enjoy the volume and expressed complete confidence that all would work out very well. And so it did, but not very fast. When the country inaugurated Mr. Roosevelt, the banks all closed and the *News*, like all other depositors, had no access to any money at all. But in a few days the Holiday ended and the banks reopened, although the Iowa Trust & Savings had been wounded. Business continued under an arrangement provided by an act of the legislature known as Senate File 111. The act enabled a bank to remain open while the state superintendent of banking acted as receiver to deal with the bank's problem credit.

Back in 1927, when the Iowa Trust opened as a new bank, the directors authorized it to assume $50,000 in loans of the old Iowa Savings regarded as good but slow. That assisted the Iowa Savings receivership with ready cash to divide as dividends but the slow paper taken over proved a burden to the new bank. An additional problem to the bank was the $281,000 it had invested in state bonds to offset its postal savings deposits. The bonds were of unquestioned good quality but to have cashed them then would have meant a severe penalty because the bond market was depressed, like everything else. Provisions of Senate File 111 permitted orderly liquidation of both the state bonds and the slow-pay loans. The bank reorganized and began to grow. No losses resulted from the experience.

In 1934 K. J. McDonald was elected president of the Iowa Trust, and he served in that capacity until 1950, when the assets totaled $3.9 million. McDonald then told Mack Groves he wanted to obtain a controlling interest in the bank or to sell his shares. Groves perhaps surprised McDonald when he said that he would buy. This led to an arrangement in which Groves, Lloyd Stockdale, Paul Gray, and some other shareholders placed their stock in trust so that a new management could take control.

Several years before our Chicago trip, Francis Shadle had become manager of Greig & Company, a feed-milling concern into which John Greig had expanded his grain business in 1940. Then when Greig & Company sold out to Honeymead, Shadle went to work for the Brenton Bank group, opening and developing the organization's bank at Eagle Grove, Iowa. When offered the chance to return to Estherville to run and acquire ownership of the Iowa Trust, he immediately recognized it as the sound opportunity it proved to be. He was not influenced by those who feared otherwise.

It was during Shadle's regime that the Iowa Trust underwent its major growth. He and John Greig owned controlling interest in the capital stock until they both sold their interests in 1971 to the Associated Bank Corporation. In 1973 Francis retired and his son George became president. Wayne C. Currell, president of the Emmet County State Bank at the time of the 1933 Holiday, continued to head that bank until his death in December 1959. The bank accumulated a substantial reserve of surplus and undivided profits. Robert Knight succeeded Currell as president, and upon retirement of Knight, Wayne Currell's son James became president and son Richard vice-president.

The mood in 1933 was anything but happy. The county treasurer twice found it necessary to postpone the annual sale of property on which taxes were delinquent. No bidders. A nasty blizzard caused no casualties but it added hardship to the winter. When 250 farmers crowded menacingly around the sheriff and his deputy as they prepared to foreclose on the chattels of a High Lake Township farmer, the sheriff saw little else he could do than call off the sale. Incidents of that sort were common throughout the grain-raising counties of Iowa. However, few incidents of farmer lawlessness occurred in the Emmet community. Even efforts of liberal groups to prevent marketing of farm commodities got little support. But poverty was everywhere.

No sooner had $2,500 been made available by the state for works projects in the county than 70 persons applied. Relief workers built a rock garden in Riverside Park, beautified and built permanent improvements in Fort Defiance State Park, and completed other public projects. Sixty men put to shoveling snow earned 36¢ an hour. By June, 4,370 hours of project work had been logged. Authorities approved $24,242 for CWA schemes and 238 men were employed.

Farmers took a look at prospects of gas-alcohol at a local demonstration and wondered if they would ever really grow fuel to fill their automobile and tractor tanks. Following the cold winter they had endured came a heat wave: 97° to 103° Fahrenheit during one week in which farmers saw their crops dry up. A frightening thunderstorm ended the drought but the crops had already been seriously damaged. Farmers reaped about half an oats crop.

Although farm commodity prices were improving — 35¢ for oats and 37¢ to 39¢ for corn — dry, hot weather shrank the crop. So the better prices didn't help much. But in the fall, Secretary of Agriculture Henry Wallace announced that farmers could seal their corn at 45¢ a bushel. By the end of 1933, Emmet farmers had banked $285,000 from government corn loans. This was money to buy groceries, clothing, and farm operation needs.

Although Emmet County residents always seem to have about the same kind of thirst as other people, they voted dry when the rest of the country opted to repeal the Eighteenth Amendment. Emmet dries polled a majority of 424 votes, as the bootleggers continued to do business. Although the hooch peddlers lost many gallons of liquor to the sheriff, state agents, and the feds, the supply never ran completely dry.

Businessmen cheerfully agreed to cooperate with the NIRA, but they would have more than enough of price regimentation before they were done with it. No segment of the community escaped irritations, hardship, or even downright poverty. But Mrs. R. L. Caldwell did her part to cheer up the folks and uplift them spiritually. She organized a Little Symphony Orchestra, despite rather limited resources of talent that a community the size of Estherville could supply.

In the midst of the worst of things — in the same week as the Bank Holiday — June Caldwell tuned up her orchestra and delivered a joint production with the town's Philharmonic Society. No admission fee was charged for hearing *The Crucifixion* and the *Tannhäuser* "Chorus" in Roosevelt auditorium. During the next few years, production of the *Messiah* was an annual Christmastime event in Estherville.

In 1934 high winds swept the plains, eroding millions of tons of topsoil. The dirt eventually settled in road ditches and drifted along fence rows; it reached the tops of the posts in some places. Although

539 farmers pocketed $353,105 in cash from government corn loans in 1934, and corn sold for as much as 80¢ a bushel, poverty persisted. One hundred families welcomed direct relief. The delinquent tax sale had to be postponed for want of bidders. Farmers in overalls who were members of the Farm Holiday Movement disrupted foreclosure of an $11,000 mortgage, thus keeping a family on its farm one more year. County Attorney William Bale prosecuted thirty-nine criminal cases during the year, obtaining thirty-one convictions.

Bands of gypsies, who traded horses and roamed the country, brought color and mystery whenever they camped near town. Fortune-telling was a specialty of the gypsy women. Housewives found it hard to overlook even petty thievery during hard times, though. The sheriff of Hamilton County detained a band of fourteen gypsies when a woman reported that her purse was missing after the gypsies told her fortune. Stickups, robberies, and safe blowings plagued police, who demanded faster autos to catch criminals.

To discuss the depressed price of haircuts, barbers met one evening in the shop of Carl Boyster, who cut hair in the basement of the Orleans Hotel. During a spirited discussion of hours and prices, barber Boyster suffered a blackened eye and abrasions of his left cheek. The meeting had not gone amicably. Host Boyster was not only painfully wounded; he was formally charged with assault with intent to commit great bodily injury with a sharp razor upon the persons of barbers Bob Penn and Pat Mauck. The conferees ultimately reached a settlement of their conflicting views by fixing a penalty of $200 to be assessed against any barber breaking the truce at future sessions. All the barbers lived to die natural deaths.

The Orleans Hotel, besides providing quarters for barber disarmament conferences, supplied a smooth floor for the lively and ablebodied who chose to escape their economic troubles by dancing the polka and other fancy steps. They could polka to the one-and-a-two-and-a-three rhythms of Lawrence Welk, who regularly hauled his musicians from Yankton, South Dakota, in a small black bus. It provided sleeping quarters of a sort when needed for such stops as those at Estherville. Often on my way to work I saw it parked near the post office beside the outside stairway to the Odd Fellows Hall.

Sometimes the bus tipped over, and more than once it rammed into deep snowdrifts and had to be dug out. Their possessions buried deep in the snow of a 1928 storm, Welk's orchestra members attired themselves for their performance that evening in overalls supplied by an Estherville clothier. Auctioneer Ben Burns dug out the bus. On another occasion, musicians Terry George, Jack Soakie, and Leo Fortin suffered injuries that required medical attention when the Welk rig flipped over one-and-a-half times on the way from Yankton when three miles out of Estherville.

On the second anniversary of Roosevelt's nomination, the news was a mixed bag. The bad news was the number of persons yet on relief — 796 families receiving surplus commodities as well as cash — and severe snows that stranded trains as long as nine hours in snowdrifts 2,000 feet long. The good news was that, even though Joe Steele's bootlegging operation had been thrown out of commission once again by forces of law, order, and rectitude, thirsty Esthervilleans would not have to wait much longer before they could walk into a state-owned liquor store and order the booze they wanted.

The other good news in the paper was promise of a planned four-day rodeo. Nobody working in the business part of town could avoid wearing a ten-gallon hat to remind passersby that Clyde S. Miller and his wife would soon provide a thrilling program of bucking broncos, cowboy ropes, and daredevil clowns to take people's minds off their hunger and their debt. For appropriate introduction of the rodeo, Governor Clyde Herring rode a white horse in a two-mile-long parade, which was led by Harley Lambert, Vern Tredway, and the versatile Irving Ellerston.

So far as we know, Ellerston was the first, and possibly the last, to ride a steed right into the lobby of the Gardston Hotel. Innkeeper Herb Drey, who like Leo Sanders was an energetic and consecrated promoter of the rodeo, reserved doubts about the propriety of riding horses inside his premises. This was perhaps narrow-minded and inconsiderate of the rights of horses. But when the beast showed no aptitude whatever for climbing the stairs, horse and rider were escorted to the street, and the incident came to a satisfactory conclusion.

One day Al Smillie, a *Daily News* reporter, told me that the city was planning to build a disposal plant and quit pouring raw sewage into the river. When I asked him what this improvement would cost, he said that councilman Ed Stockdale told him the bill would come to $4,000 or $5,000. "Come off it, Al," I said. "This may be a depression, but $5,000 won't build anything at all. You'd better check back." Al stuck by his facts until he finally telephoned for confirmation of the figure. Ed meant $45,000. Such mistakes are easily made, particularly over the telephone, even though reporters try to be accurate. Communication becomes imperfect between lip and ear. The sewage plant was built, and it cost $67,229, only the beginning of a long series of improvements to purify and render odorless Estherville wastes, including those of its industrial plants. A recently completed and entirely new facility, located a discreet one mile from town, cost $9 million. The city doggedly determined to deal effectively with sewage and to banish its smells.

Hard times notwithstanding, amusements could be found in the community. Off and on, the attorney general ruled theater bank nights as legal. Both theater promoters and their audiences favored these share-the-wealth events. Few ticket purchasers, by the law of averages, found riches at the movies, but when the bank-night pot of cash grew to several hundred dollars, customers could find standing room only to be present at a drawing.

On Thursday evenings Jesse Cox gathered his musicians and the town band tooted a concert in the Square. Listeners who sat on the lawn applauded each selection by clapping their hands; those who listened in their parked automobiles expressed approval by honking their horns. A band shell was built in Riverside Park in 1934 to supersede an ancient round bandstand in the Square, but this innovation never proved quite the success it was intended to be. Unlike the band shell, the tennis courts built in Riverside proved popular, as did the addition of floodlights at Sunderlin field so that high school games could be enjoyed in the evenings.

By 1935 the corn-hog program was pumping as much as $650,000 a year to farmers, but despite improving times, thievery persisted. Burglars stole 283 men's suits, 46 jackets, and $230 in cash from Denny Bagan's clothing store. The county government doled out $30,300 in cash assistance, but the supervisors thriftily arranged for the County Farm to put up 16,000 cans of vegetables and soups at a cost of only 10¢ a can.

If anyone consuming the home canning died of botulism, the news was successfully suppressed before it reached the newspaper office. After Everyld and I were married, Everyld canned asparagus to stretch our budget. We escaped agonizing death only because the

Bandstand in west central part of park, about 1913.

asparagus blew up, like a bomb, spewing glass jars and vegetable all over our basement. Providence works out these things in its own mysterious way.

Few Esthervilleans could forget the year 1936. A bitter cold winter was followed by a capricious spring and by an unfriendly summer that added insult to the injury of empty stomachs. Heavy drifting snows snarled railroad traffic, and the cold soon emptied the coal bins. As coal trains stalled in mammoth snowdrifts, the community ran perilously low on fuel. Mayor Fred Ehlers recruited volunteer shovelers, who rescued a train loaded with coal that got almost as far as Estherville when once again it was stalled in a deep cut. Daily bulletins published in the paper kept anxious readers informed on the progress of the train bringing them coal, which finally reached the town as residents were steeling themselves for cold houses. Fears of empty coal bins were no more than allayed when other fears replaced them. On Thursday, April 30, a funnel cloud roared in from the west over the bluffs along the river.

Fred Olson, who replaced George Phillips as advertising salesman and who wrote a funny column on the editorial page of the

News, was just returning to the office as I approached the building from a different direction. Fred had been watching the strange behavior of the clouds. As I looked up, it was apparent that low clouds were scurrying in four directions. The sure sign of a twister, I thought. The two of us had no more than entered the office when the town's fire siren began to wail. A tornado had struck nine blocks north of the plant. It was 4:30 P.M.

Remaking the front page of the paper, we were able to report to readers that evening a summary of news about a tornado that had approached from farther away than the Okoboji lakes area. As it approached Estherville it divided at the hills across the river and, after doing a moderate amount of damage in the city, united to sweep through the county in a northeasterly direction nearly as far as Fairmont, thirty-eight miles distant. No lives were lost in Emmet County, but four persons died in the outer area of the storm. About fifty persons suffered injuries. As the twister cut a narrow path through the north side of Estherville toward the east, it blew out all the windows of the hospital's operating rooms and smashed 500 panes of glass in the Estherville Greenhouse. It severed power and telephone lines, uprooted trees, and knocked houses off their foundations. Before roaring into the country to play havoc there, it made a shambles of Jesse Cox's uninsured scenery-painting studio.

Logan Anderson, a glazier, was too busy finding a supply of glass needed to replace hundreds of windows to lament the destruction of his own home on North Sixth Street. He quickly comforted his wife, Violette, by promising they would build a new one and then he went about his business of getting the hospital's operating rooms back in commission. Mrs. Anderson wanted a smaller and more modern kind of house anyway.

A farmer southeast of Estherville in the path of the storm's south fork was lifted out of his barn and tossed gently into a manure pile as the wind demolished the building in which he had been working. Over a broad area, livestock were killed, trees were torn out by the hundreds, houses and barns were leveled or wrecked, and chickens were picked of their feathers. We beefed up our small newsroom staff with every person we could find who was capable of handling a notebook or a camera. The reporters and photographers could easily follow the storm's wide strip of desolation and strewn debris.

Logan Anderson house after a tornado, April 30, 1936.

By the next day the *News* had collected many columns of details. Lives had been spared because farmers saw the storm approach and hurried to basements, storm and vegetable cellars, or other security. Total damage was estimated at $1 million. The Red Cross moved in, asking for $25,000 of immediate relief assistance to victims. Mayor Ehlers promptly took necessary steps to prevent looting. Little took place, although a washing machine and some chickens were stolen. On Monday afternoon, four days after the tornado, the newspaper could report that during the weekend local citizens had already given $1,080 for relief. Rehabilitation plans were well developed, and CCC workers were helping clear farm fields of wreckage.

Troubles sometimes come in bundles. After farmers had removed wreckage from their fields and planted them to crops, more disaster followed. A prolonged period of heat and drought scorched the growing grain. During a period of eleven days the thermometer registered nothing cooler than 98 degrees Fahrenheit and for three days showed 100 degrees or warmer. The mercury climbed to 106 degrees one day. A few days later, during a period of six days of intense heat, the mercury shot up to 108 degrees. The elevators could offer 40¢ for oats and $1.10 for corn because the supply was short. But, because of the drought, farmers had little crop to offer. That's the sorry story of farm economics.

But there was enough good corn left in some fields to hold a cornhusking contest, and Secretary of Agriculture Henry Wallace came from Washington to speak on the occasion. When at a press conference I asked Wallace what he thought of some of the far-left legislation sent over to the Congress by FDR's brain trusters, he said that England was far ahead of America in getting society socialized. That said volumes about Wallace's political philosophy. He was more liberal than his fellow Iowans had realized. But farmers appreciated the corn-hog checks that bailed them out.

Sam Naas, who had picked more corn than anyone else in the contest a year before, was beaten by a Kossuth County farmer, but Sam's brother, Dan, finished second. Sam won two years later, though, when he pitched 2,040 pounds of corn in his wagon as Dan, close behind, husked 1,990 pounds during the 80-minute contest period. However, mechanical pickers were coming on fast. Farmers lost fingers, hands, arms, and even lives to the monster robots that could beat Sam, Dan, or anybody else as they chewed through corn-fields and tossed cleanly husked ear corn into a wagon. J. E. Wilson, a successful baker who also owned a farm, lost his life to a farm machine. Huge combines that shell as well as pick the corn, all in one operation at unbelievable speeds, are in common use now.

The thirties taught us to enjoy pleasures simple and inexpensive, like those we learned in our youth. A fairly large group—mostly bachelors—that included Delbert Hinsch, Francis Shadle, and George Brunskill found exercise, companionship, and good sport at the river or on Swan Lake, where we gathered for ice-skating parties. Bill Reid and a few other farmers of the area who also liked to skate sometimes cleaned snow from patches of ice.

When the lake froze smooth and the moon accommodated us with bright illumination, we could skate all the way around the lake's island. Often we built a bonfire near the shore.

Usually when Fred Olson had finished his morning round of soliciting advertising for the *Daily News,* he closeted himself in a cubbyhole of a room originally equipped as a photographic darkroom. Fred used it for his office. After rolling and lighting a Bull Durham cigarette, he stood at his venerable Oliver typewriter, placed on the waist-high table before him, and produced a column. He called it "Around the Town." Unlike columnists eager to impress readers with their own literary assets or their acquaintances in the social register, Fred wrote about the people in our town.

He turned out some of his best work in the winter, when he was not distracted by what he called snarled underwear. One of his favorite subjects was Alex Johnston, one of the two partners who founded the Gardston Hotel. Fred lived a block and a half farther from downtown than Alex, on the same side of South Eighth Street. Because Alex lived on a corner lot and therefore needed to shovel substantial mileage of walk, he usually cleared only a narrow, one-scoop-width path after a heavy, back-breaking snowfall.

On his way to work the next morning, Fred would seek to thread his way through the narrow slit of a path that Alex had carved with his "fudge knife," as Fred called it. The path was not always handily negotiated by the fun-loving Fred, especially after an evening with the boys to whom he made frequent contributions at poker. Alex's paths became widely known, even in the outlying precincts, for Fred's column was perhaps the paper's most popular feature.

By the time 1937 rolled around, our community no longer experienced the exquisite pains of depression, but temporarily depressed were customers around the Square who found Carl Moser's drugstore in the Gardston Hotel, at George Bale's old stand, a convenient source of drinking alcohol. Sheriff Cliff Fredericksen, his deputy Ernest Huckaba, and policemen Merle Moller and Ed Case raided the store and deprived parched townsmen of sixty pints.

The board of supervisors discontinued all relief, assuring that work was plentiful. Within a year the need for assistance had been reduced to only 0.8 percent of all Emmet County residents. But the WPA went ahead with its project to plant a quarter of a million trees in the county.

Rural electrification boosted the economy as the REA began building 182 miles of lines that revolutionized farm living. By 1970 more than 3,000 farms were electrified. Juice from Estherville's municipal plant soon displaced farm families' kerosene lamps, windmills, vegetable cellars, and gasoline engines. Every yard was flood-lit. Farm homes became as convenient as those in town, and more restful. For gracious living, the migration was now toward the country, not away from it. The flow of REA electricity, like the migration, eventually reversed as Corn Belt Cooperative's electric plant was able to produce electricity cheaper than Estherville's municipal diesel power from rationed supplies of natural gas and expensive fuel oil. Coal-fired steam plants, along with nuclear and water power, reversed the flow of current over the grid of co-op lines into the city.

A $185,000 beef-killing plant proved more than a mere shot in the arm to local employment; the new industry became the town's leading source of jobs. F. M. Tobin of Rochester, New York, and Walter Casteel of Fort Dodge were on hand to open the Estherville Packing Plant in November 1936. L. E. Palmer was manager and H. C. Kibler handled sales. After the plant failed to make money, despite changes of management, Tobin sent Donald D. Mackenzie to study the problem. After hearing his report Tobin hired him to run the plant.

With the help of Ben DeKock, Mackenzie soon succeeded in saving wasted fats, instituted sound cattle-buying practices and quickly put the operation into the black. By that time the Tobin company had taken over the independent company. Tobin sold the plant in 1954 to John Morrell & Company. Two years later Morrell began slaughtering hogs in a plant acquired from the Hill Packing Company. The plant was built in 1939 for the slaughter and processing of horsemeat for dog food and foreign consumption. Esther-villeans who sampled horsemeat when the Hill plant was in operation found it sweet and acceptable, but most persons could not erase the picture of a beautiful thoroughbred taken to slaughter. Little of the meat was consumed locally.

In 1960 the Morrell company bought the Golden Sun Milling Company, a highly successful feed-manufacturing concern started in 1925 by H. N. Jensen and developed and expanded by his two sons, Lawrence and Herman (Jack). Lawrence retired in 1969. Jack, who became chief executive officer of the Morrell feed division, which included four plants, didn't retire until 1971, when Bob Hammond took the reins. The company built an entirely new, highly automated plant in 1975 that cost about $2.5 million just

Tobin Packing Plant, later sold to Morrell.

south of Estherville by the Rock Island track. Since the retirement of V. A. Gibbs in 1961, Chester Pierson has directed Morrell's beef and pork operations, now employing nearly 700 workers.

Fortunate for me personally was a classified advertisement that our newspaper should not have published but did. An employment agency placed an ad for schoolteachers. A Dolliver schoolteacher needing a job was suckered into sending money to the concern upon reading our newspaper. The young woman was swindled out of $5 she forwarded to the agency at Salt Lake City. One day a United States marshal from Fort Dodge walked in, presented his credentials, and said I was wanted in Ogden, Utah. When I had recovered from the shock, he said I was wanted as a witness in a mail fraud case. We had received the advertisement by mail and the school-teacher replied to the ad by mail. A federal case.

This trip to Ogden turned out to be my only good vacation since Francis Shadle and I had gone to the World's Fair, the Democratic convention, and had an interview with the Polish credit manager of the Butler Paper Company. It took me little time to pack my bag. I journeyed to Ogden on the posh UP train, the City of San Francisco, to help indict the conniving placement bureau manager who had sent us the fraudulent classified advertisement. I enjoyed the round trip, on which I had an opportunity to see the Rocky Mountains. Shortly after returning home from Mormon country I was called once again to testify, this time before the petit jury at Salt Lake City. To convict the rascals, I chose to ride the Burlington Zephyr and the Denver & Rio Grande, through incomparable Colorado scenery. My testimony consisted of saying "Yes, I publish the *Daily News,*" and "Yes, the ad was received by U.S. mail," and "Yes, we published the said advertisement on the said date." The government won its case and cheerfully paid my expense check, which did not include reimbursement for a relaxed evening at the Hotel Utah with Byron Vedder, whose Urbana, Illinois, newspaper had also published the offensive placement ad.

A short time later I received a cordial invitation to attend a "Russian" party at Lake Forest, Illinois. There I could greet many old friends and share a bill of fare featured on the invitation as "vodka and foodka." I decided to accept and thought it appropriate to acknowledge the invitation in Russian. Vladimir Petcoff was at the time removing a tree from my father's yard, and I persuaded him to frame a suitable reply. Vladimir obliged by dictating his best Russian and I mailed my acceptance.

But nobody, including a Russian countess who lived across Waukegan road, could decode it. Fortunately, however, the hosts decided I probably meant to accept, knowing my weakness for sociability, and they met the Milwaukee train at Roundout. What I didn't know until after I got home was that Vladimir couldn't write Russian any more than I could. He was a Bulgarian, whose language the countess was no more familiar with than Sanskrit. While living in Estherville, Vladimir mended shoes, as I recall, and then went to Detroit for employment as a die maker. But he possessed still other talents. He urged me to plug two songs he wrote: "Dear Christmas" and "Back to Iowa." *Daily News* circulation didn't stimulate much active sale of his phonograph records and sheet music. Nor did my help make him rich on the recipe he concocted for an ointment that when applied to the eyelids was guaranteed to prevent a drowsy motorist from running off a cliff. I never tried his mysterious potion, which may have been super. Vladimir's Russian wasn't.

Once mechanical corn pickers displaced Sam Naas and other huskers who harvested corn by hand, the pheasant population began to dwindle. The community lost one of its favorite autumn sports—hunting Chinese ring-necked pheasants. These wily birds provided good sport and superb eating. My very silent partner customarily came up from Fairfield each autumn to hunt three days of open season with me—and ostensibly to discuss our financial situation. We always hunted, but never got around to finances. Don always said we'd do that on the "next trip."

On one of those hunting trips McGiffin said he'd like to try his luck at ducks as well. I had never gone duck hunting in my life. It wasn't that I held any special brief for sparing the ducks. Simply, it was a sport carried on at an indecent time of day. Pheasant hunting, on the other hand, always started at noon, by which time I was usually wide awake. I asked Ralph Rogers—who fished, hunted, and minded the telephone company in his spare time—to recommend a place to hunt. He suggested a blind at Swan Lake, not far from my skating haunts, which was his favorite shooting ground.

Through snow, fog, darkness, and in bitter cold, we found the blind and settled down to freeze to death. Eventually, what seemed like several months later, a flight of two something approached. Don whispered, "You shoot." I whispered back, "Hell no, you're the one who wanted to kill a duck." He whispered a convincing and final "You!!!!!!" So as the pair of ducks flew overhead I raised the barrel of my borrowed shotgun, stuck it straight up, and fired. Boom. Plunk. A duck fell on the ice a few feet away. Apparently the explosion of my gun shell-shocked the creature, which then died of concussion of the brain upon striking the frozen lake.

Thus I came to have the most perfect duck-hunting record in the county—maybe in the world: one shell, one duck. It was my only adventure in that sport, which I regard as indecent exposure of humanity, less hazardous to waterfowl than to newspapermen. In 1939 Don, who had always seemed utterly relaxed and easy going, suddenly died of a coronary thrombosis. I thereupon purchased his half interest in the *News* from his estate with the bank's money. Again I was on a treadmill of loan payments.

At about the time the *News* published the fraudulent classified ad, the paper needed office help. We needed someone who could read, write, and learn how to keep books. The high school principal, Walter Cresap, recommended a young woman who had subsequently attended college and showed promise. I hired her. It was her family's house that a year before had been blown off the foundation by the tornado. She hadn't worked in the office long before she turned out to be such an efficient and attractive employee that I soon persuaded her to go on my permanent payroll. In the summer of 1938 the Reverend Claude Fausnaugh presided over matrimonial proceedings in the new house that Logan Anderson had built Violette when the old one got badly bent up in the storm. The Reverend Fausnaugh discreetly asked if there were any objectors present; when none showed up, he tied the knot and told us it would be all right now for us to kiss each other.

Everyld was probably not overpaid at $10 a week. She managed the social items quite well, but her forte was in the bookkeeping department. She didn't know how to cook, but she could read a cookbook, and that's where everybody else finds the recipes. I helped her to learn to play bridge but she's much better than the teacher. And if my golf gets much worse she'll beat me at that, too. Life for us has been more than adequate. Without Everyld I would be a lost cause.

I allowed her to get off to a shaky start at the office, however, when I acceded to Lloyd Stockdale's request that we collaborate in one of his many practical jokes, most of which were pranks on his mother-in-law, the wife of trainmaster Frank Martin. This time the target was Lloyd's wife, Aline, a fussy housekeeper, who the day before had placed a classified advertisement in the *News* to sell a bedroom furniture set. Lloyd prevailed upon Everyld to call his wife about the bed, pretending to be interested in buying it. Following his instructions to the word, Everyld placed a call on one phone while Lloyd listened at another: "Mrs. Stockdale," Everyld began, "I understand you have a bed for sale." Yes, she certainly did. "Well, is it in good shape?" Indeed it was. "Could I ask, have you recently been troubled with bed bugs at your house?" At this point the rather plump Stockdale began suffering from convulsions, nearly rolling out of his chair onto the floor. But poor Ev was still on the line hearing Lloyd's spouse say, "Everyld, I never thought you'd be party to one of my husband's scabby practical jokes."

She had instantly recognized the voice as that of the young woman with whom she chatted every now and then about the fortunes of Duo Decim, Entre Nous, and other earth-shaking news on the contract bridge circuit. After our marriage, the two women became close bridge and golf companions. No one was ever kinder to both of us than Lloyd and Aline. However, both suffered in community popularity because Lloyd, unlike many others, went to work and built a new, successful business career after the bank for which he was cashier closed its doors.

Dr. A. I. Reed was another incurable practical joker. During one Christmas season when City Electrician Harry Sims, a caustic, firm-jawed fellow, was suspended against his will on a skyhook hanging municipal holiday decorations and stringing colored electric light bulbs, Dr. Reed approached. Looking almost straight up at the unpredictable Sims, the mischievous M.D. began singing "Jingle Bells." It was of course a foolhardy act, from which the good-natured doctor was fortunate to escape from having a pair of pliers dropped on the skull.

The prankish doctor on another occasion treated a patient friend for sore throat. Reed's patient was a pool hall operator respected for the sharp discipline he kept at his premises. George Smith upon emigrating from Patras, Greece, to America changed his name from Phahos to the more pronounceable "Smith." After finishing his education at the University of Chicago, George opened a pool hall in Mason City and then came to Estherville. Dr. Reed was among the many good friends upon whom Smith lavished bottles of his homemade wine, fillets of walleyed pike he caught in northern Minnesota, and generous samples of Mabel's toothsome cooking.

When George went to Dr. Reed's office, complaining of an uncomfortable throat, the doctor told him to sit in his patient's chair and tip his head back. The doctor, who specialized in ailments from the neck up, then asked George to open his mouth wide. After peering at what he could see, the doctor seized a pair of pliers and made motions as though he intended to use them inside George's mouth, possibly to remove his tonsils. In a split second the powerful Smith had shoved the doctor aside, reached for something to throw (which proved to be the telephone), and hurled it out the window. In time the Smith-Reed friendship was recemented.

Now that the city fathers felt the treasury could afford it, they ordered workmen to construct a swinging suspension bridge across the river, near the railroad bridge, about where grandfather and I once fished for bullheads. The swinging bridge removed temptation from children living in the northwest section of town to use the railroad trestle, more conveniently located than the highway-pedestrian bridge on Central Avenue. Walking the railroad bridge was regarded as unhealthful. Later the city went so far as to place a swinging bridge also farther south, handy to the swimming pool, playgrounds, tennis courts, and other recreational facilities of Riverside Park.

Less important to life and limb than footbridges, but necessary to the sanity of downtowners, was action of the council in 1937 to forbid loudspeakers. One, operated by Kirt Allen from his *Enterprise* office with horns atop the Gardston Hotel to amplify radio news and broadcast such items as he might choose, drove merchants and shoppers to the point of distraction. The nuisance could be silenced only by a special ordinance.

At about the same time, the city council got around to providing the stop-and-go signals at Sixth and Central that Frank Carpenter in the beginning stages of his dementia praecox back in 1926 imagined that his fellow townsmen urgently needed.

The aldermen also, upon the suggestion of chamber of commerce president Dr. George G. Griffith, renamed the streets. Lincoln Street became Central Avenue and all the other east-west streets became numbered avenues. All north-south thoroughfares remained numbered streets. This change temporarily confused many people living on Roberts, Howard, or Emory, who sometimes forgot their own addresses. But it was a windfall to postmen, newspaper carriers, meter readers, deliverymen, and strangers.

As the decade of the painful thirties came to a close, the tempo was upbeat and relaxed. In the final two years of the thirties, which started out in necessary thrift, close to $1 million of new construction and additional paychecks of beef-packing employees poured spending dollars into the cash register tills. Frosting on the cake came as the United States Navy band arrived in town for a spine-tingling concert at Roosevelt auditorium. And to memorialize Iowa's centennial, Mrs. T. C. Mann slaved over the script of a pageant performed on Sunderlin Field. Janice Lilland, who married Eddie Burt, was voted the prettiest girl in the whole state of Iowa.

Once torn by factions that largely polarized in the banks, business and professional men of the community organized themselves into Rotary and Kiwanis clubs, carefully avoiding factionalism. They skillfully blended membership in the groups to assure community harmony. Businesswomen had already organized a Wa-Tan-Ye Club. Other service clubs soon followed: a Lions Club and Town and Country Kiwanis.

Joyriders slid down a steep toboggan slope in Fort Defiance

Park, to the annoyance of the ecologists, even though it fractured several legs. The Deemer Lees, also reckless, went deeply in debt to build a house and buy out a partner, all in the same year; they would be making weekly and monthly payments on their debt for years and years to come. The newspaper was making money, but not printing it. For $500 the Lees bought a lot from Ralph McKay. For $5,000 they built a Cape Cod house on the lot, and for $500 more they seeded the yard and poured some needed concrete surfaces. They moved in to stay, and they're still there. The editor was back once again at his favorite kite-flying grounds, next door to the capable Tom Sunde, who built the house. Vermaine (Ole) Sidles, who lived on the south of the Lees, painted and papered the place. Unfortunately, Tom and Ole are no longer among the quick.

Tears and Cheers

AFTER Estherville voters first rejected a twenty-five-year franchise to Northern Natural Gas by 248 ballots in an April election, they changed their minds and gave Northern a 600-vote majority in a second go at it in June. If nothing else of progress occurred in 1940, housewives were grateful that the city turned over its gas plant, even though recent conversion from manufactured gas to butane was regarded as an improvement. But it was still a low-pressure system that Northern's retail subsidiary, Peoples, would have to rebuild to provide dependable service. The company's purchase price of $42,500 was only the beginning of the capital needed to improve the system. Fear of the new fuel, aroused by the coal dealers, helped defeat the first election, and householders could not believe that natural gas would prove as economical and efficient as promised.

Don Mackenzie then volunteered to lead an advertising and publicity effort that changed wavering public opinion. J. P. McDermott, who represented Northern, told me that if our newspaper plant would substitute natural gas for heating oil in our furnace the gas bill would be no more than we had been spending for gas just to heat the pots of our typesetting machines and remelt furnace. I didn't believe him but he was proved right.

An unseasonable snowstorm on Armistice Day, 1940, rivaled the 1936 tornado for personal hardship and loss of livestock. The blizzard, striking in the county without warning, stranded cattle in unprotected open fields and destroyed thousands of dollars worth of farm animals. Reminiscent of many pioneer-day blizzards, the storm smothered turkeys, chickens, pheasants, and other birds.

Nothing much could be wrong with Estherville's credit, the citizenry decided the next year, when the Emmet County State Bank bought $110,000 worth of electric revenue bonds issued by the city to install a new diesel engine for the power plant. The bonds sold competitively at 1.5 percent interest. Since 1935 the city had reduced its electric rates by 43 percent. If any further confirmation of the town's good credit was needed, it came a year later when the same bank bid successfully for $28,000 of airport bonds at 2 percent interest. The city sold the bonds for the purpose of acquiring land east of the city for development of the extensively developed air facility that now serves the area. With an additional $55,000, the city bought 400 acres. In 1962 the airport became the first municipally owned OMNI station in the United States. The improvements included hard-surfaced runway and taxiway, landing lights, hangars, administration building, manager's dwelling, and shop.

Flight training began in Estherville before America entered World War II and before the new airport had been purchased. In 1939 Warner Kirlin coordinated a junior college program under which the school provided instruction in navigation, meteorology, and other courses. Harry Coffie, an attorney who after graduation at the University of Iowa had been a bush pilot in Alaska, liked flying better than trying lawsuits. He ran the airport part of the program, which continued four years with Ralph Bryan as chief pilot. Don Sunde, William Yule, George Bryant, and William O. Anderson were other instructors. Anderson, a lawyer, had worked for me as a reporter after finishing junior college and before starting law school.

Organization of the flight-training program was timely, preceding by one year County Auditor Gladys Bringle's registry of 1,733 men in the peacetime manpower draft. Hazel Ross was the first secretary of the draft board, followed by Mrs. Leonard Hackett. Irving Ellerston, the first draft board chairman, resigned in disgust a year later when John L. Lewis called a mine workers' strike that Ellerston thought was counterproductive of the defense effort. Joy Horswell, who had served on the World War I draft board, was called upon to act again. When the Japanese bombed Pearl Harbor, Lieutenants Robert Irwin and Forrest Brandt were at Hickman Field; Ralph Boone at Midway Island. As a major, Irwin later flew two bombing missions over Tokyo. Many other men of the community soon became active, and in January Donald Swartz of the navy became the first local casualty. Soon the draft board was sending a succession of contingents to training camps. By May 1945, a total of 1,433 men had been sworn into service. A canteen organized to serve refreshments to men on troop trains counted 7,100 men aided.

Emmet's sacrifice in World War II was fifty-five dead — more deaths relative to population than any other county of the state. In addition to many wounded, the county lost 4.1 men per 1,000 persons; the state average was 2.31. Every day the *News* reported recruitment, camp news, casualties, men taken prisoner, and other war service events. A large wooden arch erected at the southwest corner of the Square to display the names of servicemen needed constant enlargement. Gold stars often replaced blue ones on the board.

Those who stayed home became proud of oversubscribing every one of eight war-bond drives conducted under the able leadership of Ed Stockdale, who made none of the tragic Liberty Loan errors of World War I. There was no ugly yellow slacker board this time. The United States Treasury and the local community learned by experience. One drive, for $440,000, was oversubscribed by $11,000. Asked on one occasion to raise $722,000, the committee took in $820,000. Purchasers responded to one quota of $760,000 with $950,000. The seventh request, for $850,000, produced more than $1 million. Special entertainment, appearance of the Coast Guard band, and similar attractions spurred interest in the drives, but the sales resulted largely because of a deep sense of responsibility to support the war and particularly the local men engaged in military action.

Those on the home front also found other ways to make themselves useful in prosecuting the war by gathering scrap iron, food for shipment abroad, scrap rubbers, tin cans, and other items. They gave liberally to the Red Cross — $10,600 in one drive for which the quota was $7,600. Although not always pleased to do so, the community complied with rationing of fuel oil, tires, gasoline, sugar, butter, and fats — even shoes. Businessmen helped farmers harvest their crops. Surplus clothing was collected for the Russians. A committee recruited WACs. Curtailed outdoor lighting saved some precious fuel oil used to generate electricty. The home folks also tried to accord departing servicemen a warm, friendly gesture fitting of their role in the war. We soon missed Dr. J. P. Clark, the town's chief surgeon, who enlisted and went to Europe to mend soldiers. His departure broke up the Clark and Johnston partnership. Dr. Barklie Johnston was the son of Annie and Jay and grandson of Robert Barklie Callwell. The two doctors had an enormous practice. Dr. Clark came back after the war and continued to see and serve many patients.

As disrupting to the home scene as rationing and other inconveniences was the manpower shortage that occurred when many left their jobs. The news desk of our paper was one of those vacancies, when Hoyt Luithly joined the quartermaster corps. He had become an extremely popular sports figure and a reporter who enjoyed wide respect in the community. A succession of reporters and editors followed him, some staying only until they too joined the military. One young man showed particular promise because he was well experienced, but he developed a serious flaw. His career at the *News* ended when he was attacked by a roomful of snakes. For two or three weeks his fellow workers had observed him acting strangely, likely under the influence of liquor. But we all were mystified about where he hid his hooch and when he drank it. When delirium tremens cracked him up, the mystery was solved; the young man carried a small bottle of alcohol strapped on his leg. From that supply he nipped on trips to the toilet room.

He wisely and soberly told me that I ought to put Dorothy Story on the desk, and I did. She capably held the fort and then stayed on when Captain Luithly returned early in 1946 to become managing editor, after a distinguished record of action in the Mediterranean theater leading black troops. Three years after death cut his newspaper life short in 1964, the community honored him by naming the school's new athletic facility Hoyt Luithly Field.

Like other businesses, the *Daily News* found itself employing young men who were light for the job. That led to laborsaving devices and ways to utilize substitutes for the hardier manhood they replaced. This made many of us realize that improved material-handling equipment should have been used long before.

One office replacement made during the war developed into a permanent situation that changed the ownership of the *News*. Brother Bob, an Oberlin-trained musician, left his college teaching position in Mississippi to enlist in the army, which strangely assigned him to the signal corps. That was the perfect example of putting a round peg in a square hole. The army soon cheerfully gave him a medical discharge and sent him home. Because it was then the middle of the school semester at Mississippi State College for Women, where he had been teaching, I urged him to come to our office and perform some of the needed labor there. He liked newspapering almost as much as teaching piano and pipe organ, particularly when he began working in the advertising department. He later ran it, and I sold him an interest in the paper. We remained compatible partners until we both sold the paper in 1968.

Robert N. Lee.

William Olcott was one of the talented young men recruited by the *News* in its procession of replacements. Two of his news stories won top honors in Associated Press contests. His special field was science; but he could do almost anything. On his morning news beat at the county auditor's office, while asking the auditor what was new to report, he toyed with the office adding and posting machine. A few minues after he left, I received a frantic call from the courthouse. All the keys were locked and the machine had gone on strike. Olcott, of course, knew how to remedy that, which he cheerfully did.

It was unsafe for the soda clerk at the Estherville Drug to mix a chocolate malted milk after a visit to the store by Olcott, who had likely reversed the spouts so that chocolate squirted into the clerk's face instead of into the shaker. He also knew how to punch the telephone buttons so nobody could call in or out. This made the office quieter but proved awkward to the staff. He committed his worst misdemeanor one day upon borrowing brother Bob's green Chevrolet sedan for an urgent news trip over icy pavement to Wallingford. Bob cautioned him to be careful, and Bill understood. But an hour later he returned with one of the headlamps, attached to part of the fender, tucked under his arm. He and a bridge abutment had encountered a problem. Bill wound up in New York at a publisher's office, writing a book.

Among the *Daily News* alumni from whom we hear now and then besides Olcott are Jay Gildner, working with the United States Foreign Information Service; Liz Van Nostrand, writing editorials for *Newsday;* Jim Van Nostrand, researching in Congress; Bernice Palmer, editing publications in North Dakota; Ralph Darrow, teaching young journalists at Kent State; and Bill Olcheski, performing various Washington chores.

Not long after the hysteria of VE Day had subsided and all of us soberly wondered how long the war against Japan might go on, Colonel Munson piloted General George Marshall to Potsdam. General Marshall and President Truman had more insight than all but a few scientists about how long the Japanese might hold out. Newspapermen of northwest Iowa listened to an "informed" speaker warn them that the war against Japan might stretch out a fearfully long time. He apparently didn't know about the atom bomb, which exploded a few weeks later on Hiroshima. Surrender came quickly, which triggered an impromptu Estherville parade and celebration. A snake dance down the street halted traffic. Firemen hoped that the bonfires set by ecstatic celebrants wouldn't reduce the town to cinders.

After returning home from the war and turning apparel merchant, Harmon Veldey entertained Rotarians with an account of his career in command of an LST. A native of Fergus Falls, Minnesota, Veldey had done all his previous voyaging in a rowboat on Otter Tail Lake, when his war vessel cleared New York harbor and set out to sea, headed for Norfolk, Virginia. Inexperienced in the skills of navigation, the crew carefully observed instructions to follow the coast, keeping points of shore reference in view. But a 30-degree compass error by the navigator during the night caused the helmsman to steer in the general direction of Nigeria. Upon regaining the sight of North America once again the next day, the crew could find no landmark it could identify. So Commander Veldey

decided to beach the ship and, on the pretext of stopping to buy a
Sunday newspaper, learn on what part of the coast they might be.
The scouting party learned they were at Virginia Beach.

That meant the ship had overshot the mark a bit so the crew
headed back north in search of Chesapeake Bay, which they found
shrouded in dense fog. When the fog finally lifted, the LST steamed
into Norfolk, welcomed by blinking signals that beamed their docking instructions. However, the crew couldn't keep up with the rapid
transmittal and asked for a repeat—several repeats, in fact. At last
Norfolk slowed the signals down enough for the green sailors to read
them. Now they knew where to berth and soon approached the
designated wharf. "Back the engines," the bridge signaled. But the
confused engine room instead sent the clumsy LST full speed
ahead. The ship came to rest after ripping out 150 feet of dock.

Commander Veldey's superior officer eagerly awaited explana-
tion of the midwesterner's traumatic style of docking a ship but
spared him from loss of command. The LST had proved sturdier
than the pilings and was yet seaworthy. There being no ready
replacement for the greenhorn captain, Veldey was permitted to
take his LST on to the Pacific. It was in the South China Sea that
punishment was at last meted out to the error-prone crew. All on
board said their prayers and prepared to expire as a monsoon tossed
the vessel hopelessly out of control. But the good ship Veldey
possessed a charmed hull.

Returning soldiers, sailors, and marines found they had missed
some excitement when the old Tom & Jerry bridge collapsed under
traffic, which it dunked in the river, but the county promptly arranged a replacement. A wave of strikes greeted the peace as coal
miners, packinghouse workers, railroaders, steelmen, telephone
workers, seamen, postal employees, and others sought more wages
in the wake of a regimented war economy. While servicemen had
been away, seeds for thoughtful city planning were sown, and they
were encouraged by the *Daily News*. Soon after the peace, the city
council approved the idea of planning and appointed a commission, which elected G. H. Raife chairman. A comprehensive zoning
plan was then adopted after extensive study and debate.

City garbage hauling began and other progress came. At the
beginning of the decade, Estherville thought it had seen the
ultimate in low interest charged on its bond issues, but it had seen
nothing yet. Wayne Currell again stubbornly bid his Emmet Coun-

ty State Bank for more Estherville municipal securities, buying a $150,000 issue to expand the light plant, at 0.91 percent interest, and $220,000 of school district bonds at 1 percent. The $220,000 was used to construct a school building named Maniece in honor of Principal Margaret Maniece, who taught forty-one years at Jackson school. The new building replaced superannuated Jackson.

The defenders of America were home in time to participate fully in celebration of Emmet County's centennial. Fireworks, a pageant, displays, and related events commemorated the founding in 1856 of the first settlements along the Des Moines River and at High Lake.

Returning servicemen from overseas soon became active in the John W. Brawford Post of the Veterans of Foreign Wars. The VFW's center, first on Central Avenue and then at the old A. C. Brown house, ultimately moved into a new building. The post continually improved and expanded its quarters into a clubhouse that became so successful it has enabled the organization and its active Auxiliary to make substantial contributions to almost every cause in the community needing support. The VFW's community hall serves numerous functions, while social members frequently join the regular members in eating at the facility's dining rooms, particularly on Tuesday evenings to enjoy the tasty fried chicken and shrimp.

Women of the community found additional employment opportunities when in 1946 the Shakespeare Company opened a plant of its subsidiary Soo Valley Company to make fishing lines. Under the experienced direction of Ernest W. Robinson, the plant manufactured a variety of lines in a building vacated by the Estherville Grocer Company. The Soo Valley plant gave work to 110 women. Women found other employment at the long-established Gray Produce Company, founded by Paul G. Gray in 1918 and continued by his son Paul Gray, Jr., until the time of his death in 1957. Tony Downs's Wadco food-processing plant followed the Gray operations. Women also found work at the Butterfield Produce Company, which moved into the building vacated by Soo Valley in 1956 and was followed there by Farmers Egg Company, Land O'Lakes, and Estherville Foods. Until the Hogett cigar factory shut down in 1947 after thirty-nine years of operation, it also had given jobs to women.

In his later years, John Hansen was known to most of his customers and friends as a dry cleaner and as an expert whist player. Actually, his name was Jens, born at Jutland, Denmark, but nobody knew him as Jens. In his younger days he had clothed a good many of the town in suits tailored in his shop. C. W. Hansen, not a relative of his, came to work for John as a tailor, and the two of them sat cross-legged on a bench stitching garments they had cut from bolts of fabric the shop stocked. Later C. W. and his daughter Eliza ran their own shop, in which Mrs. Hansen and son Robert also helped. When John Hansen died in 1947 and C. W. died ten years later, nobody in the community could replace them. Once John made a suit of clothes for me that draped loosely on my frame when I went in for a try-on. Obviously his tape measure had slipped. He jokingly told me I would probably grow into it, which was prophetically all too true.

The town's most uninhibited beer drinkers appeared to favor the bar of the Broadway Inn, operated by a red-faced man by the name of Herman Golla. His brother Harry distributed Hamm's beer and his brother Clarence ran a pool hall. The Broadway Inn enjoyed a prime location on the south side of Central Avenue, across the street from the *Daily News* office, Emmanuel Stavros's shoe-mending shop, and a ladies' Fashion Shop. Retail stores flanked the Broadway at either side.

Nobody could be sure what would happen in the Broadway or in front of it. Herman was not fussy about the manners or the deportment of his customers, who might be observed pitching woo in the back booth or urinating between parked cars in front of the establishment. It was for Emmanuel, who learned on the Western Front to fear nothing, to head up a petition to the city council asking for a reformation at the Broadway. Everybody in the block signed the petition except Fred Ehlers, who said that as mayor he ought to stay neutral.

The council recognized the place for the disgrace it had become and decided to ban all drinking places in the retail area. Once again ladies might walk up and down the street without fear of what they might have to look at. But two of the Broadway's staunchest clients, overcome with grief, found Emmanuel at work during the evening at his bootshop and invited him to join them in the alley. One of them carried a long knife, but Emmanuel promptly raised his challenger's bid by dancing a .45-caliber bullet be-

tween his legs. That settled the argument for the moment but both
filed complaints in justice of the peace court. County Attorney
William O. Anderson took the complaints to the grand jury, which
decided that the two men had already resolved the situation
satisfactorily and returned no indictments. The Broadway closed.

During a period of several years many Esthervilleans received
vocal greetings on their birthdays from Annie Cole, the widow of a
plumber, who sang "Happy Birthday" to a select list of friends. In
1947 she made the front page of the paper, which reported that
during the year Annie had sung greetings to no fewer than sixty
people in the community. Mrs. Cole was possessed of a warm heart
but not infallible pitch. She kept herself out of mischief by minding
the young ones of Mrs. Gray, Mrs. Everds, and other young mothers
when they socialized.

The same year that Annie Cole felicitated sixty of us on achieving one more birthday I almost lost a longtime friend. N. E.
Demoney, who long served the school system as principal, then
superintendent, and still later as a teacher and debate coach, was
one of the last of stern disciplinarians. One day he got his name in
the paper under circumstances that Ned did not appreciate. Upon
escorting a young woman by the name of Bessie Hupp from an
assembly program because he thought she was diverting attention
from the platform, he found himself charged with assault and bat-
tery.

He told me he thought the newspaper could surely dredge up
items more wholesome than an account of this incident, but there
was no news that day more interesting than Ned's fix. He found
more relish in the newspaper story a short time later, after he had
won acquittal and even spontaneous applause of the courtroom
spectators. I always thought it fortunate that Ned was not sentenced
to the Gulag, because later, when he voluntarily chose to relinquish
his superintendency after fourteen years in the office for less
traumatic employment, he developed one state championship high
school debate team after another and proudly escorted them to national meets from one coast to the other. When the Iowa Lakes
Community College moved into new, larger quarters, the Rotunda
building it had occupied reverted to the Estherville School District
for elementary use and the board of education appropriately

named it for Ned Demoney. His son, Edwin, assisted me from his position with the Federal Reserve in quarrying material for my chapter about Estherville bank failures.

Emmet took a forward step in 1947 when it established a soil conservation district. John Greig, who at about the same time sold his feed-manufacturing plant and hatchery business to Honeymead, had been advocating the need for such a service. The choice of George Chipman as conservationist could not have been more fortunate. He and Gene Helle contributed vast wealth to the county by designing contours and terraces, setting up sound rotation and fertilizer plans, engineering needed tile lines, planning grassy waterways, designing farm ponds, and instituting other conservational practices. Farmers and landowners were the direct beneficiaries of these programs, which also added prosperity indirectly to Estherville businesses. Less successful that year was a bus line that couldn't make it for long in Estherville's modest population of 6,500.

An unwelcome epidemic of polio changed living habits and threw terror into the community. When the Maurice Olesons held a party in 1948 for those who had been stricken, including three of their own sons, sixty-nine victims and their parents attended. That didn't include all of those afflicted. Despite spraying with DDT, attempts at isolation, and raising $23,000 to fight the disease, the epidemic subsided only after it had taken a serious toll.

The Estherville Eagles of the thirties were revived in the late forties as the Red Sox. An Eagles catcher, Jerry Wegs, who had stayed on to run a tire shop and had become a substantial member of the community, organized the Red Sox, recruiting material at the start mostly from local talent. Gene Morris, who later served as chief of police and who then went to Alaska, developed a team that won forty games while losing only eighteen. Steve Gerkin, a pitcher who threw with classic style but was unaware of the need to train, drew wide attention. Directors besides Wegs were Guy Tibbetts, who ran a clothing store; Floyd Gustafson, proprietor of Butterfield Produce; Dick Everds, a road builder who had helped construct the Alcan highway; and Willis Sandin, a furniture dealer and embalmer. Ernie Johnson promoted membership in the Iowa State League. The team under various managers, including Jim McNulty and Dick Schultz, continued until 1955. Familiar names on the rosters were Bob Gibson, Sid Langston, Dick Bertell, Stan Gwinn,

Ken Retzer, John Ewaniak, and Rex Barney. Don Hall, John Andeits, and John McFadden were Red Sox ballplayers who settled down in the community. Some of the Red Sox became big league players. Beating the Storm Lake Whitecaps in the 1953 playoffs was an exciting climax. Our family, as hundreds of others, attended virtually all Red Sox games, young son Bob sometimes substituting to keep the official box score. Sitting out in the cool evening air, sipping pop, rooting for the Sox, and bemoaning a shortage of umpires with 20-20 vision provided regular and dependable local amusement.

The city hall also provided entertainment. One of the engines the city bought, as was frequently necessary to supply energy for its municipal electric plant, developed faults that proved so discouraging and expensive that the company couldn't deliver on its contract. The city fathers thereupon began suit against the Fulton Engine Company for damages of $177,000. But the city only recovered $55,000, and the councilmen were in for a merry time of it at the next election, in the spring of 1951. All but one councilman were relieved from further responsibilities at the council chamber. The voters didn't like what they read and heard of engine dealings, but the accusations developed more smoke than blaze.

After six years in the legislature, George Robb, whose business had been livestock buying and operating a sales pavilion, was elected mayor in 1949. His wife, Nell, received one vote—probably George's. Both of them were remarkably energetic in public affairs and became fast friends of Governor William Beardsley and his wife. The two couples shared kindred thoughts about politics and they both subscribed to the religion of John Wesley. For a time, Mrs. Robb wrote a column for the *Daily News;* she was as active as George, pursuing all sorts of public activities. George had not served long as mayor when the governor invited him to fill a vacancy on the state tax commission. He died about a year later, in 1951. Nell lived on, still energetic, until 1967.

Urias Uptagrafft was one of the interesting persons I remember. When the 1936 tornado blew Logan Anderson's house off the foundation and made it a derelict, the one person in town who thought it held possibilities of salvage was Urias. He made something of it for a residence out east on Fifth Avenue North, where he sold off much of his acreage for future school use and for what became spacious Ed Thoreson Park. Urias made the front page one day. Thinking that he detected a gas leak in the cookstove, Urias investigated it by lighting a match. He promptly found the leak, and Estherville's seldom idle fire department rushed out to save the neighborhood from devastation.

Martin Berge, a carpenter of unusual talents, shared his time writing steamship tickets for the Norwegian Line. He liked to swim and sail at Tuttle Lake, as it was called before it took on the Indian name of Okamanpadu. He also found time to arrange gatherings of a Sunnhordland organization of Norse who had emigrated to America from a region between Bergen and Haugesund. We chose Martin to develop an upstairs in our Cape Cod cottage attic; our second bedroom was getting too full of progeny. Bob was nine and Bill was four when Everyld said we needed more room. Martin put a lift on the back side of the roof and built us two more bedrooms and another bathroom. He was sixty-five years old when he told our boys that the upstairs project was complete and that he wanted them to witness a special ceremony he always held when he had finished a house job. He thereupon climbed to the roof, reached the ridge, threw his legs in the air, and stood there on his head. Better than any act at the circus. His early training in Norway's busy North Sea maritime trade made Martin comfortable at any height.

County Engineer F. E. Macdonald, a Scottish civil engineer of good competence, had a son, Robert, who provided our circle of friends with supernatural entertainment whenever he came out to Estherville from Chicago to visit his father. Bob was a pianist who gave concerts, accompanied prominent singers at recitals, and managed the Columbia School of Music before he retired and moved to San Diego to head the university's department of music. Bob possessed amazing extrasensory powers.

Blindfolded, he could find any object in a room that had been hidden while he was out of it, correctly add several six- or seven-digit numbers, and guide himself through a room full of furniture and people. He and my brother Bob, both blindfolded, could operate a homemade ouija board made of a sheet of cardboard on which we had printed letters and numbers. Using an inverted jelly glass as a vehicle, they "received" reams of nonsense in three foreign languages. Nobody ever explained the phenomenon adequately; but it happened.

When John Horswell moved to Washington, D.C., in 1950, I

lost my most persistent writer of letters to the editor. With strong liberal leanings, Horswell was a supporter and admirer of Henry Wallace. From time to time John commented on the political philosophy of the editor of the *News,* which was always somewhat right of John. A lonesome individual, John liked to practice singing at the Methodist church. He found the church's acoustical proper ties suitable for unlimbering his vocal chords, until one evening someone came by the church and, not knowing what caused the decibles, became alarmed that violence was being done inside. Investigation revealed John's presence in the area of the choir loft and led to an estrangement between him and the followers of John Wesley. He thereupon transferred his devotions to the Presbyterians, diagonally across the street. It was then up to the followers of John Calvin to fit his tenor register into the group singing as best they could. The Horswell pitch was sometimes a shade off that of the organ tuner's.

The State Conservation Commission and the landowners of Emmet County did not always share identical views. When Bruce Stiles announced in 1948 that the state planned to drain Swan Lake and revitalize it, Mack Groves, Watson Herrold, and a large group of other owners in the vicinity had doubts about the announced commission intentions to restore the lake to present water levels. Was the lake to be restored and refilled or would it become a shallow waterfowl refuge? Objectors filed an injunction but the commission decision prevailed. The objectors' suspicions were well founded and the lake only recently achieved a more normal level. Conservationists blamed lack of rainfall for not restoring former depth, but it was apparent that my old favorite skating rink was destined for a different type of management. Mack Groves and others admired Swan Lake as they had first found it. They were depressed to see it drained.

The State Conservation Commission and a group of farmers, this time of High Lake Township, again disagreed sharply on policy—of how Ingham and High lakes should be managed. In May 1951 the dispute erupted in a dynamite blast that was heard as far away as district court. The two lakes rose to high levels behind an earthen dam and concrete control structure, built in 1945. Runoff water from heavy snows inundated low surrounding land and submerged a Spear-owned peninusla. Summoned to the damsite when angry farmers threatened to take the situation in their own hands, Conservation Officer Harold Johnson arrived just after a dynamite explosion ripped an opening in the dam, but the rupture was not low enough to empty any water out of the lake. Johnson said that a second charge of explosive was about to be set when he arrived to support Sheriff Emlet Twito. William and Nicholas Spear and Dale Young each paid a $300 fine along with some costs, but Judge Gerald W. Stillman, a native of the small town of Dolliver, a few miles north of the dam, compassionately suspended a year's sentence imposed on the commission dissenters indicted for conspiracy. Meanwhile, dredgers finished deepening the two lakes, which improved them by emptying them of silt and mud and pouring it in the sloughs. A peaceful resolution on lake levels resulted.

On a happier and more melodious note than TNT, Alec Templeton arrived in Estherville to perform a piano concert for the Community Series at Roosevelt Auditorium. On the way to Estherville, his auto and a cock pheasant collided. Alec said it struck the car in the pitch of E flat. After innkeeper Ward Greer's Gardston Hotel chef roasted the luckless pheasant, Mr. and Mrs. Templeton and Alec's secretary, Stanley North, devoured the bird in nothing flat. Inasmuch as Bach had written a peasant cantata, Alec quipped, perhaps he should write a pheasant cantata. Hunters that season had less luck finding pheasants than the talented Templeton, who scintillated that evening at the concert.

After the performance, the three came up to our home to join us and a few friends to celebrate Mrs. Templeton's birthday, for which Everyld's mother supplied an angel food cake. Alec and my brother Bob played duets and improvised popular tunes as Bach, Beethoven, Brahms, or Stravinsky might have written them. From the memory of merely meeting our guests on arrival, Alec composed witty rhymes about them, for which he invented melodies. The unseeing Alec could never have been more charming than the day he and a Chinese ring-necked pheasant came to terms.

Less fortunate guessers surmised that Mrs. Edward Anderson was clairvoyant or a mathematical wizard when she estimated that contractors poured 11,233.27 cubic feet of concrete in rebuilding Central Avenue. She was wrong—by 4.27 cubic feet. That guestimate won her $100. The city schools closed and celebrants paraded down four lanes of new street, illuminated now by bright new mercury vapor lamps. The highway commission spent

$354,300 on a street that I remembered as a boy when horses and buggies on drippy days splattered mud from sidewalk to sidewalk.

One evening after we and most Esthervilleans had placed milk tickets on the porch for the dairyman and retired for slumber, a terrific explosion occurred. Dynamite had exploded on an elevated water storage tower two blocks up the street from the house. As police pointed their spotlights upward they saw a human shape dangling by a rope from the high structure. Dashing to the rescue, an intrepid policeman climbed the tower and retrieved the lifeless form.

What the brave rescuer found was a human shape in man's clothing stuffed with old newspapers and magazines, some of which bore the mailing address of the father of one of the hangmen. Keepers of the peace soon fitted together the story of the most explosive observance in Estherville's long history of attention-getting Halloween celebrations. For ingenuity, it rivaled the puzzle of how a cow was once somehow levitated to the old courthouse cupola.

Neighbors near the water tower wondered for several days how far down the street they might have floated if the dynamite had ruptured the 400,000-gallon tank and flooded the environs. Parents were grateful their progeny hadn't destroyed themselves, and the juvenile court judge sentenced the three stars of the show and six other teenagers of the supporting cast to full restitution of the damage. One of the conspirators later became a lawyer, another a geologist, and a third took up the study of theology.

The water tower incident was not the only local "hanging" that took place; another lynching in effigy once occurred at the south railroad underpass. Nor was it the only time that Halloween evidence proved easy to unravel. A youngster in our neighborhood once soaped his mother's windows, upstairs as well as down. He told her he hadn't the faintest idea who might have committed the crime. But Mother Ruth could imagine no one as likely to have done the soaping as her own son. She could think of no one else who might have done the job from the inside.

Emlet Twito was one of the most likable men I have ever known. He possessed the charisma that elects men to public office and wins undying loyalty. When I first knew him, he was running errands and tidying up the courthouse, at liberty to do as he pleased, although answerable to Sheriff Brown because of some problem of keeping his checkbook balanced. It was not long until Brown found Emlet so obliging that he made him a deputy. When W. G. Gordon succeeded Brown and then when Cliff Fredericksen was elected sheriff, Emlet was again the choice for deputy. Then Emmet County elected him sheriff in 1948 and he served six years.

When he won his third term, he defeated his opponent by 4,000 votes, outpolling even President Eisenhower. This was an amazing feat because he had survived a charge of drunken driving filed a few days before election. The voters were not about to turn him out just because the city police had ticketed him. Like the voters, the grand jury also believed in Twito. It returned no bill. Two years later Twito was reelected sheriff, unopposed, but on the same day a grand jury indicted him for driving while intoxicated after his auto collided with cars driven by Mrs. Selmer Amdal and Mrs. Tenner Lilland, who subsequently filed a $31,000 damage suit against the sheriff. Twito, suspended as sheriff, resigned. After a $500 fine and a 60-day jail sentence he turned over the office to Joe Betty. The judge suspended the jail sentence and Twito went back to work at the packinghouse, where he had been employed when the plant first opened. Still possessed of unshakable friends, he retired four years later after twenty years of employment—never late to work.

Newspaper coverage of the county board of supervisors was a long, continuing problem of our staff. Supervisors preferred not to discuss county business in the presence of reporters, who might be critical of their trades for new road machinery and other dealings. Some of these matters were obviously resolved by board members on their field trips to inspect drainage and roadbuilding projects. Public bodies liked to hold what they called "executive sessions," a word that I banished from newsroom use. I said it was a mystifying word that dignified ugly secrecy. We began calling them "secret" meetings, which soon ended the popularity of so-called executive sessions. Readers didn't like secrecy any better than reporters.

On a few occasions we had to threaten to splinter the door to a polling place when clerks and judges decided they wanted to count and record votes in private. But those were rare exceptions. All of us worked on election night prowling precincts scattered throughout the county to tabulate the results as rapidly as we could for our special election night coverage. County Auditor Dorothy Klopp and her successor Gladys Bringle kept night-long vigil to receive the books and ballots of precinct officials when they had finished counting. Machine voting did not come to Emmet County until 1970.

Even after the advent of a radio station in 1952, the *News* continued to gather and tabulate election returns, but we shared results with KLIL when it began operation as we had with station KICD when it operated an Estherville studio from 1946 to 1950. A new station, KILR, succeeded KLIL in late 1967, and it continues to operate on AM frequency and since 1969 on FM frequency as well. A former reporter and photographer at the *News*, Barry Huntsinger, runs the station, in which Governor Robert Ray and Attorney Dan Sanderson are financially interested.

High floodwaters in 1953 threatened security of the electric plant on the Des Moines River bank and temporarily caused distress to families across the stream near the site of the old gristmill. The city was alerted to the need for diversifying its power source. Although a serious flood had never devastated the town, Estherville saw the desirability for an interconnect with REA lines that could be highly valuable in an emergency. As the price of diesel fuel skyrocketed, power purchases from the REA became feasible on a regular basis. In 1969 the city built a protective dike along the river as cautionary insurance.

The city council's discussion of a proposal to spend $262,000 for a water-treatment plant ended in a stalemate that was broken only when Dr. Stan Ewen as mayor voted for the needed improvement. Frank Rodger, who had originally abstained, reluctantly made the mayor's vote legal by joining Ronald Prior and Dr. Hoffman, while Verne (Squeak) Kilgore and Horace Soper steadfastly voted against the plant. Estherville water, pumped from deep wells, is with treatment now less of a laundry problem. The supply of safe, drinkable water is ample.

Dr. Stan Ewen, a dentist who lived next door to my family home, had served only one term as mayor when Linn Foderburg impishly circulated nomination papers before the 1954 election for Kirt Allen, the controversial editor of the *Enterprise*. If the good mayor had made any serious mistakes, they were judgment calls. During a certain period of Estherville history every mayor had difficulty retaining the goodwill of both those who insisted that dogs should not be permitted to roam through their yards, and particularly their vegetable gardens, and the dog lovers who fumed if the dogcatcher netted their pets and confined them to the pound, or did worse. Another mayoral problem was keeping peace between the policemen—who arrested speeders, drunks, and other violators of the code, insisting that all arrested offenders should be fined or sentenced—and those who argued that to be accused of a crime is not tantamount to guilt.

Dr. Ewen, my father's longtime golfing companion, was never quite reconciled to his 173-vote defeat in the '54 election. He took it even harder than forking over a dime lost at golf. Kirt as an editor offended so many readers that Doc was incredulous Kirt could be elected mayor, or even dogcatcher. But Kirt had his supporters. An old buddy of City Superintendent of Public Works Ford Connelly, the *Enterprise* editor drank coffee with Ralph Rogers, Bill Clark, and many other sports lovers. Kirt befriended ring-necked pheasants, tied his own casting flies, and talked the language of outdoorsmen. So the voters added up his good points, decided to forgive or overlook his transgressions in print, and hoped he would come down on the "right" side of dogs-versus-gardens and policemen-versus-accused.

In the mayor's chair, Allen presided over several stormy sessions. One time he refused to sign the warrants approved by councilmen. Sometimes a reporter had to censor the dialogue for print. After Allen's one term, Leo Sanders, elected in a landslide, tried his hand as mayor and did better. He lasted six years.

According to a census taken in 1955, the town had accumulated 7,500 population and probably deserved the automatic dial telephone service installed by Northwestern Bell. Like everyone else, I found it a convenient improvement—when I got accustomed to it. But of course I lost all my alibis for ringing wrong numbers, a specialty of mine. And no longer did my favorite "hello girl" help me run down elusive people whom she knew how to find better than I did. Dial gadgetry service simply didn't know enough to try calling Joe at the pool hall or to understand that Jim usually lunched at Stafford's hamburger shop. And robots are utterly devoid of folksy charm.

The woman who tried to organize an Estherville Sex Club got no place at all. But it's about the only kind of club I can think of that has not been organized in our town. We have gotten together in the town to eat pancakes, fly kites, shoot marbles, catch fish, barbecue slabs of beef, and eat breakfast at the airport when enthusiasts from far away point their flying machines once a year toward Estherville and drop in for a morning of ham, eggs, organ music, and ceremonies. But sex never came off in our town on an organized, community basis. The woman who thought up such an idea was carted off to the state hospital for a mental examination.

In 1957 the town lost a valued friend of flying and a good friend of mine. Harry Coffie, Bill Maher, and I had debated Philippine Independence and Paved Roads for Iowa while in high school, preparing for tournaments in a cubbyhole over a stairway. When Harry died suddenly of a strange malady, he was only fifty and at the height of developing the town's elegant airport. Ralph Bryan was capable of carrying on, but Coffie's death was a tragedy that saddened many persons. The only wrong he ever did me was to invite our family of four to a spin in his airplane over Okoboji and Spirit Lake. Everybody in the family was ecstatic on the ride except the born-too-soon printer.

If Harry had lived just a few more months, he would have marveled at the new Estherville high school building which included a little theater, a spacious gym, music rooms, and a more comfortable space for debating than the cubbyhole we once occupied. Three years after constructing the new high school building, the district built a large addition to it and a charming replacement for McKinley School in the native woods of the west hills.

Watching Esterville Grow

IN one of the Estherville community's most generous moments, the people contributed $300,000 in 1957 to help build the finest hospital facilities that money could buy.[1] The project cost $1.3 million, of which a federal grant supplied $434,000, to add to the local gifts and funds of the Sisters of the Sorrowful Mother.

The Catholic order had acquired the hospital in 1944. Following the death of Dr. R. C. Coleman in 1933, when he despondently ended it all after hopelessly struggling with financial woes, the hospital had continued operation under the management of the Upper Des Moines Valley Association. This was simply a group of public-spirited men, led by L. M. Christensen, Ed Stockdale, John E. Greig, Paul Gray, and Roy Buckingham, who employed Magnus Wolden as superintendent. A number of Lutherans, organized as the Concordia Hospital Association, had attempted to raise sufficient funds to purchase the facilities, but despite promotion and newspaper help fund raising fell short of the need. At that point the Sister order decided to purchase the property and called it Holy Family Hospital.

Upon acquiring the property, the Sisters made immediate improvements, adding a lobby, a four-floor east wing, mechanical and laundry facilities, a fourth floor on the main building, and a chapel. A few years later the order appointed a lay advisory board, while an Auxiliary to assist patients with extra services became active in '54. But the order saw need for a much more modern plant, and ambitious plans were drawn. No more ideal an administrator to carry out the improvement and to obtain community accord could have been found than Sister Irenea Whitmann, a woman of vast charm and good executive ability.

The most painful incident of the campaign for funds in 1957 occurred at a meeting called at the Gardston Hotel after a number of Protestants decided it was inappropriate to support a Catholic

Coleman Hospital.

hospital. Leaders of the drive suspended it for thirty-six hours, pending outcome of the meeting they had called. Supporters of the hospital as well as conscientious objectors attended. Discussion covered the Spanish Inquisition, the political stance of Catholic priests in Spanish America, and aspects of Papal government unacceptable to Lutherans and Protestants.

Paul Gray, the chairman, was stunned by the pointless, ugly remarks. Suffering from a severe heart ailment that killed him before the end of the year, he gasped for breath and threw a quick and unexpected lateral pass to me. How jolly. Irrelevant though some of

Holy Family Hospital.

the rhetoric was, the meeting proved fortunate because unhappy dissenters had their say. Silent opposition was brought into the open, and in the end, members of the community largely convinced themselves that money invested in the project would not enrich the Papacy. Rather it would simply provide a safer, better place to mend the community's own sick.

Between 3,000 and 4,000 donors made pledges of help, some of them contributing enough individually to furnish one whole room. John Morrell & Company gave $30,000 to the cause. With the community's donations, the funds supplied by the order, and the federal grant, the hospital built the finest facilities obtainable. The new construction, along with more facilities added later, provided five new operating rooms; two delivery rooms; recovery, intensive, and coronary care rooms; isolation; emergency center; oxygen to all rooms; more elevators; an ambulance entrance; laboratory, radiology and pathology sections; a pharmacy; food preparation; cafeteria; physical and respiration therapy; air conditioning and purifying systems; and many additional patient rooms. The Sisters poured nearly a half million dollars more into the 100-bed hospital plant subsequent to the 1957 program to include facilities seen as desirable.

Since my retirement from the newspaper, I have transferred my business concerns to the hospital. No longer do I fret about meeting pressroom deadlines. Instead, as a member of the governing board's executive committee, I stew about the ever-dropping rate of occupancy and how to sustain a cash flow adequate to keep the hospital up-to-date and solvent. And Everyld, who seldom plays the organ at First Presbyterian church anymore, makes her main contribution in community service by scheduling women for activities in the busy, ecumenically supported Auxiliary. It performs many patient services and with its small profits helps to fund new items of equipment that Administrator Don Schmaus hints the hospital could use to advantage.

Convent Sisters who once held almost all the hospital's responsible positions are now nearly all replaced by lay professionals. Looking back on my own minor surgical experience in Ethyl Walker's first city hospital, I realize how far the community has come in providing a suitable place to treat the ill. Members of my family and I have been X-rayed, sliced, and treated a good many times in the immaculate, accredited hospital for which we felt privileged to contribute a few bricks and bits of stainless steel back in 1957. Holy Family is our town's most vital asset, serving not just some of the people but all of them.

Although the hospital provided in its plant comfortable extended care facilities, unfathomable federal and state regulations made use of them financially impractical. Other hospitals have had the same problem with regulatory bodies in attempting to provide two levels of care in the same building. However, the people of Estherville are fortunate in having two residential and nursing homes and a growing number of comfortable units for elderly persons at low-cost rental. The $1 million Good Samaritan Center, established in 1956, has been expanded on several occasions and now includes beds and dining space for 141 persons, in addition to 16 apartment units. Rosewood Manor, built in 1968, accommodates 55 residents in similar quarters.

I am comforted by the fact that all the aged and the ill are housed in modern, fire-resistant, clean quarters. This was not true in the early days of Estherville nursing home care. Meanwhile, the town's builders did not neglect the churches, almost all of which now occupy spacious, attractive, well-appointed buildings, and also provide comfortable and suitable homes for their clergy. In recent years attractive, masonry apartment buildings have gone up in town, filling a need for those families choosing to save themselves the chores of home ownership. Estherville's most recent housing development is the Gardston building, no longer a hotel, which with the aid of a $400,000 federal grant is to be remodeled and adapted for occupancy of senior citizens, with housing and meeting rooms for them.

All in the same year that members of the community dug into their pockets to help build a better hospital, they also attended open house at a spanking new high school facility, and the county laid the cornerstone for a new courthouse. But Emmet never built a new courthouse the easy way. The supervisors soon disposed of differences of opinion about what sort of building ought to be constructed, dismissing appeal by a fairly substantial group of us who thought we made a convincing argument in favor of a Colonial type structure. Architect James A. Dougher of Des Moines did not share our enthusiasm for the type of building that to us seemed ap-

Emmet County Courthouse, 1884–1958.

propriate for a Square platted by the first settlers, who came from New England. Dougher told the board that a Colonial building to replace the quaint courthouse of 1884 would prove too expensive; he had in mind a set of plans used at Algona that he thought would do nicely. He described the plans' clean lines and was unimpressed when I said in rebuttal that hen houses, tool sheds, and privies also have such attributes. But the architect compromised; when he provided information for a brochure after the building was completed, he announced the style as "Modified Colonial." Well modified, but a good building, nonetheless.

Style of the building was not the only problem. In 1954 the voters approved a $350,000 bond issue, sold at slightly under 2 percent interest, but the supervisors in two tries could get no contractor to build it for that. When the supervisors asked for an additional $100,000, the voters expressed pique and said no. But in 1957 they yielded, and in June, supervisors laid the cornerstone. The three-story stone-and-brick building, erected by Lundquist Construction Company of LeMars, was finished a year later. Colonial or otherwise, it graces the Square: a solid, fire-resistant home for county business and its records. A wide street now cuts through the Square where the 1884 courthouse stood.

Emmet County Courthouse, built in 1958.

One salesman, trying to sell the city of Estherville a Fairbanks-Morse engine to generate power at the municipal light plant, suddenly found himself nailed to the cross. Councilman Cliff Hedrick, a dry cleaner, laid a tape-recorder trap for Clyde Critchfield, who found himself charged with trying to buy Hedrick's vote for $5,000. When the case went to district court, Critchfield pleaded guilty of "offering a gratuity" and paid a $500 fine. That same year the council bought two Cooper-Bessemer engines for $763,000. By then the plant needed its handsome new building to house a stable of eight powerful workhorses.

At the same time that members of the business community were busy organizing an Estherville Industrial Development Committee to buy an industrial park and to supply capital for buildings to improve it, fire completely destroyed a local industry. The Super-Sweet Feed mills, originally built by Greig & Company and later sold to Honeymead, became ashes. Flames that shot high in the air and puffed up vast clouds of smoke provided action for beautiful color photography. In maturity, I viewed this costly destruction through different eyes than when a firebug during my boyhood touched the match to the barns in his neighborhood. In 1967 Kent Feeds supplied the city with its second feed-manufacturing plant, located near the Golden Sun's big new plant and close to the Swift fertilizer plant, which was originally built in 1955 by the Virginia-Carolina Company.

Destruction of the old George Lyon home made a spectacular fire from which the Frank Fuhrman family was lucky to escape. The quaint old house surrounded by an iron picket fence was being used as a funeral home when it lit the Estherville sky one cold February night in 1962. My thoughts raced back to Virginia and her red pony cart and the dining room table that couldn't be persuaded through the front door.

I have always felt a deep sense of pride in the way the Estherville community has responded to appeals for good causes. Sometimes it has been buying war bonds; voting to build improvements; or making gifts to the Red Cross, donations for tornado victims, or contributions to provide medical assistance for unfortunate persons. In the rural areas it is the common practice of our community for neighbors to plow, cultivate, and harvest crops of farmers who have been injured or are ill or deceased. Helping other people is the way of rural life. When the Ed Thoresons' twelve-year-old daughter was bitten by a rabid skunk while on a western vacation trip, Estherville folks responded with $5,000 of help so quickly that the Thoresons were emotionally touched. But the Thoresons' grief was deep; Janis died after nine months in a coma.

Jerry Galvin, a man of modest build, was one of Estherville's most durable citizens and workers. At the time he was still active unloading and reloading heavy lifts of lumber at the yard operated by Jim Harker and Verne Beauman, his age was variously estimated. He gave up work at the yard at ninety-nine years of age, when he underwent amputation of his right leg. In 1961 he celebrated his 105th birthday, and he held a press conference—with our reporter. He recalled that in his youth he worked for two sisters who rode bareback in the Barnum & Bailey Circus. He cared for the horses, a job at which he had gained familiarity as a groomsman for an Englishman. He also revealed he had sought gold in Alaska and traveled in a number of foreign countries. Regular dosage of distilled spirits not only agreed with this remarkable man but it apparently was the elixir of longevity. Jerry carefully avoided a state of being parched. He finally surrendered this life after 106 vigorous years.

By 1962 the *Daily News* was growing out of its square brick building west of the Iowa Trust & Savings Bank, which had become its home in 1930, when the *News* began daily publication. A mezzanine floor to expand the news department and a photo lab temporarily helped, but larger quarters were needed. And besides that, the bank was anxious to expand its installment loan department into an addition on the location. So we searched for a new home. We found a suitable building at 10 North Seventh Street, beside the Gardston Hotel. It had been built by Mrs. Charles Anderson to replace the dilapidated old wooden structure in which her husband and Henry Mahlum had operated a furniture store for many years.

After remodeling by Stanley and Roland Fagre, who had erected the structure in 1954, the fine building was ready for newspaper occupancy on my fifty-seventh birthday, March 31, 1962. Moving day was as hectic as publication of the first daily issue thirty-two years before. The Fagres' forty-five years of experience in constructing various public and business buildings in the community were valuable to us, while Howard Heidke solved difficult problems in providing the illumination and flexible outlets of power needed for a modern newspaper plant. And Orval Clark saw that we got plumbed, heated, and cooled. In making our improvements we came to appreciate the convenience of ready-mix concrete; readily available supplies of hardware, plumbing, and electrical items; and fast service from an electric motor shop. We even found need for machine parts stocked by the auto supply wholesalers. Progress had been good since our previous move in 1930.

We spent more money on the plant than necessary, but Bob

and I wanted to create a plant not only useful and convenient but pleasant for everyone to work in. At about the same time, we asked the Estherville Library to join us in microfilming all the newspaper files we had acquired through the years: the *Northern Vindicator,* the *Broad-Axe,* the *Republican,* the *V. & R.,* the *Democrat,* and the *News.* The up-to-date microfilmed files afford the most complete history that the community possesses. The library retains duplicate films of the newspapers.

Always experiencing a sense of pride in the achievements of staffers who moved on from our newspaper to bigger fields, I was easily persuaded by the telephone company to make the first direct dial telephone call from Estherville's new Northwestern Bell plant. Jay Gildner, a University of Minnesota journalism graduate, who moved on from our newspaper to the state department, was serving as a press secretary for Mrs. John Kennedy when we dialed the White House. All I could think of to say was to ask if Beverly was as pretty as ever. I have to admit that direct dialing has some advantages.

Ben Reeves, an auctioneer, wrestled other musclemen during his young days in thirty-two different states, more commonwealths than most folks of the town ever visit. Ben frequented the *News* office to bring in auction sale bills or to place ads for selling guns, which he collected as a hobby. Shortly after we moved to our new plant, Ben stood on his head to observe his seventy-sixth birthday. This was a quaint brainscrambling custom he had been following for more years than he could remember.

Having lived through Estherville street mud in my boyhood, I was particularly pleased when the city began a systematic plan of curbing, guttering, and hard-surfacing every street in town. The city accomplished this job by sharing its road use tax funds to defray a fourth of the cost of improvements. The balance came from reasonable, long-term assessments against adjacent property owners. When the Roy Rohlin asphalters established headquarters in town, these facilities, along with those available from the Everds company and Maurice Boggess, enabled the city to make rapid progress. With $152,000 the city paved thirty-seven blocks of streets in the one year of 1964, the start of a five-year plan. Street and parking lot surfacing planned by the city engineering services and later by private engineers, Jacobson-Westergard, took Estherville out of mud and dust.

"Pop" Munson would have been impressed with the plant put up by his son Dick to carry on the family's Crystal Springs Bottling Works. Richard, voted "Mr. Estherville" in 1965, called his business Dix Bottling, adding Pepsi and other flavors besides my favorite cream soda that Pop Munson bottled. Like his brother Homer, Dick had become a flyer and piloted a bomber in World War II.

Jack Kint was another son who carried on the family business—food distributing—with updated equipment and headquarters for his K & M Sales. The K stood for Bert Kint and the M for Joe Marsell, two retreaded managers of the Gamble-Robinson fruit house, whose history in Estherville produce wholesaling dated back to 1917. Gamble transferred its district headquarters to Mankato in 1975.

In 1965 I lost my golfing buddy and insurance counselor when John Stockdale forsook the insurance business his father had built to go back to school. At the University of Iowa he acquired a doctorate in economics and began teaching the truths of insurance and other facts in Sacramento, where I have to go to get a game with him. His brother, Jerry, continued in the business, which he expanded, but he has no time for golf. To some extent I overlook this flaw in his makeup because he inherited his father's fun-loving charm. But Pappy Lloyd apparently passed on to neither son his addiction to practical jokes. Eyebrows were lifted at the time the state revised its liquor law when Jerry built the Black Coach Restaurant on Okoboji and served the first legal Iowa liquor-by-the-drink highball to his brother. From Mother Aline, Jerry acquired his restless need for adventure in conquest of the new and different.

It may be the climate. Or the water. Maybe it is simply the joy of living that has stimulated so many Estervilleans to defy the actuarial tables. A *Daily News* reporter one day caught Charlie Werling, ninety-eight years old, laying a slab of concrete at his home. If the exercise injured his health, he was slow to suffer ill effects, because he lived another three years before laying down his trowel, hammer, and saw. That was after he had built 150 houses, besides crafting untold numbers of cabinets, chairs, tables, desks, pulpits, and other items of exquisite furniture. He was a craftsman in the use of both woodworking and upholstery tools. He gave up hunting pheasants upon reaching his centennial, when over birthday cake he said his sound health might be attributed to good food and rest.

With special friends, Charlie often divided the wine he fermented. But, personally, I rated Charlie's greater flair his woodworking talents. At those he was a pro.

As farming became more and more specialized in Emmet County, few farmers continued to raise their own chickens, keep cows, and raise a few pigs. As local poultry production declined, so did the hatchery business. The well-equipped hatchery of Don Woodley and one that the Doolittles and later Greig & Company operated simply went out of business. But turkey growing was still going strong in 1966, when Gordon Barsness on the west fringe of Estherville was marketing from 25,000 to 30,000 Thanksgiving fowl every year. But eventually even turkey growing became restricted to areas of specialization.

The year before brother Bob and I sold the *Daily News* we lost the services of a longtime contributor, B. O. Wolden, whose notes about flora and fauna of Emmet County published in a column called "The Observer" received good readership. He was a recognized and highly respected ornithologist. When Wolden died we had no one to replace him, although Olaf's widow, Ida, was a knowledgeable biologist who continued to be helpful to the newspaper on nature subjects.

In 1967 Everyld and I paid a brief visit to son Bob, yet in Columbia University graduate school, where we met Susan, his intended, and amused ourselves at a show or two. At Philharmonic Hall to hear Steinberg conduct Mozart, Dvorak, and Bruckner, we suddenly found ourselves localized. There we came upon Joe Salyers, general manager of the hall, a grandson of I. N. Salyers, who in the dim past had built the post office and many other Estherville structures. Joe's theatrical experience had been extensive. After working in New York theaters as a designer and production manager, he involved himself in President Kennedy's cultural exchange program. When Joe left New York and went to the West Coast and the Hollywood Bowl, we lost track of him.

As letterpress printing of newspapers lost favor to offset printing because of that process's superior reproduction of photographs, the *Daily News* saw the need to change. To do so represented a substantial investment, for which the newspaper had accumulated some reserves in bonds. But it seemed more feasible to make use of underused facilities of a modern offset plant at the town of Spirit

Lake, only fifteen miles away. Our newspaper needed an offset plant and the Spirit Lake Beacon needed more newspapers to print, so in December 1968 Bob and I sold our newspaper to William E. Beck of Spirit Lake.

We would not have done this if any of the sons in the family had wanted to continue the newspaper. But two of Bob's boys, Joe and Jim, became pilots and Nelson studied law. One of mine, Bill, turned out to be an aeronautical engineer after MIT, and the other, Bob, finally decided to be a college political science teacher after considerable vacation-time writing for our paper and for the *Minneapolis Tribune* and a degree from Columbia's Graduate School of Journalism.

It was the plan that after selling the paper to Beck I would act as a consultant and do some opinion writing, and brother Bob would manage the paper. But different owners have different ideas, and these plans didn't last long. Bob, under superintendent Richard H. Blacker, became information and publications director for Iowa Lakes Community College, where he continued until retirement. I contented myself with putting together facts and recollections of Estherville life and history and following agreeable pursuits and hobbies. In the spring of 1971 Beck turned the paper over to Mid-America Publishing of Des Moines on a long-term contract arrangement. Fred Williams became the publisher.

Fifty years too late for my participation, Estherville held the first of its winter sports festivals in 1969. One of the many events in the competition was skiing down Holiday Mountain, a hillside south of the river, just west of the bridge toward Wallingford. On that natural site, Don Sievers had developed an elaborate facility of runs and lifts, with a capability of manufacturing snow whenever the weatherman neglected his obligations to produce the stuff. Activities at the winter festival ranged from dog races to snowmobiling, skating, and outdoor sculpture of figures made of ice and snow. The festival has attracted wide participation and attendance. Indoor activities at the annual event are not neglected. These include musical productions, banquets, and other pursuits that I find more acceptable now than neck-breaking games.

Guy Webber finished his life at eighty-nine in the Good Samaritan Center in 1970. Before he was examined for admission to the center, Chief of Police Clarence Hackett and Dan Sanderson conspired to give him a bath in the city jail's shower stall. An inmate of the jail was sentenced by the chief to give Webber a thorough scrubbing. After this renovation, Hackett dressed him in some clothes brought from across the alley at the Penney store.

Shaved, washed, and cleanly dressed, Webber was not recognizable. He had lived in squalor amid rubble in a tarpaper shack close by the stockyards. He owned an old Essex coach, the roof of which he more or less waterproofed with a thick coat of asphalt. After the roof collected a certain amount of dust and leaves it looked as though it had been tarred and feathered. On Sundays, Guy delivered papers for the *Des Moines Register;* the pay was the only earned income he had, although he collected any discarded items and scraps he found in the alleys. Guy may or may not have included cat and dog meat in his diet as generally suspected— nobody was sure—but he frequently salvaged food from grocery store back rooms. That's the Webber almost everyone in town knew.

But there was another Guy Webber people didn't know. He subscribed for the Wall Street Journal and Barron's weekly, read other periodicals of financial interest, and made careful investments. Upon his death his lawyer found in his safety deposit box scores of certificates of ownership, many for as little as one share, in common stocks of ACF Industries, INA, Western Union, Pepsi-Cola, American Cyanamid, electric public utilities, and several investment trusts and funds. Bank certificates of deposits, promissory note receivables, and bonds rounded out the portfolio of citizen Webber, whose estate upon his death was inventoried at $49,000. Now, each year, an Estherville high school graduating senior receives a four-year scholarship worth about $600 a year. These are awarded by the Emmet County State Bank, largely on the basis of need, paid from the income of a $40,000 Guy Webber trust fund. Webber, the scavenging hermit, bequeathed an infinite gift to the community from which he asked only its unwanted leftovers.

When I was a boy, I always looked forward to the Fourth of July with about as much pleasure as Christmas. I always had a plentiful supply of firecrackers, torpedoes, and other effective weapons with which to get burned and maimed. On one Fourth, the chamber of commerce, or perhaps the city, shot off fireworks for the common amusement, at an unwisely chosen missile site on the southeast corner of the Square. After watching the display, mother, father, and I had just left the Square and were walking home on North Seventh Street when a skyrocket slithered off the launching pad and jetted straight up the street, shoulder high. That was the fastest that anything ever went up that street, before or since. The Lees were understandably frightened out of their wits. Such dangerous practices were looked upon as just one of the hazards of life until a fireworks accident burned down much of the city of Spencer. Then the state legislature passed a law that banned private sale of fireworks, a Chinese invention long depended upon to commemorate the signing of the Declaration of Independence.

However, so that Estherville youth would not be totally deprived of patriotic participation, it became the practice of the city each Fourth to purchase a supply of bombs, rockets, and Roman candles, often arranging for a municipal display at the Estherville Golf & Country Club and in later years at the ball park. But the firemen, who always handled the combustibles, ran into a problem with its 1970 spectacular. William Rosenau, a sixteen-year-old boy, suffered injuries from what appeared to be a dud three-inch firecracker. He carried it with him from the ball park, where he found it, to a picnic at Tuttle Lake. There, when ignited, it blew off three fingers of his hand. A petit jury awarded him $83,500, a verdict sustained by the Iowa Supreme Court. Total cost to the city for the misadventure proved to be $99,000. The only fireworks exploded in the city since have been contraband merchandise smuggled in from less enlightened states.

In a clean, neat new building near the Good Samaritan Center, thirty-four persons of the county have found new meaning in their lives as they fashion ceramics, mend furniture, knit, and perform many other tasks. No longer do they sit at home or stroll without purpose or direction. The community generously contributed funds to make possible this institution in 1974. It is known as ECHO. That stands for Emmet County Handicapped Opportunities, Incorporated. Staffed with personnel who understand problems of handicapped persons, ECHO has not only rebuilt the lives of those persons and their families but also has become a source of pride and satisfaction to others who feel rewarded by the accomplishment. Four years after ECHO was started, Project Challenge, a program for gifted students, got under way in the fifth,

sixth, seventh, and eighth grades. This recognized the need for attention to those who are especially advantaged as well as those persons who are disadvantaged.

As the nation went through a trying period of streaking, a
group of Iowa Lakes Community College students chose the quiet
hour of one o'clock in the morning for a nude sortie around the
courthouse. The bravest of the streakers soloed around the library
as well. So far as I know they received neither grade points nor a
sentence of free lodging in the keep.

Somewhat later, the daughter of Paul and Alice Neppel,
Peggy, ran like a streak while a student at Iowa State University to
win medals as the county's most talented woman athlete. She competed and won many meets as a distance runner, competing with
the International United States Women's cross-country team at
Rabat, Morocco. The Neppels are some of the county's most successful grain and livestock producers. Paul's parents and other
members of the family, which had German origin, spelled the name
Neppl. But after doing some research, Paul decided that a distant
ancestor accidentally omitted a useful vowel, so he added an "e"
before the "l."

Although I had known Hiram Albee a long time, it was not until I employed him to resurrect a superannuated warehouse by the
M.&St.L. tracks we acquired for newsprint storage that I got acquainted with him. I soon found I had chosen the right workman;
he wasted not a nail, board, or scrap of metal to produce a transfor-
mation in the old building at unbelievably little cost. On a few occasions when I called at his bungalow to consult with him about our
project, I observed that the old bachelor was also frugal in his own
home. He lived largely on vegetables he grew in the backyard,
cooked his own meals, and apparently laundered the dishes only as
impulse moved him. He was absorbed in a wide variety of reading,
catching up on the high school education he hadn't finished and the
college career that never started. Modern science intrigued him.

Several years before Hiram died at eighty-nine years of age he
asked Bill Anderson to help him make up for the education he had
wanted himself by planning to spread much of it around to those
not advantaged with funds for schooling. So when his will was probated upon death in 1975, there were gasps of surprise. First off, he
bequeathed the Emmet County Historical Society $80,000, which,

Hiram Albee.

together with his lifetime gifts to the society of $20,000, supplied the $100,000 needed for the new fire-resistant building it then put up in 1977 to house records, photographs, antiques, and relics.

That wasn't all, by any means. With a little more than a half million dollars left after paying probate expense and after his gift to the Historical Society, his estate provided a trust at the Iowa Trust & Savings Bank for scholarships to worthy students, based on academic performance, to study at the Estherville campus of Iowa Lakes Community College. When the bank received the estate proceeds, it included $215,400 in bonds, certificates of deposits, and cash; $20,400 of contract receivables; and $284,800 worth of farmland — $520,600 in all — that the bank in accordance with Hiram's wish reduced to bonds and C.D.'s. During their lifetimes, each of his nine nephews and nieces receives $50 a month from the trust and all the rest of the income is perpetually available for ILCC scholarships through the Iowa Lakes Scholarship Foundation. There was serious purpose in Hiram's thrift and frugality.

The college has also received many other gifts, such as one from the Clyde Sanborns, retired from their furniture store, who

have established an educational trust, and who make $3,000 to
$4,000 available on the basis of need for scholarships each year to
Estherville area students at the Estherville campus. A gift from
Hallie Drake provided $18,000 worth of books for the library.
Twenty other gifts of individuals and organizations in the city pro-
vide scholarships worth $4,500 to $5,000 annually.

In a meaningful observance of the nation's 200th birthday, the
Emmet County Historical Society arranged publication of volume
III of a county history. It consists largely of biographies of families
in the community, together with sketches of organizations and a few
of the commercial enterprises, with generous use of photographs.
Ivadell Ross and Louis (Pete) Obye headed up the effort. Besides
the ringing of bells, the planting of time capsules to be opened in
100 years — activities deemed appropriate to the Bicentennial —
Iowa Lakes Community College, with a sense of local history, arranged a chautauqua. Some of the program was held in a tent — just
like long ago. Other events took place in the auditorium and other
facilities of the Methodist campgrounds on Lake Okoboji. Like an
old-fashioned chautauqua, the entertainment included music, lectures, programs for youngsters, and drama. A chorus sang, and local talent as well as professionals performed. Even a flea market was
arranged.

Estherville's Avenue of Flags is an impressive sight on Memorial Day each year. Around the library and courthouse square and
along each of the walks through the two parks are the battle flags of
575 men who gave their lives in the nation's wars. Permanent recep-
tacles, spaced six feet apart, hold the battle flags in breathtaking
reminder of the community's military contribution in manpower.
Of the 575 flags, 5 are those of Civil War veterans, 3 of the Spanish-
American conflict, 365 of World War I, 172 of World War II, 14 of
Korea, 8 of Vietnam, and 8 of peacetime.

Howard Hughes's will No. 16 was mailed by someone who
dropped it in the Estherville post office. Apparently spurious, it was
supposedly mailed to Estherville in 1931 from London and then
held there in a bank safety deposit box. The joker didn't make it
stick; no one I ever knew got a share of the Hughes fortune.

As retail outlets sought more space around their stores for
parking automobiles, Estherville, like almost all other cities, expanded outward from the Square. Industrial development went

south from town, and there was a limited residential expansion to the west, but most of the extension was toward the east, closer to the population center of the county. Although other new subdivisions had already been established in that area, a major development in 1977 added a grocery supermarket, a discount store, and a general department store. To round out the merchandise selections, the state moved its liquor store there and converted it to self-serve. Through Estherville's long history of saloons, drugstore prescription whiskey, bootlegging, and tavern operations, the supply of spirits to quench the thirst was never so plentiful and in such wide selection as found now in a help-yourself Estherville boozery.

For quite a while now, Estherville has enjoyed a respite from the devastating fires it experienced through past years. Improved construction, effective prevention, and superior defense techniques have bettered the batting averages. But volunteer firemen, with no intention of resting on their better luck, persuaded the city council not long ago that the department ought to spread out into much larger quarters. The new facility is the town's most recently built structure. Through its five wide doors the firefighters can simultaneously speed their red trucks on the way to trouble. And where, do you think, the town fathers chose to build this new hangar for its fire engines? Don't be surprised to learn that they picked a vacant lot by the Rock Island tracks, close to where an immense billboard during the days of my youth invited all lookers to WATCH ESTHERVILLE GROW. And appropriately, I thought, in the light of a long history of expensive blazes that incinerated much of Esther's town, the city government cautiously built its new engine house of steel. It's fireproof.

It's All Progress,
One Might Suppose

AS I sit comfortably in my living room and reflect on the changes I have seen take place in my lifetime and those changes that took place during the years before that, it's apparent that the Estherville of today is indeed different. The store buildings are bigger and more elegant and the merchandise they offer is remarkable. The homes are spacious and comfortable, in settings of immaculate lawns. The public buildings are impressive. This adds up to progress. But I liked some of the old. I miss hearing the voice of the telephone operator when I become frustrated in searching for the number of someone in or out of town I'm trying to reach. That shows what an old-timer I am.

The new supermarkets are nice but I liked shopping for steak at Oehrlein's meat market. We bought groceries by telephoning our order to Barbara or Glenn at Sconberg & Kilgore. A pleasant young man delivered our purchases. We settled accounts once a month. Now, when Everyld entrusts me to grocery shop for an item or so, she supplies me with a crude map of the store and even sometimes notes the aisle number where I might likely find the olives, breakfast food, canned soup, or other eatables. When I become lost in a drugstore, Mary Ann or Joyce leads me by the hand to find the insect powder, hidden perhaps behind piles of groceries, tools, hosiery, and other items that in my day were never found in a pharmacy.

Certainly the modern high school building is better than the one where I studied geometry in Clara Brees's room or where I puzzled over Latin with Lucy O. Pingrey. One time a mouse got loose in John Lytle's somewhat primitive chemistry and physics lab and I heroically captured it. The new high school is better lighted and equipped, and the floors don't squeak. Even the chairs are more comfortable and the desks are engraved with fewer autographs. But I am disturbed that many of the graduates of this and other schools speak such unutterables as "he gave it to Marge and *I*." Latin had long been a dead language in my day but was yet useful in learning something about the declension of nouns and the conjugation of verbs. We were taught that prepositions took pronouns of the objective case, and we learned other useful knowledge about language.

In this age of true-and-false and multiple-choice testing, the essay test is neglected. It is a pity that many teachers do not mark their papers for grammar as well as subject content, thus cheating their students of training they need in English. Pocket calculators will not, I hope, displace geometry, which I loved and which I thought helped me learn to think logically.

In the park, where grandfather and I ate pears, is a paved parking lot close to where I once watched tadpoles in a water fountain. A wide street runs through that section of the park where the quaint 1884 courthouse stood. The massive elms in the park are gone because disease imported from the Dutch has killed them all. The young saplings aren't big enough to shade anyone wanting to eat pears — or to watch girls. The wide street where the courthouse stood permits more autos to pass through the commercial area, but it also produces more carbon monoxide and other poisons. Two-tone auto horns and motor bikes make more noise than the traffic of grandpa's time. Worth Schloeman and "Squeak" Kilgore owned the only motorcycles I remember in my boyhood.

Nobody sits on the old dam to fish any more. It's largely washed away. Anyway, the fish moved out when progress arrived and more people moved in. Maybe the millions spent for pollution control will restore the Des Moines River to game fish that once lured anglers to drop bait in the deep holes. Few cities have spent as liberally as Estherville to filter wastes and to remove the smell of sewage from the noses of its residents. That fight is being won at enormous expense, but other pollution along the river still persists.

It has been a long time since we have had to light a candle or a kerosene lamp. The city-owned power plant and a grid of connecting transmission wires assure uninterrupted light and energy. And piped-in natural gas is far superior to the manufactured gas Estherville once produced by burning coke; in the old days mother fretted about getting enough heat at mealtime to cook dinner when all the other households turned on their burners. The water pressure is better, too. The water is safer than that once supplied by shallow wells along the river. And Holy Family Hospital with its impeccable housekeeping is infinitely superior to Ethyl Walker's city hospital, where I was drugged with ether.

I should enjoy the well-equipped airport and hard-surfaced runways, prepared for arrivals day or night, with planes waiting for hire. But I don't. I liked trains. I found it exciting to ride a first-class train that hauled passengers in comfortable Pullmans, observation lounges, and dining cars. I can still hear in my ears the tinkle of silverware and of ice cubes in water tumblers on the dining car tables of the City of San Francisco as it rolled through the Rockies. The scenery that unfolded past the window was magnificent. What I see mainly from my seat in a flying machine is a paper bag to use in case I am overcome by nausea. And I puzzle over incomprehensible instructions of how to jump out of the plane if the pilot decides to ditch it. Although in driving my automobile there is a sense of comfort in knowing that the ground is not far away, I am aware that mayhem lurks around every hill and curve. I liked it best when a locomotive engineer did the driving.

There is more employment security now in Estherville, as there is in almost every other American community, than in the old days. Too much security. Perhaps it is progress that no longer can a person be dismissed from his job without good cause. But now it is difficult to discharge a person when there is indeed excellent cause. In the age of employment hearings and rehearings it has to be proved that a public employee has committed a felony or serious misdemeanor if he is to be replaced by a more capable and suitable worker. This has subtracted something important from the gross national product and the quality of government, teaching, and private enterprise.

Fortunately, in my writing and editing of newspaper copy it had not become the practice to use such inane expressions in print as "chairperson." I cannot see that abolishing "chairman" has enhanced womanhood. I liked "Mrs.," "Miss," and "Mr." and I still do. Using only a woman's last name in print offends my sense of politeness and good usage.

In the eyes of small-towners and country folks, extravagances of the federal government are appalling. Bureaus and agencies multiply and none of them is ever abandoned. Particularly shameful is the proliferation of congressional payrolls and never-ending expansion of office space. There is no effective check on the Congress itself to curb abuse of privilege. Meanwhile the primary cause of inflation—the spending of billions of dollars more money than the federal government's income—is unrestrained. The president and the Congress both insist on huge spending programs that unbalance the budget and pump an oversupply of money into the economy. It is more important to both the president and the Congress to win votes and pay off campaign promises than to stem inflation.

I am baffled that in a free-enterprise system our nation seeks to deal with problems of scarcity—such as that of crude oil and natural gas—while regulating the price. This country editor can't see how the gap between supply and demand will ever be closed under such abuse of regulatory power. I am no less discouraged by such federal blundering than by news from astroscientists that they suspect a few fickle stars of the universe have collapsed into Black Holes of nothingness. I can believe almost anything, now that man has walked on the moon and put rockets on Mars. Maybe the universe was born in a Big Bang fifteen or twenty billion years ago and maybe it wasn't. Numbers in billions are beyond the scope of my limited imagination.

I am nonetheless comforted by the forecasts of physicists that the universe is unlikely to consume itself convulsively in one vast super Black Hole before another fifty billion years go by. This still gives our society some bargaining time to work on its most perplexing problems. I simply decline to take sides in quarrels about quasars, collapsing stars, exploding galaxies, and sundry extraterritorial affairs of the Milky Way; we have so much to worry about in Washington. As the president and the Congress ponder the inscrutables of federal debt, inflation, abortion, ecology, and crude oil, we don't have to peer into a powerful telescope to observe cataclysmic collapses taking place that are less remote to the concerns of Estherville and Emmet County than tentative speculation about exhausted stars consumed in nothingness.

Despite all the faults I can discover in the new, I like much of it. Life is more comfortable. I enjoy its conveniences. I could not have imagined as a boy that the average American would ever have it so deluxe. Dependable automobiles, household appliances, calculators, tools, typewriters, mechanical equipment, and furnishings abound. Homes, offices, stores, and industrial plants are well lighted, ventilated, heated, and cooled, and they are attractively appointed. Even though I still prefer fresh air over refrigerated air (which plugs my sinuses), I know this all sums up to progress.

What I am less sure of is that Americans are wisely using all their advantages and resources. I am encouraged that Estherville and the nation are developing awareness of the country's improvidence and wastefulness, but a happy mix of imposing environmental control and meeting needs of the economy has not been easy to achieve.

The new music that I unavoidably hear from my neighbors' windows or at inescapable public programs is loud. I find it unpleasing, ear-splitting, and inferior to what I play on our stereo record player. A small treasury of Brahms, Beethoven, Wagner, Rachmaninoff, Mozart, and other musical geniuses soothes my inner self. But I also enjoy sweet melodies played by the great orchestras of my younger, dancing days. One side of my nature allows me to relish even such performances as two records of Bobby Short's recordings that my special friend Mari Ann Blatch presented to me after we heard Bobby play and sing a few years ago at the Carlyle Hotel in New York. I guess what I do not like are loud dissonance and monotonous, pointless tunes. Perhaps a reformation of musical composition is around the corner.

In glancing back at my forty-one years of publishing a newspaper I can think of no deathless prose that the *News* wrote or edited, but our newspaper did record quite reliably and objectively—occasionally with entertainment—considerable current history. Our newspaper's encouragement of systematic city planning—along with zoning, park enlargement and improvement, and tree planting—affords pleasing reflections during my relaxed retirement from frustrations of a busy past. Behind us are agonies of press breakdowns, fractured deadlines, undelivered or misdelivered newspapers, subscribers unhappy because their names were misspelled or omitted or included, and advertisers who preferred that the news not be told the way it was. We prefer to forget all that and to remember gratefully a few posies gathered along the way that made the turnips and cabbages easier to accept.

Everyld and I have been enjoying our trips to both coasts, to Texas, the Gulf, and Florida since I relinquished responsibilities of the newspaper to others. Visits to see our two sons, their wives, and a grandson are special treats. Too brittle to ski and skate, we have sought sunshine and exercise where we could find it. Never in my life did I learn to enjoy blizzards and other asperities of Iowa winter climate; the short, pleasant summers seem too brief. But no way would I want to live anywhere else I can think of than Estherville. I like Esther's town. The drugstore, the hardware, the grocery, city hall, courthouse, and post office are only blocks away. The golf course for my foursome of Paul Pearson, Dr. J. B. Osher, and Delbert Hinsch is but eleven minutes from my home.

Robert and Esther Ridley laid out the town sensibly and with foresight. Planners have since expanded the parks and have legislated thoughtful zoning. The result is an environment that is pleasant, law-abiding, and wholesome. In Estherville there is opportunity for those willing to work conscientiously to earn a good livelihood. And if they so desire, they can acquire savings to make themselves comfortable in old age. Although the town has experienced adversity, it bears no lasting scars of ill will. Except for bitterness in the frustrating twenties, there has since been a good measure of peace and harmony, perhaps valued all the more for the breach of it back when economic misfortune befell.

As in most ambitious towns, an industrial development committee has been active. Expansion has made jobs available; population growth has taken place, but not so rapidly that anyone trying to WATCH ESTHERVILLE GROW could actually see the blooming take place. Fortunately, Estherville has not grown into an ugly town robbed of its small-city charm and quality of life. Other cities, even whole states, have regretted excessive expansion that polluted, crowded, and overtaxed them. Estherville's growth to about 8,500 souls has been just right.

To prevent casualties from such a tornadic windstorm as destroyed one million dollars worth of property and threatened life and limb in 1936, the community has provided effective defense against tornadoes and other outrages of nature. A highly audible alarm system that can be heard not only in the city's environs but for miles around is one of those safeguards.

When a funnel cloud was recently reported nearby, defense

personnel put the noisemaker to work. On that signal the inhabitants were supposed to retreat to their cellars or to other relative security. Many persons did, as they had been instructed. Others
looked at the sky and second-guessed the official observers. At least
a few absorbed in their tennis game didn't seem to notice the din
emitted by the screeching sirens. One young lady strolled over the
Central Avenue bridge enjoying her ice-cream cone. A woman sitting in a card foursome said to one of the other three at her table,
"It's your bid." Defense director Al Conlee was shocked. But he was
kidded, because the tornado did not strike Estherville at all but hit
nearby instead. Al rationalized, "If we blow the sirens and there is
no tornado, all we're out is a false alarm. But if we don't blow and
then it hits, we've got dead people." He spoke the truth. His problem is that Estherville in its 120 years has never suffered a first-rate
disaster; a good many Esthervilleans are not convinced it ever will.

As increasing numbers of Estherville business and professional
men move their families to the attractive shores of Okoboji and
Spirit lakes, the city faces possibilities of decay. Plans for extensive
downtown renewal and beautification can languish if those in business and in offices around the Square neglect generous support of
development. This is a concern shared by all those undivided in
their loyalty, and who feel deep pride in the community as heirs of
Esther Ridley and her husband. The first platters and planners
were unstinting in their gifts to the settlement they founded and
which has flourished.

The successful agriculture and livestock operations upon which
Estherville prosperity has been built are different from what they
were only a few decades ago. The 80-acre and even 160-acre farms
of the twenties are no longer typical. Farmers plant and harvest
their record-breaking crops in rows frequently a mile long. Soybeans have replaced oats and other small-grain crops; only the steep
slopes are planted to green-manure crops such as alfalfa and red
clover, with oats as a nurse crop. Common rotation of Emmet's
level, fertile prairie is corn-beans-corn-beans. The use of huge
quantities of chemical fertilizer, herbicides, insecticides, hybrid
seed corn, and improved drainage and tillage practices makes simpler rotations practical and produces record-breaking yields. Farmers were once proud of 50 bushels of corn an acre; now they expect
150. Top farmers produce considerably higher yields than the 100

bushels of corn and 35 bushels of soybeans reported as the 1975 Emmet County average of all farmland, including the least productive.[1] The 1975 crop on the December 1 market was worth $2.52 for corn and $4.60 for soybeans.[2] Many tenants pay $100 an acre—much more than the land sold for in the thirties—in cash rent.

To become efficient, farmers utilize modern equipment for which they pay as much as $50,000, $60,000, or more for single machines. With such monsters they are able to plant, cultivate, and harvest hundreds of acres, with little extra help. Feedlots of 500, 1,000, or more head of cattle convert corn and silage into choice and prime beef. Other farmers find conversion of grain into pork more profitable than selling grain. A Cattlemen's Association organized in 1966 and a pork producer's group founded in 1956 and reorganized in 1973 have helped stimulate achievement in high production standards. The 4-H youth movement, other County Extension and Farm Bureau efforts, County Fair judging, carcass grading, and vocational agriculture courses in high school and Iowa Lakes College have combined to accomplish high standards of livestock feeding. Golden Sun's research and proving grounds at Estherville have also contributed to quality meat achievement.

Intensive, large-scale farming has resulted in fewer but much larger farms. The 1,281 Emmet farms of 1934 had consolidated into only 761 by 1974. The average-sized farm of 194 acres in 1934 had grown to 315 acres in 1974.[3] The trend still continues. Many operators farm two or more 640-acre sections of land. Farm population has decreased somewhat as farmers retire to town, but a growing number of families retire on the land, where rural electrification and improved telephones provide them with all the comforts of city dwelling in the pastoral setting they enjoy.

That Emmet County's primary wealth is in the soil rather than in industries, stores, businesses, service institutions, buildings, homes, and other urban improvements is evident as one looks at the assessor's valuations. In 1977 the assessor put a tax valuation of $70 million on Estherville property and $22 million for other town property in the county. As compared with $92 million of urban valuation, the rural wealth was placed at $186 million, or more than double all other taxable assets in the county. What lured Norwegians, Danes, Germans, Irish, and Yankees to Emmet County in 1856 and throughout an ensuing period of rapid settlement was rich, black soil. This fertile prairie on which buffalo once grazed is today, as it was 100 years ago, sustaining and enriching the community. The settlement founded by the Ridleys and their intrepid companions has shared that prosperity.

A large wooded acreage along the west side of the Des Moines River has expanded the city's Riverside Park as far as the north bridge. It was appropriately named for druggist Joe Hoye, an ardent conservationist and lover of nature's wonders. And Thoreson Park is all that Ed, the agriculture teacher and park commissioner, hoped it would be. Places abound in Estherville for opportunities to ice-skate, ski, play baseball and tennis, swim, swing, tumble, and picnic. With the persistence of Cato demanding the destruction of Carthage, Hattie Rhodes at every opportunity urged the preservation of a native woodland area that ultimately became Fort Defiance State Park. The park, close to the lovely setting chosen by the Ridleys, attracts hundreds of picnickers, hikers, and campers eager to enjoy the beauty of unspoiled timber. The county's own conservation board, organized in 1964, developed with county tax monies twelve acres of park area at Okamanpadan Lake and an extensively improved Wolden recreation area between High and Ingham lakes, near where the Lutherans built and developed a summer Bible camp.

Several waterfowl preserves delight bird-watchers, sportsmen, and other outdoor recreationists. These treasures, along with lush golf courses and the vast Okoboji-Spirit Lake playground nearby, preserve for successors of the pioneering settlers a general inheritance of rich natural resources for common enjoyment.

When I'm asked by a stranger to spell the odd-sounding name of the town in which I say I live, I sometimes hear a snicker, and I get a questioning look. "Yes, Estherville!" I repeat. Why not? "Estherville" — the only one in the world. After all, if Robert Ridley had married someone other than Esther, this could have been Phoebeville, Lenaville, Kittyville, or Daisyville. Esther is a pretty name for a pretty ville, nestled along a meandering river under bluffs wooded by native oak, walnut, maples, and other dense timber. Esther's town escaped the scalping knife and the hazards of frontier childbirth; her town survived blizzards, fires, a visit from outer space, a county-seat squabble, locusts and even bank failures.

The people of her town and the farmers who developed the surrounding rich prairie joined in achieving a prosperous and livable
Estherville.

Prairie fires, the scourge of grasshoppers,
Indian frights, and blizzards
did not deter the hardy who came first.
Those who ventured in 1856 to settle
and till Emmet's fertile black soil
founded undreamt wealth
in yields of grain and fattened livestock.
They were destined to build and sustain
a vigorous and compatible community.

APPENDIX

OFFICIAL CENSUS OF EMMET COUNTY

	Estherville	Emmet County
1860		105
1863		160
1865		308
1867		708
1870		1,392
1875		1,436
1880		1,550
1885	701	2,781
1890	1,475	4,274
1895	2,498	7,619
1900	3,237	9,936
1905	3,650	10,105
1910	3,404	9,836
1915	4,123	11,360
1920	4,699	12,627
1930	4,940	12,856
1940	5,651	13,406
1950	6,719	14,102
1960	7,927	14,871
1970	8,108	14,009
1975	8,500*	

*Estimated.

EMMET COUNTY MEN ELECTED TO STATE OFFICE

Those who have served Emmet County in the Iowa legislature are Howard Graves, 1865; Harwood G. Day,* 1869; W. M. McFarland, 1887, 1889; J. O. Kasa, 1891; J. C. Myerly, 1893; Martin K. Whelan, 1895, 1897; B. F. Robinson, 1901, 1903, 1905; Nelson J. Lee, 1907, 1909; C. B.

Murtagh, 1911; Lewis L. Bingham, 1913, 1915; William Stuart, 1917, 1919; W. G. Gordon, 1921; Fred Himebaugh, 1923; R. S. Clark, 1925; R. B. Crone, 1927; E. O. Helgason, 1929, 1931; E. J. Maniece, 1933, 1935; Lehman C. Rovn, 1937, 1939; Harley A. Degen, 1941, 1943; George H. Robb, 1945, 1947, 1949; Max Soeth, 1951, 1953; Fred J. Ehlers, 1955; Niels J. Nielsen, 1957, 1959, 1961, 1963, 1965; Leo Sanders, 1967, 1969; Rollin C. Edelen, 1971; Terry Branstad* and Rollin Edelen, 1973; Don Spencer,* 1975.

NOTE: *Not of Emmet County but represented it.

Those who have served in the state senate from Emmet County are Dr. E. W. Bachman, 1901, 1903; Burl N. Ridout, 1949; Walter B. Hammer, 1969.

Frank P. Woods was the only Emmet County person to serve in the United States House of Representatives, 1909-1917.

The county has sent no one to the United States Senate.

Nelson J. Lee was the only district court judge, 1913-1923, chosen from Emmet County.

William M. McFarland, after two terms in the state legislature, was elected in 1890 as secretary of state and served two terms.

George E. Delevan, *Vindicator* editor, was appointed in 1894 as the state fish commissioner. When that position was abolished in 1897, he was appointed state fish and game warden, serving until April 1901.

George H. Robb was appointed to the state tax commission, 1950-51.

From the *History of Emmet County and Dickinson County, Iowa,* vol. 1, Pioneer Publishing Company, Chicago, 1917, pp. 240 and 241, with later information from the county auditor.

WAR LOANS IN EMMET COUNTY

Drive	Quota	Sold	Int.	Maturity
First	$ 227,200	$ 52,600	3½ %	6/15/47
Second	335,475	243,050	3½	11/15/42
Third	440,510	718,850	4¼	9/15/28
Fourth	815,500	969,100	4¼	10/15/38
Fifth	611,625	661,625	4¾	5/20/23
			3¾ *	5/20/23
	$2,430,310	$2,645,100		

*The 3¾ % bonds were exempt from federal as well as state income taxes. The two issues of the fifth drive were interchangeable.

This information was found in *Sale of War Bonds in Iowa* by Nathaniel R. Whitney, 1923, State Historical Society of Iowa.

ESTHERVILLE CHURCHES

The Free Will Baptist church was formally organized in the spring of 1870. The church constructed its own building in 1882. Signing articles of incorporation May 1, 1883, were J. W. Ridley, Isaac Mattson, Amos A. Pingrey, R. E. Ridley, H. A. Curtis, T. B. Mattson, R. P. Ridley, and C. I. Hinman.

The Estherville Lutheran congregation was incorporated February 11, 1871, and services were first conducted by the Rev. H. Hande in 1872. A building was dedicated in May 1891.

The Methodist Episcopal church was incorporated December 1, 1875, with C. W. Jarvis, E. Whitcomb, E. B. Soper, Howard Graves, and R. E. Ridley as trustees. A building was erected in 1879.

The Presbyterians organized a church in 1881. A building was provided in 1888 when articles of incorporation were signed by L. M. Culver, C. H. Bryant, David Weir, Howard Graves, and John Woods.

Roman Catholics built a frame church in 1888 but Father Luke Carroll had held services before that time. William Fahey, J. P. Kirby, and the Rev. Joseph J. Murtagh signed incorporation articles May 14, 1912.

The Church of Christ was organized in the spring of 1888 by the Rev. J. B. Vawter, a chautauqua evangelist. In 1890 incorporation articles were signed by trustees G. W. Hawk, F. R. Lyman, Lewis Lyman, M. J. Mattson, Charles H. Evans, J. W. Lough, I. N. Salyers, and Orlando Lough. A church was built in 1889.

Grace Episcopal church was started in 1889 with the Rev. Francis C. Berry as first resident priest. Incorporation articles were signed February 28, 1890, by G. A. Goodell, Henry Allen, E. J. Woods, A. O. Peterson, S. C. Clark, W. P. Upman, James C. Atkins, Fred N. Roberts, and H. F. Wells. A building was constructed in April 1890.

The First Baptist church was organized in 1890 and a building provided in 1899. Incorporation articles were signed in 1894 by O. J. Brown, S. H. Pelton, and D. J. Gillett.

Immanuel Lutheran church (Missouri Synod) was organized in 1892 with services held in a frame building. It was incorporated July 11, 1902.

The Christian Scientists organized in January 1899 and met at Neville Hall. The first trustees upon incorporation January 31, 1900, were Oswald Neville, Henry A. Hanson, and Minnie B. Lough.

The Free Methodist church was organized Dec. 1, 1901, by the Rev. John Sutton. Incorporation articles were signed by Ole Anderson, John Sutton, Clara Anderson, W. G. Anderson, and Hannah Anderson. The former Presbyterian church building was purchased.

Calvary Gospel Assembly held its first services January 2, 1932, and used a building erected by the Baptists in 1899.

The Fellowship Tabernacle was established by the Rev. Kenneth Fogelman in 1950. A new building was used in October 1950.

A Calvary Baptist church was established in 1952 with the Rev. Warren Steward as the first minister. A building was begun in July 1954.

Trinity Lutheran church was organized in 1955 by Phillip Bigelow. A building was begun in 1957.

Redeemer Lutheran church was established October 9, 1956, with the Rev. Robert Beckstrand as the first pastor. Cornerstone for a building was laid June 24, 1956.

Church of the Nazarene purchased the former Free Methodist building in April 1957, organized with the Rev. Kathryn Loutzenhiser as minister.

Church of the Bible and Jehovah's Witness congregations were established more recently.

From the *History of Emmet County and Dickinson County, Iowa*, vol. 1, Pioneer Publishing Company, 1917, pp. 194-99, and historical edition of *Estherville Daily News*, October 29, 1968.

FRATERNAL ORGANIZATIONS AND SOCIETIES

Masonic North Star Lodge No. 447, chartered June 5, 1884, named C. I. Hinman worshipful master; William H. Davis, senior warden; and M. K. Whelan, junior warden.

Jeptha Chapter No. 128, Royal Arch Masons, was chartered September 25, 1897.

Esdraelon Commandery No. 52, Knights Templar, was chartered July 9, 1889, with George A. Goodell, eminent commander; D. L. Riley, generalissimo; J. P. Forrest, captain-general; Alexander Peddie, prelate; M. K. Whelan, senior warden; W. L. Telford, junior warden; Joseph N. Lee, recorder; P. J. Sargent, treasurer; T. W. Carter, warder; T. J. Randolph, sentinel.

The Order of Eastern Star, North Star No. 200, another Masonic group, was organized later, with Mrs. Jennie Ellerston as first worthy matron and H. G. Pittenger as first worthy patron.

Independent Order of Oddfellows Lodge No. 423 was organized April 18, 1887. Samuel Collins, A. L. Houltshouser, H. G. Graaf, William Mahlum, S. E. Rathe, and J. D. Rutan were charter members.

Rebekah Lodge, Harmony No. 55, was organized April 23, 1889. A. O. Peterson was noble grand; Mrs. W. M. McFarland, vice-grand; Mrs. Orphia Rutan, recording secretary; Mrs. James Espeset, financial secretary; Mrs. A. O. Peterson, treasurer; Mrs. George Allen, chaplain.

Knights of Pythias Red Gauntlet Lodge No. 233 was organized June 5, 1889. T. W. Carter was installed as chancellor commander; E. B. Myrick, vice-chancellor; Charles Miller, prelate; A. D. Cooley, master of arms; E. P. Butterfield, keeper of the records and seal; G. N. Evans, master of finance; N. A. Erdahl, master of the exchequer; E. E. Goff, inner guard; Bert Miller, outer guard.

Pythian Sisters Temple No. 180 was organized November 14, 1916. Mrs. Chris Rosenberger was installed as P.C.; Mrs. Frank Wing, M.E.C.; Mrs. Frank King, E.S.; Mrs. G. H. Lucas, E.J.; Mrs. William Foshier, manager; Mrs. Frank Nelson, M.R.C.; Mrs. Vance Noe, M.F.; Mrs. George Cox, protector; Mrs. Richard Sheldon, guard.

Grand Army of the Republic, Isaac Mattson Post, was organized September 3, 1884. First officers were S. E. Bemis, commander; Charles Young, senior vice-commander; Harvey Miller, junior vice-commander; Joseph N. Lee, adjutant; and H. C. Coon, quartermaster.

Woman's Relief Corps of GAR, Isaac Mattson No. 315, was organized March 18, 1886, with Mrs. Mary G. Williams president; Eliza M. Bemis, senior vice-president; Emma Sondrol, junior vice-president; Frances Barber, secretary; Abbie Peterson, treasurer; Esther A. Ridley, chaplain, Ella Coon, conductress; and Della Miller, guard.

Estherville B.P.O. Elks Lodge No. 528 was organized November 9, 1889, with W. L. Rammage as first exalted ruler.

The Brotherhood of Locomotive Firemen, Emmet Lodge No. 288, was organized September 18, 1885, with W. S. Davis as presiding officer; F. Slayton, vice-president; P. J. Sullivan, secretary; and George Godden, treasurer.

The Estherville Young Men's Christian Association (YMCA) was organized April 5, 1897, with N. A. Lawrence, president; Albert Mahlum, C. S. Robinson, Leonard Anderson, and Edward Kline, vice-presidents; Orlando Lough, secretary; Arthur Pelton, treasurer.

Modern Woodmen of America and its auxiliary the Royal Neighbors; the Brotherhood of American Yeomen; the Fraternal Brotherhood of the World; the Ancient Order of United Workmen; Modern Brotherhood of America; and the United Commercial Travelers Post organized February 5, 1910, were other organizations of the era.

The Women's Christian Temperance Union was organized in Estherville February 10, 1884, with Esther A. Ridley as president; Mrs. G. N. Luccock, Mrs. G. H. Stafford, and Mrs. William Bartlett, vice-presidents; Mrs. H. A. Jehu, secretary; Mrs. S. E. Bemis, treasurer.

The K.K.K. cooking club was organized in January 1893.

The Woman's Town Improvement Association was organized March 16, 1896, with Mrs. F. E. Allen, president; Mrs. L. L. Bingham, Mrs. John Woods, Mrs. Jennie Ellerston, Mrs. Peter Johnston, Mrs. M. G. Willson, and Mrs. A. O. Peterson, vice-presidents; Mrs. George Letchford, secretary; and Miss Ellerston, treasurer.

The Ladies' Literary Club, the Searchlight Club, the Civic Club, and the Estherville Woman's Club in February 1900 united in urging an ordinance prohibiting spitting on the sidewalk.

Chapter AY of P.E.O. was established November 6, 1896, with Mrs. M. K. Whelan, president; Mrs. Mary Williams, vice-president; Mrs. Eva Ladd, corresponding secretary; Mrs. Helen Wells, recording secretary; Mrs. Emma Allen, treasurer; Mrs. Jessie Knapp, chaplain; Mrs. Ada Ammon, guard; Mrs. Maggie Hardie, pianist; and Mrs. Minnie Binford, journalist.

Daughters of the American Revolution, Okamanpado Chapter, was organized May 13, 1903, by Emma G. Allen, Margaret S. Alexander, Marietta Groves, Mary G. Knight, Mary B. Lawrence, Callie B. Letchford, Mary E. Maxwell, Mary G. Osgood, Mary R. Orvis, Jennie J. Randolph, Hattie C. Rhodes, Almira Ridley, Vestaline Salisbury, Iza B. Soper, and Ethel T. Woods.

Estherville Federated Woman's Club was organized in 1880 as the Monday Club with Mrs. H. E. Ballard, Mrs. W. C. Barber, Mrs. F. E. Allen, and Mrs. G. K. Allen as charter members.

Knights of Columbus, Estherville Council, organized in 1912 with fifty-six charter members of whom Louis Krier, Henry Neppl, Matt Scholtes, and John O'Neill celebrated the fiftieth anniversary.

Service Star Legion was organized October 4, 1918, with Mrs. F. H. Rhodes, president; Mrs. Ed Smith, vice-president; Mrs. H. B. Miller, secretary; Mrs. W. A. Rankin, treasurer; and Mrs. C. W. Crim, historian.

Maurice Doyle Post of the American Legion was organized in Estherville immediately after World War I.

American Legion Auxiliary, Maurice Doyle Post, was organized February 12, 1924. The Past Presidents Parley was formed December 10, 1931.

In 1919, 4-H was organized as a pig club; in 1921 as a dairy calf, poultry, and corn club; and in 1923 as a girls' committee.

White Shrine of Estherville was organized May 12, 1920, with ninety-seven members, of whom Dorothy Morton, Gladys Hunt, Clare Wilson, Vera Diltz, Grace Strong, and Nelda Echternacht are still living.

Past Noble Grands of Rebekah was instituted April 25, 1923, with Lydia Anderson, president; Minnie Nourse, vice-president; Minnie Sillge, secretary; and Maude Anderson, treasurer.

Rock Island Woman's Club was organized from Cedar Rapids with twenty-six members and Mrs. Ora Hipple as president. It recently celebrated its eighty-sixth birthday.

Wa-tan-ye Club was organized in November 1936 with thirty-three women as charter members.

The Estherville Rotary Club was organized in 1938 with George W. Thompson, president; Deemer Lee, vice-president; Henry W. Mahlum, secretary-treasurer; and Francis T. Shadle and Herbert H. Drey, directors.

Estherville Kiwanis Club, now known as the Estherville Noon Kiwanis Club, had its first official meeting July 10, 1939. Dr. C. E. Birney was elected president and F. E. Rosendahl, secretary.

The Estherville Saddle Club was organized in 1941 by C. E. Shirley, Arnold Hockett, Art Kaltvedt, William Hageman, and Adelaide Nichols.

Veterans of Foreign Wars, John W. Brawford Post, was organized October 17, 1935, by charter members of whom William Hunt, Milton Larson, Andrew Peterson, E. G. Stavros, and Francis Weir are still living.

V.F.W. Auxiliary of John W. Brawford Post was chartered August 6, 1943, with twenty-five original members.

Isaak Walton League of Estherville was organized in 1946.

Ladies of Izaak Walton, Fort Defiance chapter, was organized May 26, 1953, with Mrs. Orel Young, president; Mrs. Harold C. Johnson, vice-president; Mrs. William Recher, secretary; and Mrs. Albert Heywood, treasurer.

Emmet County Pork Producers was organized February 20, 1956, by Vernon Origer, Keith Griffith, James Simon, Delbert Ellis, Lee Shultz, Cliff McMillan, and Dick Solberg.

Toastmasters Club was formed in 1957 by thirty members. Don Hoye has been a member since organization.

Estherville Flying Club was formed March 3, 1958.

Emmet County Historical Society was organized July 27, 1964, with Henry M. Larsen, president; Henry W. Mahlum, vice-president; Ivadell Ross and Dorothy Story, secretaries; and Sylvester Berge, treasurer.

Emmet County Cattlemen's Association was organized in 1966 with William O. Anderson, president.

Estherville Federated Garden Club was organized in 1968 with Mrs. Edgar Martin, president; Mrs. Henry Larsen, vice-president; Wilma Gronstal, secretary; and Mrs. Ralph LaRue, treasurer.

Estherville Town & Country Kiwanis was organized in May 1971, with Leonard Anderson, president; Dick Potratz, vice-president; and Dick Sidles, secretary-treasurer.

Sons of Norway, Ibsen Lodge, was organized April 17, 1974, with Stanley Fagre as president.

The Emmet County Rescue Unit was formed in October 1974 by Rodney Ross, Harriet Ringsdorf, John Heckard, Harvey Enns, and Randy Cody.

Estherville Lions Club was begun in March 1975 by Davis Webb, president; Dr. Ronald Lemmons, vice-president; Ray LeSieur, secretary; Steve Olson, Lion Tamer; J. D. Webb, Tailtwister; Bob Louwagie and Steve Doty, directors.

Estherville Golf & County Club was organized September 15, 1920, electing Fred J. White, president; C. E. Tedrow, secretary-treasurer; and George A. Lyon, J. W. Morse, G. G. Griffith, N. P. Walker, Roy Buckingham, and G. H. Raife directors.

_____

From the *History of Emmet County and Dickinson County, Iowa,* vol. 1, Pioneer Publishing Company, Chicago, 1917, pp. 205-16, and *History of Emmet County, Iowa,* vol. 3, pp. 42-54.

NOTES

An Era of Bootlegging, Culture under Canvas, and Arson

1. The Grand Theater and Confectionery, $135,000; First National Bank building, $80,000; Estherville Wholesale Grocery, $75,000; Elks Lodge home, $45,000; Johnston & Bixby furniture store, $20,000; Rock Island roundhouse improvements, $30,000; high school, $35,000; city gas plant, $44,000; residential construction, $35,000; miscellaneous, $15,000. (*Vindicator & Republican,* December 26, 1917.)

Fearless Settlers and Rampaging Indians

1. The story of the massacre is told in *White Men Follow After,* by Hattie P. Elston, Athens Press, Iowa City, Iowa, 1946, pp. 10–15.
2. *Early Algona,* by Florence Call Cowles, Des Moines Register & Tribune Company, 1929, pp. 8, 9, 56, 57.
3. Members of the Northern Border Brigade were William H. Ingham, of Algona, captain; Edward McKnight of Decorah (more likely of Dakotah), first lieutenant; Jesse Coverdale, second lieutenant; Lewis H. Smith of Algona, quartermaster; Haven F. Watson, Addison Fisher, Christian Hackman, J. R. Armstrong, August Zahlten, William Crook, Thomas F. Clarke, John Hegarty, John W. Summers, James Young, James G. Greene, Andrew J. Jones, Thomas Robinson, Michael Smith, and Jacob Altwegg. (*Ibid.,* p. 163.)
4. Emmet County men in the company were Howard Graves, first sergeant; Amos A. Pingrey, third sergeant; Morgan Jenkins, second corporal; Thomas Mahar, fourth corporal; Ruel Fisher, farrier; Robert A. Ridley, wagoner; and privates Peter S. Baker, Hiram Barrett, Ira Camfield, John H. Clark, Hogen Gilbert, Willis C. Jarvis, George Palmer, Judah Phillips, Eugene G. Ridley, Otto Schadt, who was promoted to third corporal; and Elbridge Whitcomb, promoted to fourth sergeant. (*History of Emmet County and Dickinson County, Iowa,* vol. 1, Pioneer Publishing Company, Chicago, 1917, p. 74.)
5. When Company A was mustered out on September 26, 1863, it was reorganized as Company F, with William H. Ingham, captain; Jerome M. White, first lieutenant; and Lewis W. Estes, second lieutenant. In the reorganization, which was completed on October 20, 1863, Emmet County furnished the following members of the company: Edward Altwegg, Henry Archer, Peter S. Baker, William Carter, Jerry Crowley, John D. Goff, Erwin Hall, John W. Hewitt, Patrick Jackman, Gunther Knutzen, John A. Lucas, James Maher, Thomas Maher (or Mahar), Joseph T. Mulroney, Keiran Mulroney, William J. Salisbury, and George F. Schaad.

Dickinson County furnished a large part of the company: Hudson D. Barton, Franklin Bascomb, Jacob Bossert, Alexander H. Burd, Charles Carpenter, David N. Carver, William W. Collins (promoted bugler), Joseph Courrier, John H. Evans, Samuel N. Guilliams, William A. Harden, Roderick Harris, Charles W. Hathaway, Silas R. King, Joseph R. Line, Jonathan N. Lyon, Eben Palmer, John W. Rose, Robert Seeber, Joseph W. Sharp, Milan E. Sharp, Miles R. Sheldon, John Striker, John D. Striker, Harrison L. Thomas, John L. Thomas, William H. Thrift, Robert F. Turner, and Crosby Warner. The company was mustered out in December 1863.

Soon after the Northern Border Brigade was mustered out of service, a detachment of Company I, Sixth Iowa Cavalry, under the command of Captain Wolf, was stationed on the frontier. Captain Wolf made his headquarters at Estherville and part of his command was sent to Spirit Lake under Lieutenant Benjamin King. In the spring of 1864 Captain Cooper's company of the Seventh Iowa Cavalry relieved Captain Wolf. This company remained but a short time, when Captain Daniel Eichor came with Company E, Sixth Iowa Cavalry, and continued on duty until the spring of 1865, when he was succeeded by a detachment of Minnesota troops under Captain Read. This was the last miltary force stationed along the Iowa border. (Ibid., p. 76.)

Blizzards, Prairie Fires, and Grasshoppers

1. Description of early pioneer life drawn from the *History of Emmet County and Dickinson County, Iowa*, vol. 1, Pioneer Publishing Company, Chicago, 1917, pp. 95-102.

2. Ibid.

3. Voyage and experiences of a Norwegian emigrant, from *Frontier Mother* by Gro Svendsen, Norwegian-American Historical Association, 1950, pp. 12-26.

4. Ibid., p. 53.

5. Preceded by attempts to organize agriculturally in 1868 and 1869 (records of which were lost), an agricultural society was founded July 19, 1872, with G. M. Haskins, president; C. A. Prosser, vice-president; J. W. Cory, secretary; Isaac Skinner, treasurer; and H. W. Halverson, John Crumb, and Isaac Mattson, the executive committee. The directors, representing each township, were D. W. Perry, Armstrong Grove; R. E. Bunt, Center; Horace Meeker, Ellsworth; W. Barker, Emmet; James W. Ridley, Estherville; Ammi Follett, Fairview; E. Mulroney, High Lake; and Peter Larson, Peterson. (*History of Emmet County and Dickinson County, Iowa*, vol. 1, p. 203.)

An Invasion from Outer Space

1. *History of Emmet County and Dickinson County, Iowa*, vol. 1, Pioneer Publishing Company, Chicago, 1917, p. 85.

2. Ibid., pp. 229, 230.

3. Commissioners officiating in locating the county seat were Lewis H. Smith of Kossuth County and Orlando C. Howe of Dickinson. They were appointed by Judge A. W. Hubbard of Sioux City. The first county officers were Adolphus Jenkins, county judge; Jesse Coverdale, clerk of the district court; R. E. Ridley, treasurer and recorder; A. H. Ridley, sheriff; Robert P. Ridley, superintendent of

schools; and Henry Jenkins, surveyor. (*A. T. Andreas' Illustrated Historical Atlas of the State of Iowa, 1875,* Andreas Atlas Company, Chicago.)

The *Vindicator* reported, however, that Stanley Weston was the first treasurer and recorder, that D. W. Hoyt was sheriff, Robert Z. Swift was drainage commissioner, and R. P. Ridley, the coroner.

The first term of district court held in Emmet County was May 30, 1862, with Judge Asahel W. Hubbard presiding. At that time Emmet was in the Fifth Judicial District, which included all of northwestern Iowa. Cave J. McFarland was judge in 1859, but no court was held until 1862. Adolphus Jenkins served as county judge, the only one to hold that office until the position was abolished by the county board in 1860. (*History of Emmet County and Dickinson County, Iowa,* vol. 1, p. 186.)

4. *History of Emmet County and Dickinson County, Iowa,* vol. 1, pp. 87–90.

5. The Andreas 1875 atlas showed Emmet County to have nine townships: the north tier, left to right, was Emmett [*sic*], Ellsworth, and Fairview (later divided into Lincoln and Iowa Lake); the center tier was Estherville, Centre, Swan Lake, and Armstrong Grove; and the lower tier was Peterson (later mostly 12-Mile-Lake), High Lake (later the east part became Jack Creek), and Armstrong Grove (later Denmark). The postoffices in 1875, according to Andreas, were Emmett in Emmett Township, Iowa Lake in Fairview Township, Estherville in Estherville Township, Swan Lake in Centre, Armstrong Grove in Armstrong Grove Township, and New Bergen in Peterson Township.

6. *History of Emmet County and Dickinson County, Iowa,* vol. 1, pp. 91, 92.

7. The first officers to occupy the new palace of justice in 1884 were H. W. Halvorson, auditor; ———— Knudson, recorder; S. H. Mattson, clerk of court; Knuet Espeset, treasurer (who worked in a room at the post office during winter months to save fuel); M. K. Whelan, sheriff; and E. H. Ballard, superintendent of schools.

8. Petitioners for incorporation were F. E. Allen, Frank Davey, C. J. Wilson, E. S. Wells, Howard Graves, Lyman S. Williams, A. O. Peterson, W. J. Pullen, W. C. Barber, G. I. Ridley, W. E. Riggs, Henry Coon, J. L. L. Riggs, C. W. Dillman, Knuet Espeset, James Maher, S. E. Bemis, A. H. Stone, R. E. Ridley, W. H. Davis, J. W. Plummer, D. M. L. Bemis, Tolliff Espeset, E. H. Ballard, and D. A. Painter. (*History of Emmet County and Dickinson County, Iowa,* vol. 1, p. 129.)

9. Mayors serving under the town government were E. H. Ballard, 1881; F. E. Allen, 1882; S. E. Bemis, 1884; E. J. Woods, 1885; J. H. Barnhart, 1886; A. O. Peterson, 1888; and M. L. Archer, 1892. Allen and Barnhart served two 1-year terms and Peterson four. (Ibid., p. 130.)

New Life in the Town

1. At a meeting February 22, 1870, at which Howard Graves was elected to preside and Dr. E. H. Ballard was chosen secretary, a resolution of protest against the Parsons Bill before the legislature was voted. O. C. Bates of the *Northern Vindicator* prepared a series of resolutions to the legislature, which defeated the Parsons Bill. (*History of Emmet County and Dickinson County, Iowa,* vol. 1, Pioneer Publishing Company, Chicago, 1917, pp. 165, 166.)

2. Ibid., p. 164.

3. Account of railroad history drawn largely from *History of Emmet County and Dickinson County, Iowa,* vol. 1, pp. 167–72.

4. The masthead of the paper by the next spring, 1883, was changed to carry the names of G. F. Shaad and C. M. Thompson. In August, after a year of publication, the *Broad-Axe* became the *Emmet County Republican* when sold to Reynolds, Lough & Company, with Frank Davey as editor. In May 1884, Peter Johnson and H. I. Wasson bought the paper, changing the name to the *Emmett* [*sic*] *County Herald.* Sometimes "Emmet" in the news columns was spelled right; sometimes not. (From the newspaper's files.)

5. Jenkins and Mulholland succeeded Woods. In 1891 George Nichols purchased Mulholland's interest, and in 1900 he bought out Jenkins. (*History of Emmet County and Dickinson County, Iowa,* vol. 1, p. 181.)

6. Editor Northrop, partner of O. C. Bates, retired from the original firm of the *Northern Vindicator* on October 14, 1869, selling his interest to Frank A. Day. On November 11, 1871, the masthead became H. G. Day and Frank A. Day. Henry Jenkins later took the place of H. G. Day. Then it was Jenkins and Charles W. Jarvis who became the publishers until 1876, when they sold to Frank Davey. Six years later Davey conveyed the paper to Logue and Mattson. Later, Mattson took in his son and it was Mattson and Son. In 1895 the paper was owned by McFarland and Jarvis, then W. T. Heacock and George Gruwell, with Heacock selling to Frank P. Woods. (*Northern Vindicator* files.)

7. *Rock Island News Digest,* October 1952, p. 24.

8. Reorganized January 1, 1917, with $100,000 capital, the First National Bank's officers were John P. Kirby, president; M. K. Whelan, vice-president; and Ralph H. Miller, cashier. (*History of Emmet County and Dickinson County, Iowa,* vol. 1, p. 146.)

9. The private Rhodes bank was incorporated with a capital of $35,000 May 1, 1916, as the First Trust & Savings Bank, with F. H. Rhodes, president; W. T. Rhodes, vice-president; I. C. Stanley, cashier; and C. D. Tedrow and E. A. Albright, assistant cashiers. (Ibid.)

10. By 1917 the Iowa Trust & Savings Bank had capital stock of $50,000 and the officers were Mack J. Groves, president; M. D. Miller and A. D. Root, vice-presidents; Lloyd E. Stockdale, cashier; and Frank G. Crumb and F. G. Parsons, assistant cashiers. (Ibid.)

11. Mayors of the city of Estherville were A. W. Dawson, 1893; E. E. Hartung, 1897; E. J. Breen, 1898; Mack J. Groves, 1903; W. P. Galloway, 1907; H. C. Coon, 1909; J. E. Stockdale, 1911; B. B. Anderson, 1913; Mack J. Groves, 1915; B. B. Anderson, 1919; John C. Lilley, 1921; M. H. Schloeman, 1927; M. K. Whelan, 1931; Fred Ehlers, 1935; W. R. Sidles, 1947; George H. Robb, 1949; Dan S. Howard, 1950; Dr. S. G. Ewen, 1952; G. K. Allen, 1954; Leo Sanders, 1956; Henry Schroeder, 1962; Jack B. White, 1962; Dr. James P. Clark, 1965; Larry Jacobsen, 1970; Kenneth Meadows, 1971; Linn Foderburg, 1971; and Elmer Jacob, 1974. (Ibid., pp. 130, 131, and files of city clerk.)

12. Members of the fire department were Chauncey Ammon, M. L. Archer, C. L. Bartlett, W. A. Beecher, T. W. Carter, H. C. Coon, C. W. Crim, C. W. Dillman, N. B. Egbert, James Espeset, C. I. Hinman, J. D. Hoover, H. A. Jehu, C. B. Little, A. O. Peterson, Warren Pullen, G. I. Ridley, and William Stivers. (Ibid., p. 132.)

13. On April 4, 1892, the Rescue Fire Company elected John Dygert chief; L. E. White and Samuel Fritz, assistant chiefs; A. O. Peterson, foreman of the engine; H. O. Sillge, foreman of the hose cart; W. J. Pullen, foreman of the hook and ladder brigade. A. O. Peterson was elected president and H. G. Graaf, secretary. (Ibid.)

14. Provisional officers and directors were R. K. Soper, president; C. A. Williams, vice-president; O. A. Meade, secretary; A. J. Penn, assistant secretary; J: D. Wilson, treasurer; and A. O. Peterson, H. M. Rhode, Samuel Reaney, C. S. Byfield, and H. W. Woods, directors. Permanent directors, representing each township, were P. H. Burt, Armstrong Grove; I. C. Wildfang, Center; Morten Petersen, Denmark; Nels Anderson, Ellsworth; S. B. Weir, Emmet; E. L. Brown, Estherville; Joseph N. Lee, High Lake; Ammi Follett, Iowa Lake; J. C. Mollison, Jack Creek; Cornelius Anderson, Swan Lake; and L. L. Bixby, 12-Mile Lake. They were elected following a campaign for funds to hold county fairs, interest in which waned after a few years. In 1916 the Emmet County Fair and Agricultural Association was incorporated, with G. E. Moore, president; R. G. Ross, vice-president; H. M. Lambert, secretary; James Rainey, treasurer; L. H. Heinerich, R. S. Harris, S. M. Reed, George W. Murray, J. S. Peterson, P. S. Anderson, J. R. Horswell, John Thompson, and I. Coleman, directors. (Ibid., pp. 204, 205.)

Progressives versus Standpatters

1. M.&St.L. stories and facts drawn from *Mileposts on the Prairie*, by Frank P. Donovan, Jr., Simmons-Boardman Publishing Corporation, New York, 1950.

2. In 1916 the office personnel included a postmaster, assistant postmaster, four clerks, four city carriers, six rural carriers, a janitor, and a charwoman. Estherville postmasters in order of service were Adolphus Jenkins, Howard Graves, Peter Johnston, Lyman S. Williams, John W. Randolph, M. K. Whelan, George C. Allen, Frank Carpenter, Fred Robinson, Clara Kennedy, Louis Obye, and James Matre. (*History of Emmet County and Dickinson County, Iowa*, vol. 1, Pioneer Publishing Company, Chicago, 1917, p. 133, with later postmasters added from newspaper files.)

War Days and Happier Times

1. *Sale of War Bonds in Iowa* by Nathaniel R. Whitney, State Historical Society of Iowa, 1923, pp. 14, 15, 17, 19, 21.
2. Ibid., p. 24.
3. Ibid., p. 92.
4. Ibid., p. 167.
5. Ibid., p. 86.
6. Ibid., p. 126.

When All the Banks Failed

1. *Thirty-fifth Annual Year Book*, Part XIV of Iowa Department of Agriculture.
2. *U.S. Treasury Annual Reports*, 1920, p. 120; 1921, p. 69; 1922, p. 58; 1923, p. 60; 1924, p. 68.
3. Bank receivership files in Emmet County District Court.
4. Ibid.
5. *Report of the Comptroller of the Currency*, October 31, 1932, pp. 214, 215.

6. Bank receivership files in Emmet County District Court.
7. Ibid.

Eleven-Cent Corn, 108-Degree Heat, and a Twister

1. *Thirty-fifth Annual Year Book,* Part XIV of Iowa Department of Agriculture.

Watching Estherville Grow

1. On the Holy Family Hospital fund-raising committee were Paul Gray, president; V. A. Gibbs, vice-president; Leo Fitzgibbons, secretary; Wayne Currell, M. P. Graves, John E. Greig, Joe Hoye, Francis Kennedy, Deemer Lee, Charles Reed, Mrs. Lloyd Stockdale, James Stillman, Herman Elsenbast, Stanley Fagre, DeWayne Fisher, and C. M. Robinson. (*Estherville Daily News,* October 19, 1956.)

It's All Progress, One Might Suppose

1. Iowa Crop and Livestock Reporting Service of Iowa Department of Agriculture.
2. December 1 elevator prices for 1974 to 1978 were:

	Corn	Soybeans
1974	$3.37	$7.27
1975	2.52	4.60
1976	2.23	6.44
1977	1.97	5.40
1978	1.95	6.15

(Superior Co-op Elevator Company quotations.)
3. Iowa Weather and Crop Bureau comparisons of Assessors' reports. Iowa Department of Agriculture.

INDEX